TALES FROM A KENT VILLAGE

Hildenborough

As seen through the Parish Council Archives

Compiled by
Maurice Nairne
from the archives of
Hildenborough Parish Council 1894 to 1956

Tales from a Kent Village
Hildenborough
As seen through the Parish Council Archives
First published 2017

ISBN:978 1 5272 0607 6

Front Cover: photographs of Mr & Mrs John Francis, Mr M C Morris,
Mrs Kingswood, Rev'd L G Chamberlen, MC, Hildenborough Station
and the Jubilee Fountain on the Village Green

Back Cover: St John's Church, The Old Barn,
The Platelayers' Memorial Stone, the Pavilion, Presentation of The Shilling,
the Jubilee Fountain on the B245, 4 prominent buildings in Hildenborough

Printed by
Scarbutts Printers, Winsor Works, London Road,
West Malling, Kent ME19 5AN

TALES FROM A KENT VILLAGE

Hildenborough

As seen through the Parish Council Archives

Preface

In 2013 Hildenborough Parish Council published a little booklet "Notes from Hildenborough Parish Council's Minutes 1938-1952". Following a study of the Council's Minute Books covering the period from 1894 together with the separate books covering Parish Meetings and celebrations from 1894 to 1956, five more booklets were produced. These have not been published before but the Council has decided that the six booklets should be put together and printed in one book as a contribution to the history of the Village. Production costs are being met privately so that the proceeds from any sales will be for the benefit of the Parish Council and the parishioners of Hildenborough.

The Parish Council was established in 1894 and various documents have been deposited for safe keeping at the Kent History and Library Centre, James Whatman Way, Maidstone ME14 1LQ. Amongst these documents are the Minute Books for the Council and for Parish Meetings and celebrations.

This book is dedicated to the Councillors and Clerks who served the Parish at various times from the very first Council in 1894 up to 1952. Their names are listed at the beginning of each of the Parts Covering the Council Minutes.

The book is divided into seven Parts:

Based on the Council Minutes:

Part One	1894-1908
Part Two	1909-1924
Part Three	A selection of Historic Photographs
Part Four	1924-1938
Part Five	1938-1952

Based on Minutes of Parish Meetings and Celebrations

Part Six	1894-1924
Part Seven	1925-1956

A complete list of original subscribers is printed at the back of this book.

Hildenborough Parish Council thanks the subscribers without whose support publication would not have been possible. The cost of publication has been underwritten privately at no charge to the Council.

* * *

Acknowledgements

Special thanks are due to Pam Gow, Clerk to the Parish Council for the immense amount of time she spent in preparing the book for publication.

Photographs by kind permission of:
Hildenborough History Society
Hildenborough Village Hall Management Committee
The Parish Church of St. John the Evangelist
Stuart Gow
Nigel Simpkins
Robin Oakley
J L Allwork Ltd.
Tonbridge Free Press
The Kent Messenger
The Kent and Sussex Courier

In some cases we have been unable to trace the copyright holder but have made every effort to do so.

The Story of "The Shocking Railway Accident" is reproduced by kind permission of the Editor of "Keys", the Parish Magazine.

Assistance with research in the History Society's archives from Pat Davies and Tracy Chandler is gratefully acknowledged.

The help of the Kent History and Library Centre in making documents available is acknowledged with thanks.

Hildenborough Parish Council acknowledges with thanks the advice and help received from Scarbutts Printers.

Text by Maurice Nairne

Printed by Scarbutts Printers

Published by Hildenborough Parish Council
2017

TABLE OF CONTENTS

PART ONE: 1894 – 1908 1
List of Councillors and Officers 1
Introduction...1
The Local Government Act, 1894.....................................2
The Early Councils 2
Pounds, shillings and pence (£.s.d.) 4
Charities..5
Overseers 8
Allotments 10
Technical Education 12
The Institute and the Recreation Ground 13
Fire Brigade Problems 17
Tonbridge Burial Board 20
Road and Footpaths 23
Mount Pleasant 27
Lighting the Village..29
The Coronation of Edward VII, 1902 29
The Licensing Act, 1904 31
Drainage Problems at Oakhill..31
A "Bathing Place" for the Parish? 33
Telephones...33
Powder Mills 34
Snippets from the Minutes 34
Postscript 35
"Shocking Railway Accident", 1898 35
PART TWO: 1909– 1924 39
List of Councillors and Officers 39
Introduction..39
Pounds, shillings and pence (£.s.d.) 40
The Coronation of George V, 22nd June 1911 41
The Protection of Wild Plants..41
The School...42
Housing 42
The Fire Brigade 46
Allotments 51
Roads and Footpaths 57

The War 62

After the War 63

Leigh United Charities 65

Water 65

Snippets from the Minutes 67

PART THREE: A SELECTION OF HISTORIC PHOTOGRAPHS 69

Mount Pleasant 69

"The Poplars", Watts Cross 70

Mr and Mrs John Francis outside "The Poplars"..70

The Jubilee Fountain 1887 71

Junction of Coldharbour Lane and B245 72

The Post Office 72

The Half Moon 73

Mr M C Morris, Headmaster of the Village School 73

The Charles Fitch Kemp Memorial 74

Rev'd R L G Pidcock 74

Rev'd James Stone 75

Rev'd H Warde 75

The War Memorial 76

Noble Tree Corner 76

Tug of War at the 1919 Peace Celebrations 77

Peace Celebration procession 77

William Castle's bakery vehicles 78

The Windmill, Watts Cross 79

Webber's Garage 79

Mrs Kingswood 80

Edwin Hendry 80

Flat Cottages 81

The Flying Dutchman 81

Mr Walter J King 82

Shipbourne Road (Riding Lane)...82

The Recreation Ground 83

The Pavilion in the Recreation Ground 83

Rev'd L G Chamberlen M C 84

Rev'd W H Bass..84

The Shilling 85

Presentation of The Shilling 86

Rev'd E H Wade 86

Masters Tea House 87
The Green Rabbit 87
The Cemetery for Dogs and Cats 88
The Village Fire Brigade..88
Home Guard in 1944 89
Inspection of Special Constables...89
Extract from Minute Book 18th January 1943 90
Rev'd E W E Fraser 90
The Drill Hall and Institute 91
The Old Barn interior..92
The Old Barn Tea House 93
The Stocks at the Old Barn Tea House 93
Mr Frank Burton presents cup to Mr Ted Francis 94
Mr F G Balcombe as School Lollipop Man 94
Mr A G T Oakley with his children 95
Sketch of Oldhouse Farm 1959..95
Hildenborough Station 1875 96
Hildenborough Station 1947 96
The Gate Hotel 97
Plaque commemorating rail accident on 1st April 1898 97
Memorial to "London Jack" 98
Memorial to platelayers killed on 1st April 1898 98
The Upton Family at the unveiling of the memorial plaque 16th July 2016 99
PART FOUR: 1924 -1938..101
List of Councillors and Officials 101
Councillors and Clerks 101
Pounds, Shillings and Pence (£ s. d.) 105
Finance..106
The Village Fire Brigade..107
Allotments 115
The Jubilee Fountain..118
The War Memorial 118
Seats at Bus Stops 120
Telegraph Poles 121
The Village Green 122
The Recreation Ground 126
Footpaths 133
Public Health 135

Housing 138
Lighting 139
Traffic Matters 141
The Approach of War 143
Snippets from the Minutes 143
PART FIVE: 1938 – 1952 147
List of Councillors and Officials 147
Introduction...147
Hildenborough's Fire Brigade 148
The Years 1938 and 1939 148
"There would almost be a riot …" 149
Money Matters...149
The Outbreak of War 150
The Years 1940 and 1941 150
The Stirrup Pump Controversy 151
The Pavilion...151
The Impact of War on Footpaths 151
From the Wartime Minutes..152
"Dig for Victory" 153
Elections...153
The Victory Celebrations 154
Raisins, Sultanas, Peas and Pears 154
Welcome Home! 155
The War Memorial 155
"Vicar prefers Sunday Games to Cinemas – Better Than Watching Bad Films,
He Thinks" 155
The Underriver Bus 156
A 30 m.p.h. speed limit through the Village? 156
Pedestrian Crossings 157
Rejection of a Plan for Playing Fields 157
The Drill Hall and Institute 157
The Library 158
80 Applicants for the post of Caretaker 159
Oakhill House 159
Post War Housing Schemes...159
Improving the Pavilion 160
Lighting up the Village 160
The Recreation Ground 161

Gang-mowing for the "Rec" 162
A Miscellany from the Minutes 162
PARISH MEETINGS 165
PART SIX: 1894 – 1924 165
Hildenborough's first Parish Meeting...166
1895 – 1896 167
The Diamond Jubilee, 1897 168
1898 – 1903 171
The Celebration of the Coronation of King Edward VII and Queen Alexandra 172
1904 – 1911 174
The Coronation Celebration of George V and Queen Mary, June 1911 177
1912 – 1924 179
PART SEVEN: 1925-1956...183
1925 – 1930 183
1931 – 1936 186
1937 – 1939 188
1940 – 1956 192
List of Subscribers 206

Part 1 – 1894-1908

List of Councillors and Officers

Those who served the Council as Members and/or officials are listed below. In the first years of the Council the Clerk and the Treasurer were Councillors but the first Chairman was not. Under the Local Government Act of 1894, which established Parish Councils, the Council was free to choose any qualified elector to be the Chairman.

Note: In the Minutes there are sometimes different spellings for some names eg Louis and Lewis, Basset and Bassett.

Mr Thomas Bassett, Junior
Mr Richard A Bosanquet
Mr George Castle
Mr William Clarke
Mr Thomas Collins
Mr Charles Crowhurst
Mr Roger Cunliffe, Treasurer 1894-1898
Mr John T Fellowes Wilson
Mr John Francis
Mr Edwin Hendry
Mr Henry Hills
Mr Charles Hitchcock
Mr Horace H Hitchcock
Mr Raymond Hitchcock
Mr William Holmwood
Mr Lewis Ingram
Mr George W. Johnson, Clerk 1894-1907 Treasurer 1907,
    Chairman 1907-1937
Mr Charles Fitch Kemp, Chairman 1894-1907
Mr William King
Mr Mesech C. Morris, Clerk 1907-1913
Mr John E Sadler
Mr Robert Wingate, Treasurer 1898-1907

Introduction

For much of the 19th Century local government was largely administered through the Poor Law Boards of Guardians, set up under the 1834 Poor Law Amendment Act. The day-to-day work was done by the Overseers of the Poor. In rural areas local Justices of the Peace (magistrates) played a part in local government with formal meetings every few months at the Quarter Sessions to deal with both criminal and civil matters. Parishes were grouped together into Unions, each Union having a workhouse for the destitute. That for the Tonbridge Union was at Pembury, now the site of the new Tunbridge Wells Hospital.

Boards were set up to administer various activities. For example, elected School Boards were established in most areas under the 1870 Education Act which decreed that every child should be within reach of a school. In 1880 primary education became compulsory. Locally, there were Boards dealing with such matters as sanitation and burials.

Changes in local government came about in the late Victorian period:

1. 1871 – the Local Government Board set up. This brought together various functions of local government including Poor Law administration.
2. 1884 – Urban and Rural District councils established e.g. in Tonbridge with the Rural and Urban District Councils
3. 1888 – County Councils set up. At the same time the London County Council was established.
4. 1894 – The Local Government Act set up Parish Councils.

The Local Government Act, 1894

This Act was the work of the President of the Local Government Board, Mr Henry H Fowler, M.P. (later Viscount Wolverhampton) and set up some 6,880 Parish Councils. It was finally passed on 1st March 1894, two days before the resignation of the Prime Minister, Mr W E Gladstone. This brought to an end his fourth Liberal administration – he was aged 84. Mr Gladstone was not much interested in local government and at this time devoted his attention to the problems of Ireland. Had he been more interested he might have made an effort to get the 1894 Act through more quickly. It is reported that the House of Commons devoted 38 days to it, with Mr Fowler speaking over 800 times! Sadly, the Act was flawed since, although it gave a number of powers to Parish Councils, crucially they were permitted to levy only a 3d in the £ rate, thus starving them of funds. On the positive side there was an historic step on the road to equal voting rights for women. Since 1869 women householders – not those who were married since their husbands were the householders – could vote in municipal elections although they couldn't be candidates. The 1894 Act gave the vote to all women rate payers, married or single, in Parish Council elections. As well as having the vote, women could now be candidates:

"No person shall be disqualified by sex or marriage from being elected or being a member of a Parish Council."

Hildenborough Parish Council's first Minute book covering the period from December 1894 until September 1908 only mentions two women. In 1898 Miss K Johnson was co-opted on to the Council's Technical Education Committee whilst the only other reference to women was the appointment of the Mrs Kingswood as caretaker at the Institute.

Apart from the reference to women, what else did the 1894 Act say about Parish Councils?

• The number of Councillors was to be fixed by the County Council – not less than 5 or more than 15. Hildenborough had 9 councillors.
• Councillors served only one year from 15th April. Within the 7 days following the Council must hold an Annual Meeting.
• The Annual Meeting elected a chairman from amongst the councillors or "from other persons qualified to be Councillors of the parish." The meeting also elected overseers for the parish.
• Casual vacancies would be filled by the council.
• There must be at least four Parish Council meetings a year, including an annual Parish Meeting. Meetings to be held in public.

The Early Councils

In April 1898 Hildenborough Parish Council agreed to hold quarterly meetings on the third Tuesday of every third month. The annual elections of councillors were held at the Annual Parish Meeting but with effect from 1901 Councillors were elected for a 3 year term. The councillors elected a Clerk "without remuneration" and a Treasurer, also unpaid, from within their number. Mr G W Johnson was the first Clerk and Mr Roger Cunliffe the first Treasurer. The District Auditor for the Local Government Board carried out an annual audit of the Council's work and accounts.

The first Chairman of Hildenborough Parish Council was Mr Charles Fitch Kemp who served until his death in 1907 when Mr Johnson took his place with Mr C Morris elected as Clerk. Mr Cunliffe was succeeded by Mr Robert Wingate as Treasurer in 1898, a post he held until his death in 1907. Mr Johnson held the post briefly but in December of that year the Council appointed the Manager of Lloyds Bank, Tonbridge to act as treasurer.

Mr George W Johnson and Mr Horace H Hitchcock were the only councillors to serve from 1894 until the end of the period of the first Minute book in September 1908. Mr John Francis was a member from 1894 until his death in the Spring of 1908. In the previous year the death had occurred of Mr Wingate, a councillor since 1896.

Mr Charles Fitch Kemp, J.P. D.L. was re-elected year after year as Chairman, a tribute to the high regard in which he was held. The Minutes for 19 December 1907 record the moving tribute to him which was paid when the news of his death was reported to the Council.

> "Mr Hitchcock, who spoke with deep feeling, referred to the great loss sustained by the parish generally and by the Parish Council particularly … . Speaking as one who had known Mr Kemp for over half a century, Mr Hitchcock said that never could they hope to see his like again. He had been a brilliant chairman of the Council ever since its formation in 1894, and in regularity of attendance, and in strict attention to the true interests of the parish he had always set a noble example."

Mr Kemp lived at Foxbush, now Sackville School, not far from his friend Mr J H Johnson who lived at Mountains, in Noble Tree Road. The Chairman sometimes sought the advice of Mr Johnson, a lawyer, and it was one of his sons, Mr George Johnson who was the first Clerk to the Council and then Chairman in succession to Mr Kemp, a post he held until December 1937.

Looking at the list of Councillors in those early days, other notable members included Mr Edwin Hendry who purchased what is now "One Stop" from the late Mr Kemp's estate. Mr Roger Cunliffe of Meopham Bank served on early councils and Mr John Francis, a member of the prominent Francis family was a distinguished council member for many years as well as being an Overseer of the Poor. Following his death in early 1908, the Council passed the following Resolution:

> "This Council has heard with deep regret of the death of their esteemed colleague Mr J Francis, who, as a member of the Council since its inauguration always showed the greatest interest in parish affairs, particularly in connection with the allotments."

The first impression when looking at the Council's first Minute book is that it was beautifully kept. The handwriting clearly belongs to a different era, the age of copper-plate writing using ink and a steel-nibbed pen. The Parish appears to have been blessed with a dedicated team of men (there were no women councillors) who worked hard for the good of the community. Attendance at meetings was very high – Mr Kemp for so long the chairman, hardly missed a meeting during his twelve years' service.

Whilst the council dealt with matters like roads, drainage, charities, lighting, the Burial Board and the fire brigade, it also concerned itself with matters which would improve the lives of parishioners. Much time was devoted to allotments and to the purchase of an Institute. Consideration was given to the provision of a "bathing place" and a recreation

3

ground. Education was important with "technical education" a high priority. Lectures were arranged on subjects such as gardening and "bee culture". There were concerns about poverty in the village – in November 1905 there was a discussion about unemployment with Mr Wingate expressing concern about "underfed children in the Elementary Schools". The Council took the lead in organising festivities for the village at times of national celebration e.g. Queen Victoria's Diamond Jubilee in 1897 and Edward VII's coronation in 1902.

It is clear that much of the Parish Council's work was subject to supervision by numerous organisations e.g.

- Kent County Council, Tonbridge Urban District Council, Tonbridge Rural District Council
- Tonbridge Burial Board, Tonbridge Union Board of Guardians
- The Board of Trade – which had to be consulted about matters such as gas and water supplies

Above all, there was the Local Government Board. This Government Department supervised the work of parish councils, approved loans, provided the District Auditor and held local inquiries e.g. into the state of the roads in the Mount Pleasant area. Within the village the Council had to account for its actions to the Annual Parish Meeting.

It is hard to imagine Hildenborough over a century ago and, although there are photographs of the time, it is difficult to appreciate what life must have been like for the councillors mentioned in the early Minute book. On dark evenings did they walk to meetings at the school or the Institute at a time when the usually unlit roads and pavements, if any, were in a poor state? At the council meeting on 18th April 1900 members agreed that the attention of the County Council should be drawn to the dangers of the footpath past Oak Hill "to pedestrians on dark nights". Perhaps they came by pony and trap? A pedal cycle? Possibly even one of those new automobiles! The population of the parish was much smaller then and, no doubt, they were known by all.

Pounds, shillings and pence (£.s.d.)

The present decimal currency was introduced in 1971 and it is perhaps helpful to give examples of conversions from the old pound, shillings and pence:

6d (sixpence) = 2½p   1/- (one shilling) = 5p   2/- (two shillings, a florin)
2/6 (half a crown) = 12½p   5/- (five shillings, a crown) = 25p
One guinea, £1/1/- (one pound and one shilling) = £1.05p

At each Council meeting, as nowadays, approval had to be given for various payments to be made. These examples give some idea of the monetary values at the time:

April	1895	Returning Officer's fee for election of 1895	18/1
		A deed box	7/6
June	1895	Hazledene for grubbing in allotment field	£1-18-0
		Gray for survey of allotment field	£1-1-0
July	1895	Spickett for repairs to Village Fountain	£1-6-0
Nov	1895	E Hendry for lamps	£3-6-9
		Crowhurst for stumps (allotments)	16/-
Jan	1896	Crowhurst hook for lamps	8d
		Thos Basset Ploughing Allotment field £2-9-6	
		Harrowing the same 7/6	
		(The acreage covered was 2 acres and 3 rods –	
		a rod = 5½ yards)	£2-17-0

April	1896	Water rate for village fountain	£1
Jan	1897	Sanitary rate	1/8
		Poor rate	15/-
		Watson for oil	5/6
		Watson for firing	11/-
May	1897	Sands (work on allotments)	4/2
Dec	1897	Rent for Institute (1½ years to Dec 1897)	£30
		Rates	£1-11-3
		DW Elliot (chimney sweep)	2/-
Jan	1898	Mrs Kingswood for work at Institute – 13 weeks @ 2/-	£1-6-0
Mar	1898	Income tax on Institute	6/8
Oct	1898	Francis for hedging on allotments	9/-
Jan	1901	Trustees of the Institute "for use of same for 5 meetings"	10/-
July	1901	Gorham Warner & Son – Inquiry re: Tonbridge Joint Burial Committee	£5-5-0
July	1902	W Holmwood repairing fountain	7/6
Mar	1903	Tonbridge Joint Burial Committee – towards upkeep of Tonbridge Parish Churchyard for 1902	£11
Nov.	1903	Audit stamp and rates	£2-16-9
April	1904	Gas and coals at schools	2/6
June	1908	Poor Rate	3/-
		Sanitary rate	7d
Sept	1908	South East & Chatham Railway	2/1
		Baltic Saw Mills	1/-

A Minute for the meeting of 5 March 1896 says something about the Council's finances:

"The Treasurer stated that the only receipt besides £50 raised by precept which we had received during the year was £4-7-11 in respect of rents for allotments up to September 30th 1895.

Charities

At the very first meeting of Hildenborough Parish Council held at the "National Schools" on 20th December 1894 there was a discussion about the various charities that were known to exist, some of them ancient and some relating not just to Hildenborough but also to Leigh and to Tonbridge. Where did the Council's responsibilities lie? The land which formed the old Manor of Hollanden was transferred in 1894 from the Parish of Leigh to the newly created civil Parish of Hildenborough. Hollanden covered the area between Riding Lane and Mill Lane. This first Council meeting agreed:

1. To ask Mr J H Johnson of Mountains to report "as to the interest this Parish had" in the various charities.
2. That the Vicar and Church Wardens of Hildenborough be authorised "to distribute all charitable funds that may come to their hands … without prejudice to the right of this Council in the future."
3. That the Parish Church wardens of Tonbridge be asked to "furnish the Council with full particulars of all charities in which the old Parish of Tonbridge was interested in order that proper steps may be taken to have an apportionment made between the remaining Parish of Tonbridge and the new Parish of Hildenborough". A similar request would be made to "the church wardens and overseers of the Parish of Leigh" now that part of that Parish had been transferred to Hildenborough

The second meeting of the Council was held on 17th January 1895 and the Chairman, Mr Charles Fitch Kemp, reported that he had received a letter dated "Christmas Eve" from the Vicar of Leigh, the Rev. H R Callum stating that the Leigh Charities Trust was being "administered as in former years, irrespective of recent alterations of parochial boundaries". He pointed out that the future of the charity would be considered by the Charity Commissioners during 1895.

The Church Wardens of Tonbridge had written to say that "with regard to pure Ecclesiastical Charities or those vested in the Vicar and Church Wardens alone the Parish Council has no jurisdiction whatever…". As far as other local charities were concerned, the Church Wardens were in no way involved. The Parish Council asked the Church Wardens "to reconsider the matter".

A very lengthy Report from Mr J H Johnson was then read to the Council. He stated "that the Council as a body do not take over these charities but they have the right to appoint trustees" and may have a say in who shall benefit from the charities.

Mr Johnson wrote that with respect to the various Tonbridge Charities he had obtained information from "a pamphlet published in the year 1866 (Snelling's Tonbridge)" and he lists those "from which it appears that the Parish of Hildenborough as part of the old Parish of Tonbridge is interested". By far the most significant is Sir Thomas Smythe's Charity which had an income in 1882 of £1,158. These funds were mainly used for educational purposes but also for the benefit of the poor (e.g. "furnishing outfits or tools to the poor on entering trades"), convalescent homes, hospitals and the provision of nurses. Money could be used to provide "food, fuel, clothing, blankets etc. for the poor who have not received parish relief".

A list of 19 other charities, including details of three alms houses, was provided by Mr Johnson, some ancient, which, in most cases, derived their income from property. Examples:

1. Lampard's White Horse Charity set up in the Will of Thomas Lampard dated 22nd August 1593. £25 p.a. was received in rent from "a house near the Town Hall, Tonbridge." £3 of the income went to the poor of Hildenborough.
2. Sulham's Charity set up in the Will of William Sulham dated 23rd March 1578 with an income of "£3-2-0d p.a. charged on Powner's Mead in Hildenborough." A total of £3 was distributed to the poor of Hildenborough.
3. Goodhugh's Charity set up under the Will of Robert Goodhugh dated 17th December 1662 with "40/- p.a. out of Noble Tree Lands, Hildenborough, now the property of Mr J H Johnson" for the benefit of the "aged poor people of Parish".
4. Sheffington's Charity established under a Deed dated 10th June 1695 with "£10-10-0 p.a. charged on Rose & Crown Hotel, Tonbridge". This was to provide "four penny loaves weekly to 12 poor people".
5. Children's Charity set up under the Will of George Children dated 11th November 1713 with "£10-10-0 payable out of Lower Street Farm …" This was to provide a weekly distribution of bread to the "Poor of Parish of Tonbridge". Mr Johnson notes that "for many years" this had been done by the Vicar and Church Wardens of Hildenborough.
6. The Leigh Charities. Mr Johnson writes:
   "I have not been able to get any particulars of these charities beyond those contained in Kelly's Kent Directory as follows –
   'There is property left by C. Budgeon and three cottages by Saxby together of yearly value of £73 for the use of the poor and there are other charities of the yearly value of £31 and £17 distributed in money' ".
He goes on to write that –
   "On enquiring I find that several of the inhabitants of the Club Cottages,

Hildenborough, have received small sums of money from these charities but the whole of the sums received in that part of Hildenborough, formerly Leigh, do not amount to more than £2 or £3 whilst the detached portion of Leigh now part of Hildenborough formed about one sixth of that parish".

On the suggestion of Mr Johnson the Council appointed a Committee to "pursue the enquiries with respect to the various charities with power to arrange for a proper apportionment of the income...."

It was reported to the Parish Council meeting of 21st February 1895 that the Church Wardens of Tonbridge "were willing to pay over for the benefit of the poor of Hildenborough the same proportion of various charities they had hitherto done." Hildenborough received £3 from Lampard's White Horse Charity, the income from which was divided between the parishes of Tonbridge, Tunbridge Wells, Southborough and Hildenborough. The "total amount of the money and bread doles for the whole of the old Parish of Tonbridge" for the other charities "amounted to £38-18-0 p.a.". Of this, £12-10-0, roughly one-third, had been paid to Hildenborough.

The Clerk, Mr G W Johnson, reported to the Council on 31st October 1895 that a letter had been received from the Clerk to the Leigh Charities, Mr Robert Stapley, stating that Leigh Parish Council had heard from the Charity Commissioners:

- That the inhabitants of that part of Leigh which had now been incorporated in Hildenborough Parish were still eligible to benefit from the Charity
- That Hildenborough Parish Council was entitled to elect a trustee

The Council elected Mr Roger Cunliffe to represent "such of the inhabitants of Hildenborough as are entitled to the benefit of these charities". The Council was told that an advertisement stated that applicants for assistance from the charity had to apply to the Leigh Charity Trustees by 1st November – next day. Mr Cunliffe had " ... made application for the whole of residents (22 in number) entitled under the rules of the Trustees to participate in the benefits of these Charities".

By May 1896 it was clear that the matter of the Council's responsibility for charities had been clarified: the Chairman, Mr Charles Fitch Kemp explained to the meeting held on the 21st "that only one charity came under the Council" – the Leigh Charity.

Mr Cunliffe of Meopham Bank, the Council's representative on the Board of Trustees for the Leigh Charity, left the district in 1899 and was replaced by the Vicar, the Rev. R L G Pidcock. However, there seem to have been problems with the "Leigh Charities" at this time and the Council meeting of 2nd November 1900 heard from the Chairman "of the unsatisfactory condition into which the administration of these Charities had been allowed to drift". The Clerk read letters dated 7th August and 3rd September from the Charity Commissioners who had "refused to recognise" the appointment of the Vicar. They called for a reorganisation of the Board of Trustees. Mr H H Hitchcock and Mr R Wingate were appointed to act on a joint committee with Leigh Parish Council as suggested by the Commissioners.

On 15th February 1901 Mr Wingate told the Council that he had attended a meeting of the Trustees "as representing the hamlet of Hollanden now merged into their parish, and informed the Council that they were now applying to the Charity Commissioners for a new scheme to appoint two trustees for Leigh and one for Hildenborough".

A special meeting of the Parish Council was held on 13th May 1901 to consider a scheme proposed by the Charity Commissioners for the Leigh Charities:

1. The "real estate" would be vested in "The Official Trustee of Charity Lands".
2. The trustees would number four being:
   One ex-officio trustee – the Vicar of Leigh
   Two appointed by Leigh Parish Council

One appointed by Hildenborough Parish Council

On 25th September 1901 the Council was informed that "the order for a new scheme for the administration of the Leigh Charities had been sealed on 9th August last". The Council nominated Hildenborough's vicar, the Rev. James Stone as the Parish's trustee. Mr Stone had become Vicar in place of the Rev R L G Pidcock who had died the previous December..

The Minutes for the Parish Council meeting of 7th March 1904 include extracts from the report given by the Rev. James Stone as trustee so far as it affected Hildenborough:

- "7 persons living in the part of the parish which formerly belonged to Leigh had been receiving bread quarterly".
- In "January last £48-14-0 was distributed by the Trustees of which £6-5-0 was given to 16 persons living in the Hollanden portion of this parish".
- "in a few instances orders had been given for groceries etc. from these charities."

It was reported to the Council on 18th April 1906 "that 15 persons in the parish ... had received tickets in January last to the amount of £5 in all and 10 persons were on the quarterly bread list and received two 4d loaves each quarter". Two more recipients had been added during the year. A year later, on 4th March 1907, the Council was told that 13 recipients had received £4-14-0 from the Leigh United Charities the previous January whilst "12 persons were now receiving the quarterly bread". On 21st April 1908 the Vicar, as the representative of the parish, reported that "he was of opinion that Hildenborough had received its fair share in the distribution of the Charity". On 3rd June the Rev James Stone was re-elected as a trustee for a further three years.

The Leigh United Charities have continued into the 21st Century with Hildenborough Parish Council retaining the right to nominate a trustee.

Overseers

One of the duties of the Parish Council was to appoint overseers and the first appointments were made at the meeting of 18th April 1895 when "Mr Edwin Hendry and Mr John Francis were appointed overseers for the ensuing year". Both were members of the Council. They were re-elected at the Council's Annual Meeting on 21st April 1896. Mr Hendry was still in office in 1908 whilst Mr Francis retired the previous year.

The Parish Council received most of its funds from the Overseers of the Tonbridge Union. An example is seen in the Minutes for 21st February 1895 when the Clerk reported that he had received an account from the Returning Officer "in relation to the Council – 18/1". This related to the election at a parish meeting of the first Councillors at the end of 1894 at a cost of just under £1. The Clerk (Mr G W Johnson) stated that "as other small expenses are being incurred it was considered desirable that an order should be made upon the Overseers of Tonbridge for £50 in favour of the Treasurer, Mr Roger Cunliffe".

The Council agreed to this suggestion. A similar request was approved on 18th October 1898 when ...

"The Council resolved upon a precept on the Overseers .... for £50 and this was accordingly signed by the Chairman, two councillors and the Clerk."

At this time it appears that the Council's funds were held personally by the Treasurer. Mr Cunliffe was succeeded in 1898 by Mr Robert Wingate. He continued in office, sometimes reluctantly it seems, until his death in late 1906. In his absence the Council elected Mr J T Fellowes Wilson as Treasurer but he declined to take office "owing to pressure of other work". A few months later the Clerk (Mr G W Johnson) was elected Treasurer but, following the death of the Chairman, Mr Charles Fitch Kemp, Mr Johnson was elected as his successor on 19th December 1907. At that meeting it was agreed that...

"… the manager of Lloyds Bank be the Treasurer of the Council"
When Mr Cunliffe was appointed Treasurer two issues arose:

1. "A safe for the purposes of the council" was required. On 17th January 1895 the Chairman reported that the cost would be "between £12 and £15". The Clerk was instructed to ask if it could be kept at the school. The answer was that there was no available place "until the additions to the school were completed at Easter".

2. As Treasurer, Mr Cunliffe was required to provide security. The Clerk reported to the Council on 21st February 1895 that this would be "one quarter the annual rateable value of the Parish". As Mr Cunliffe was absent and the rateable value "not having been ascertained", the matter was left for future consideration. At the Council's Annual Meeting on 18th April 1895 Mr Cunliffe reported that …

"… he had written to the Clerk of the County Council in respect of the security required and he had been told that he must provide a bond with two bondsmen which he would endeavour to obtain."

The Minutes of the Council meeting of 19th May 1898 record the election of an "Assistant Overseer" by the councillors. In the contested election Mr G T Francis was elected and it was ….

"… agreed that Mr George Thomas Francis should enter into a bond for £100 conditioned for the due and faithful performance of the duties of Assistant Overseer."

There was a discussion about the duties of an Assistant Overseer and it was agreed that …

"… he would have to do all the work appertaining to the office of Overseers of the Poor, except collecting the poor rate."

For an annual salary of £25 the record sets out the duties:

"To make out the rates, the jury lists and the Parliamentary Voters' lists, to collect the burial rate and the special sanitary rate and post all notices and generally to perform all such duties as appertain to and are incident to the office of Overseers of the poor."

Mr George Francis remained in office until the end of March 1904 when he resigned "on his appointment as School Attendance Officer in the District of Tonbridge". The Council elected "Mr C M Morris" as his replacement with the same salary and list of duties. He would be paid quarterly. (In the Minutes Mr Morris is variously described as Mr C, Mr M C or Mr C M Morris.) Mr Morris held office until his resignation with effect from 31st March 1907.

A new Assistant Overseer was required and on 19th April 1907 the Council considered two applications for the post. It was decided to appoint Mr Edwin Francis whose application was "accompanied by testimonials from the Vicar of Hildenborough, the Rev. James Stone, and Mr R J G Nevins". He was required to "enter into a Bond for £100…".

At the same meeting the Council considered the matter of the Overseers. Mr Edwin Hendry was again re-elected but Mr John Francis was replaced by the former Assistant Overseer, "Mr M C Morris". All these were councillors. Mr Francis was absent from the meeting "owing to indisposition" and members discussed his role as an Overseer. The Chairman, Mr Charles Fitch Kemp stated that ….

"… he did not think the Council ought to burden Mr John Francis with the responsibility of retaining his post, in view of his advancing years and infirmities…"

The Council agreed and Mr M C Morris was elected. A "cordial vote of thanks" was accorded to Mr Francis for his work as an overseer and "… also for the general interest he had shewn in the welfare of the Parish" (Notice the archaic spelling 'shewn' – shown).

Mr Hendry and Mr Morris were re-elected as Overseers at the Annual Meeting of the

9

Council on 21st April 1908. At that meeting the Council recorded the death of Mr John Francis. Mr Thomas Collins of Orchard Mains in Coldharbour Lane was invited to succeed Mr Francis as a Councillor.

Allotments

At the very first meeting on 20th December 1894 the Council discussed its powers with respect to allotments. It was agreed to ascertain whether there was a demand for them and to invite requests for plots from villagers. At the next meeting on 17th January 1895, 9 applications were received. Two were for "4 acres" whilst others sought plots of "15-20 rods" (a rod equals 5½ yards). Land had to be found and the Clerk, Mr G W Johnson, was requested …

> "… to write to the Earl of Derby, the owner, and Mr Thomas Bassett the tenant of Great Forge Farm and ask if His Lordship would agree to let (with the concurrence of the tenant) the field called the Workhouse Field lying between the large orchard on the Shipbourne Road and the roadway leading from that road to the farmhouse, to be used as garden allotments, and upon what terms and conditions".

"Shipbourne Road" is the old name for Riding Lane. Until 1894 it was part of Leigh Parish.

On 21st February 1895 the Clerk reported that he had met the Earl of Derby in London and that "he was favourable to the proposed lease" whilst the tenant, Mr T Bassett, had left the matter in the hands of his nephew, Thomas Bassett Junior, a member of the Council. Mr Collins, on behalf of the Earl, attended the meeting and said that Lord Derby would let the field, a little over 3 acres, for £6 p.a. Fences must be made good and maintained by the Council. The Council agreed to accept the offer of the Workhouse Field on a 14 year lease with Lord Derby fixing a gate from the main road and providing materials "(stakes and rods) for putting the fence in good repair". The Council, which agreed to set up an allotments committee, received three more applications for plots: "A Paris for 10 rods, G Woolett for 20 rods, and Rogers for 10 or 15 rods". The two villagers who requested 4 acres of land had withdrawn their applications.

The Allotments Committee got down to work within days and on the afternoon of 23rd February inspected the Workhouse Field and resolved to repair the hedges and drain the land before the allotments were marked out. The "existing shaw" (wooded area) "should not be grubbed up but might be utilised by the allotment holders who desired to erect pig styes".

The Committee met again on 6th March and heard that "Lord Derby would probably pay for the drains" with the Council paying for the labour. The hedges would be made good and the entrance gate set up at the Earl's expense. Ten days later, on Saturday 16th March, the Committee visited the allotments' site. Work was well under way and the drains "were found to be in good working order". The Clerk was asked to draw up a map showing the proposed plots which were then to be marked out. There was some discussion about the allotment rules.

The Council meeting on 18th April 1895 heard that the plots had been allocated by ballot to 20 applicants. 3 plots remained. Most tenants had already started to work on their allotments. The Committee was asked to consider the rules and the rent for the allotments. These matters were discussed by the Allotments Committee on 22nd June when it was agreed that a pond should be dug in the Autumn for the benefit of the allotment holders. An estimate for "building a tool house" would be sought but the Council meeting on 25th June heard that some holders were unwilling to incur the extra expense.

On 26th September 1895 the Council accepted the recommendation that the rent for the current year should be fixed at 5d per rod. This was after receiving details of the expenses so far incurred. Tenants would be required to sign agreements, with the rent payable half yearly.

The lease between Lord Derby and the Council was agreed at the Council's meeting on 5th March 1896. There are details regarding payments in respect of the allotments in various Minutes e.g. Mr T Bassett £2-9-6 for ploughing and 7/6 for harrowing whilst Mr Collins, acting for Lord Derby, submitted an account for £10-13-4d. On 21st May the Council agreed to the erection of "a shed on the Allotment Field free of cost to the Council".

On 21st January 1897 the Council heard that more land was needed for allotments. Members were told "that about 1¼ acres lying between Watts Cross and the Lower Cock could be procured for this purpose". The land was currently sown with wheat "and need not be obtained 'till Michaelmas". The Allotments Committee was asked to investigate. The meeting on 15th March instructed the Clerk to find out ....

"... on what terms Mr d'Avigdor Goldsmid would let the Council some land ... on Bourne Place Farm adjacent to the High Road."

On 15th April it was reported that Mr d'Avigdor Goldsmid had agreed to let the land for allotments at a rental of £3 p.a..

The Council received regular reports about "the financial condition of the allotments" which were expected to be self-financing. Inevitably there were items of expenditure and on 21st December 1897 the Allotment Committee asked for "30/- for cutting another pond" in the Shipbourne Road (Riding Lane) allotments. The same meeting agreed to meet expenses of £2-10-4 in respect of the new Bourne Place allotments between Watts Cross and the Lower Cock Inn. The lease was agreed at a Council meeting on 29th December and approval given on 4th January 1898 for "Messrs Waterhouse account for agreement for lease of land on Bourne Place Farm - £5-9-6". Later that year, on 19th July, the Council heard that the allotments "were indebted to the Parish for about £28-10-0". At the close of the financial year on 31st March 1898 the Council had a credit balance of £18-9-11. On 18th April 1900 members were told that the figure as at 31st March was £21-8-0 but that there was a deficit on the allotments of £20-8-10, £12-1-9 in respect of the Forge Farm plots and £8-7-1 owed by the Watts Cross allotments. "Various means for reducing the debt were discussed but no decision was arrived at".

Gradually the debt on the allotments was reduced and on 25th March 1903 it was reported that there was a deficit on the Forge Farm allotments of £3-12-0 whilst the figure for Watts Cross was £4-12-9. There was a problem with rent arrears by allotment holders. For example, a holder from Club Cottages near the Forge Farm allotments was reported on 25th November 1904 as being 15/7½ in arrears. The Council agreed to write to the holder asking for the arrears to be paid within three months. On 7th April 1905 it was reported that the letter had been ignored. The Council agreed that if the rent was not paid within a week "the allotment would be considered vacant and re-let". This prompted the tenant to ask that he be allowed to pay off the arrears in instalments. The matter was left in the hands of the Clerk who reported on 27th September that he had had "several interviews" with the tenant but "that little had been paid". He proposed that unless the money was forthcoming he would be given "a month's notice at Michaelmas". Matters came to a head on 13th November when it was agreed that the tenant, still being 15/7½ in arrears, "should be deprived of his allotment". It was also reported that another tenant was 4/2 in arrears.

Clearly, by 1908, there were problems with the allotments. On 8th June the Council was told by the Allotments Committee "that there were several vacant plots badly over run with weeds and that the hedges were in a bad condition". The Council agreed to the

11

employment "of a man to clean the vacant plots, and to repair and trim the hedges". It was also agreed that "Mr E Francis be appointed collector of the allotment rents". Mr Francis was an Assistant Overseer and his salary of £25 p.a. would be increased by £1 p.a. At the Council's meeting on 28th July it was reported that the work on the allotments had been done at a cost of £5-6-1 "all for labour". On 30th September 1908 the Council heard that at last "the allotments were self-supporting".

Technical Education

From its earliest days the Parish Council took a great interest in what the Minutes describe as "Technical Education". At the meeting of 21st January 1897 Mr John Francis ....

> "....enquired what steps could be taken and what cost would be incurred for Technical classes to be held at Hildenborough as arranged by the County Council ...."

The Clerk, Mr. G.W. Johnson was asked to contact Kent County Council and at the next meeting on 15th March he reported "that Technical Classes were given by the KCC in the winter months at a nominal charge." The "Syllabus of the classes" proposed for 1897-98 would be published in June.

"Technical Education" was next discussed at the Council's meeting of 29th June 1898 when details of KCC's plans for 1898/9 were considered. It was agreed to apply for classes on certain subjects whilst the Council agreed to act as a local committee with the power to co-opt additional members. On 19th July the Council decided to apply to the KCC's Technical Committee for two courses:

> "6 lectures on vegetables .... 12 lessons on wood carving"

Three people were co-opted on to the Council's local committee – The Rev. R L G Pidcock, the Vicar, Mr A F Heath and Miss K Johnson. Miss Johnson's co-option is significant as she is one of only two women mentioned in the Minute Book from 1894-1908. During that period, although eligible, there were no women councillors. The Local Government Act of 1894 which established Parish Councils stated:

> "No person shall be disqualified by sex or marriage for being elected or being a member of a Parish Council."

The Council meeting on 18th October 1898 was told that "the set of 6 lectures in practical gardening commenced on Monday October 3rd." They were well attended. The programme of 10 fortnightly classes in wood carving would begin next day "with every prospect of a full class." On 16th December the Council's sub-committee reported on ....

> "... the gardening Lectures given by the County Council and expressed a hope that steps might be taken next year to give the boys of the Parish an opportunity of learning gardening under the County Council system."

The Gardening Lectures were again discussed at the Council's meeting on 17th January 1899. Mr W P Wright, the lecturer, had delivered six talks on Monday evenings. One or more had been attended by 55 participants with an average of 33 per evening. There was a charge of 2d per lecture. 10 of those attending ....

> "... had been accepted by Mr Wright as eligible to compete for the County Council prizes which were to be on the 'penny per point' principle."

There was considerable discussion about the proposed "School Gardens Scheme" under the County Council for boys from 13 to 16 years of age. It was felt that the only expense might be the provision of a tool shed at an estimated cost of "between £5 and £6". At the next meeting, on 21 February, it was reported that the County Council's Technical Education Committee had ....

> "... sanctioned the starting of a set of school gardens ... and that the tool shed .... would be paid for by this Committee."

The Parish Council agreed to continue to act as a local committee for the County Council's Technical Education Committee at the meeting of 30th October 1899. Mr Wright would once again give a series of six lectures on "practical gardening" and lectures "in respect of the St John's Ambulance" were under consideration. At the next meeting on 30th January 1900 the Clerk, Mr G W Johnson, reported that the Technical Education Committee "did not give assistance in lectures on ambulance work." It was suggested that a Tonbridge doctor should conduct classes and it was agreed to post a notice in the village asking for the names of those interested in attending.

The matter of "Ambulance Lectures" was next considered on 2nd November 1900 when the Chairman was "authorised to engage the services of some doctor to give such lectures" at the Institute providing that a minimum attendance of 15 could be guaranteed. The lectures were "to be open, free to all men in the parish" – no mention of women! It was stated that the cost of the lectures would be about 5 guineas.

At the meeting on 4th January 1901 the Council heard that over 20 men wished to attend the "Ambulance Lectures" and the Chairman was asked to "engage the services of Dr. Ivers, or some other medical practitioner."

On 25th July 1901 the Clerk reported to the Council that he had attended the annual audit held at the Pembury Union on 4th June. (This was the Union Workhouse, now the site of the new Tunbridge Wells Hospital.) He reported that the Parish Council's income for the year to 31st March 1901 was £124-8-4 and the expenditure £82-17-2. He also reported that the Auditor had disallowed payments of £5-5-0 and £5-1-6 for the ambulance lectures. It was agreed to appeal to the Local Government Board against this ruling, an appeal which was to prove successful.

Having been held for three consecutive years, the Parish Council on 25th September 1901 heard that the Technical Education Committee was unlikely to approve a further series of "Gardening Lectures". Consent was more likely to be given to those parishes whose applications for such lectures had so far been unsuccessful. The Clerk, Mr G W Johnson, reported that arrangements had been made for a series of three lectures to be given at the Institute by Wye College "the first to be on 'soils', the second on 'seeds' and the third on 'fungoid diseases'". The Chairman, Mr Charles Fitch Kemp, commented that ....

"… if the prizes hitherto given by the County Council Committee (which amounted to £3-14-3 last year) were not forthcoming this season he would be pleased to contribute £1 towards providing similar prizes by private enterprise, and the Clerk stated that he would do likewise."

The same meeting heard that the Clerk was making enquiries "in respect applications for boys' gardens and lectures on bee-culture."

The Minutes for the meeting of 25th March 1903 record that, on the recommendation of Mr Wright (the gardening lecturer), Mr George Ford was appointed "as teacher for the boys in gardening in this parish… ." Sadly, Mr Wright reported to the Council on 7th March 1904 that he had submitted a "somewhat unfavourable report" to Kent Education Committee and that consequently the Committee did not plan to continue the class at Hildenborough. The land for the "boys' gardens", rented by the Committee, would be returned to the Parish Council. Fortunately, the scheme was saved by Mr R A Bosanquet, a former Councillor and the first chairman of the Gardeners' Society. The Council heard at their next meeting on 15th April that he was willing to be responsible "for the management and expenses", including the rent of these allotments for the boys.

The Institute and the Recreation Ground

From the earliest days of the Parish Council it was considered desirable to have "a good

Parish Room and Offices". A new building could be constructed or an existing one purchased and adapted. The Minutes record that on 21st February 1895 the matter was discussed and a committee set up to examine the possibilities. It was given the power to hire an architect and surveyor to assist in the task. Two days later the committee met to discuss several possible sites. Owners were to be contacted to see if they were interested in selling their properties.

The Committee acted quickly as on 16th March 1895 it was reported that Mr Charles Barkaway through his solicitors, Messrs Warner & Son indicated that he would ...

"... sell the Institute and 30 feet of land fronting the Shipbourne Road (now Riding Lane) by a depth of 100 feet for £550."

He stipulated that the Council "should erect a brick wall not less than 5 feet high round the land bought." The Committee decided to instruct ...

"... Mr Wadmore as Architect and obtain from him plans for the additional buildings and alterations and an estimate of the cost of the same."

The Committee reported to the Annual Meeting of the Council held on 18th April 1895 at "the Hildenborough National Schools". One of the committee Mr H H Hitchcock, stated that ...

"... he was not certain that the present plan under consideration, viz. converting the old Institute, was the most suitable and suggested purchasing another piece of land and erecting a new building."

The matter was left with the Committee.

By 22nd June 1895 the Committee had received two plans from the architect:
1. This showed "the proposed Parish Hall added to and incorporated with the house known as the Institute." Cost – about £2,000.
2. An entirely new building. Cost – "considerably more"

The Committee agreed to recommend the acceptance of Mr Barkaway's offer to sell the Institute but there should be sufficient land "to add on a hall". At the Council meeting three days later this recommendation was accepted but it was felt that to add on a hall would be at "a very considerable expense". Such expenditure should not be incurred "until the feeling of the whole Parish wasin favour of it".

On 25th July 1895 the Council heard that Mr Barkaway agreed to include in the sale of the Institute "30 additional feet from the boundary fence on the lower side of the building facing the Shipbourne Road, the entire depth of the land to be 100 feet from the frontage...." The Council would have the right to add to the depth "at the cost of £1 per foot". Mr Barkaway would not press for a brick wall to be built – a "stout wooden fence" round the property would suffice. Members agreed to accept these terms.

The Council formally appointed "Messrs J H and J G Johnson of 47 Lincoln's Inn Fields, London WC" to act for the Council in the purchase of the Institute on 26th September. On 31st October "the Agreement", approved by the solicitors, was signed by the Chairman and two councillors. At the same time it was resolved that:
1. The consent of Kent County Council be requested and "if necessary" that of the Local Government Board for a loan to be raised by the Parish Council for the purchase.
2. In support of the loan application it was stated that the building would be "used as a public office for Parish Council and Parish Meetings and other purposes connected with Parish business ..."
3. The County Council was asked to make the loan. If the Parish Council had to raise the money elsewhere would the County Council object?

Within a fortnight the County Council had rejected the loan request. At the Council's meeting on 15th November it was agreed to send the correspondence to the Local

Government Board "to ask their advice in the matter." The Board's response was reported to the Council meeting of 3rd December ....

> ".... it merely stated that the matter was not one on which they were prepared to express an opinion."

With no prospect of a loan, the Council then considered hiring the Institute: - the Parish needed a room for meetings "and where the people of the Parish could assemble ... for recreation."

Hiring the Institute presented a potential problem, according to Mr Edwin Hendry. A member of the Council, he pointed out that under the Local Government Act of 1894 the Council had the right to "use the schoolroom for their meetings". The Auditor might consider the suggested rent of £20 pa for the Institute "a considerable item to pay for a room for meeting only".

The Chairman, Mr Charles Fitch Kemp, came up with a solution which met with the approval of the Council – he would hire the Institute privately "and arrange afterwards the terms on which the Council could hire the premises."

Progress over the hiring of the Institute was reported to the Council on 10th January 1896 when the Chairman revealed that he had rented the building from Mr Barkaway on a yearly tenancy. The Council agreed to hire the Institute "on the terms settled by Mr Fitch Kemp." It was agreed that:

1. The Parish Hall Committee should draw up rules together with a scheme under which "the Institute room will be available for hire."
2. The Chairman be authorised to appoint "Watson and his wife" as caretakers, rent free, their duties to be defined by the Committee.

On February 29th the Committee produced a draft of "Rules for the caretaker and a schedule of the charges to be made for use of the Parish Council Chamber". These were adopted "subject to the proviso that no payment even when lights and firing were not required should be less than 1/-".

The Council Meeting on 5th March 1896 was held at the Institute rather than the School and members agreed to let the Parish Hall Committee make some purchases – "25 chairs and some necessary articles" for the Parish's new headquarters.

The Minutes for the Council Meeting on 28th July 1896, on the instruction of the Council, include a complete list of the "Rules for Caretaker" and details of charges. The caretaker was required ....

1. "To keep the room properly scrubbed and swept, grates blacked and windows and furniture clean.
2. To trim and light the lamps when required for use and put them out as soon as the room is vacated.
3. To arrange the chairs and tables etc.
4. To examine the ... furniture after each meeting and report any damage to the Clerk ... within 24 hours.
5. To report any disturbance or improper conduct at any meeting should the same come under the Caretaker's observation.
6. To keep the room properly secured and the key available when required."

The caretaker was also required to keep in a book details of all hiring including the purpose and the charges payable.

Applications for hiring the "Parish Council Chamber" were to be made in writing to the Clerk. Charges were payable in advance and the Council reimbursed for damage to property.

"The Schedule of Rates – per hour or part thereof"-

1. "For any Meetings of parishioners only whem there is no admission charge – 3d.

2. If parishioners were charged admission – 6d.
3. For any Meeting open to the public but without an admission charge – 1/-.
4. For any Meeting open to the public where an admission fee is charged – 2/6.
5. The minimum charge for the use of the Council chamber shall be not less than 1/-
6. Extras – lighting and firing for parishioners' meetings – 1/-."

At the Council meeting on 21 January 1897 the Clerk reported that he had received payments for the hire of the parish room:

"By Gardening Society for the year 1896   £1-6-0
By concert party for Oct 14th 1896   5-0"

At the same meeting there were signs that Members were not happy with the current arrangement as, after "some discussion the Chairman undertook to give notice to Mr Barkaway that possibly the building would not be required after the close of the year ...."

1897 was the year of Queen Victoria's Diamond Jubilee and at the January meeting the Council discussed how it should be commemorated but no firm decisions were made. Mr Horace Hitchcock mentioned "some land on the estate of Lord Derby near the village in which were some old pits". He hoped that Lord Derby would present the land to the parish for use as a recreation ground.

At the next Council meeting, on 15th March, the Chairman, Mr Charles Fitch Kemp said that he had seen Lord Derby about the proposed Recreation Ground and that ....

"....his Lordship ....wished to associate himself with the people of the Parish in carrying out any scheme they might decide upon as desirable".

The Chairman pointed out that commemorations of the Jubilee could be done by purchasing the Institute or "the building of baths" but both would entail considerable expense. A councillor, Mr Robert Wingate, suggested that ...

".... the recreation ground could be hired out of the rates, while any improvements effected might be paid for by subscriptions."

The Jubilee was again considered at the Council's meeting on 3rd May when the Chairman reported that Lord Derby....

"... had very generously offered £250 towards a permanent memorial such as the purchasing of the Institute."

He said that Mr Barkaway was prepared "to sell the building with the land for £1,500". (In March 1895 the figure quoted had been £550.) Mr Fitch Kemp said that "subscriptions might be spread over 5 years and that part of the money for acquiring the land might be raised by means of a 6d rate." The Council left the matter in the Chairman's hands "for the purpose of ascertaining what funds could be guaranteed".

At the same meeting the Chairman had suggested that, providing funds were available, apart from the purchase of the Institute "and the fields adjoining thereto", there should be "a feast for the poor". At the 4th June 1897 meeting he reported that he had promises of contributions totalling over £1,000 to purchase the Institute and adjoining land. As for the Jubilee Day "treat" for the Parishioners, this should take the form "of a dinner with fireworks in the evening" to be held on Tuesday 29th June. There was a discussion about the purchase of the Institute and the adjacent field and Mr Horace Hitchcock proposed that "a swimming bath should be included in the scheme" but it was felt that this would be too expensive.

For no apparent reason the Council didn't meet again until 21st December. In the interim the Chairman had appointed Mrs Kingswood as the caretaker of the Institute. The Council ratified this appointment with Mrs Kingswood living in the adjoining cottage rent free but with "a sum of 2/- per week" for extra work in keeping the Institute's rooms "in order". The same meeting agreed that the Parish Council Room could be loaned to the "Institute Committee" as required.

The Chairman was asked at the Council's meeting on 4th January 1898 what had been done with regard to the "Diamond Jubilee Scheme". He replied that the matter was "under consideration" but that he was not prepared to make any statement at this time. The reason for Mr Fitch Kemp's reticence became clear over a year later when the meeting of 21st February 1899 received the news from him …

> "… that the Institute had been purchased by a few gentlemen for the benefit of the Parish and that it had been placed in the hands of 4 trustees, viz: himself, Mr C W M Kemp, the Vicar (The Rev. R L G Pidcock) and Mr G W Johnson."

There was an explanation given: not enough money could be raised from subscribers. The Council Treasurer, Mr Robert Wingate, "expressed his strong disapproval of vesting the property in the hands of trustees". He wanted to see the Institute placed in the hands of the Parish Council but his was a lone voice.

Confirmation of the new arrangement for the Institute was given to the Council at its meeting on 17th April 1899 by the solicitors to the Trustees, Messrs J H and J G Johnson. They stated that "the premises had been duly conveyed by a deed dated 13th June 1898 to the Trustees" who would manage the Institute themselves and "charge a small sum for the use of the room when required." Payment of rent for a year and a quarter was authorised. The Minutes for 4th January 1901 show that the rent was 2/- per meeting. At that meeting the Treasurer, Mr Wingate successfully proposed that future Council meetings should be held at "the National Schools" as they had been until March 1896. The Council's first Minute Book is a record of meetings up to 30th September 1908 but from 4th January 1901 until that date there are no further references to the Institute or the idea of a Recreation Ground.

Fire Brigade Problems

At the Council meeting on 18th October 1898 the Clerk, Mr G W Johnson, presented a circular from the Local Government Board drawing the Council's attention to legislation conferring powers on Parish Councils. One Act was "The Parish Fire Engines Act". There was a discussion …

> "… as to the need in the Parish of some fire extinguishing appliances but no resolution was passed."

Similarly, on 30th October 1899 "no resolution was arrived at" by the Council. The Council had received offers to supply "a manual or other engine" from Messrs Shand Mason & Co and from Messrs Merryweather. It was considered that ….

> "…under Section 29 of the Poor Law Amendment Act 1867 an engine and other appliances might be provided by the Parish Council but there was a limit as to expense."

A letter from Tonbridge Urban District Council was read at the Council meeting on 16th November 1900 proposing a scheme whereby it took over ….

> "…the whole management and maintenance of the present Tonbridge Fire Brigade for their own district and for the use of neighbouring parishes."

Did Hildenborough wish to participate in the scheme?" The answer was "yes" and Mr Robert Wingate of Oakhurst, Councillor and Treasurer, was appointed as the Council's representative in any future negotiations.

The question of the Fire Brigade was again considered at the Council meeting of 15th February 1901. Tonbridge Urban District Council had produced a Memorandum proposing the amalgamation of ….

> "…. the surrounding parishes with the Rural District Council of Tonbridge for

the provision of a Fire Brigade for the whole district."
The Parish Council declared that –
1. The "outlying parishes should not be called upon to contribute towards capital expenditure" which should be a matter for "the town of Tonbridge".
2. Parishes would pay an annual sum for the upkeep of the Brigade.
3. Hildenborough was willing to contribute £30p.a.. In return, the parish would have the services of the Brigade, free.

The matter of the Fire Brigade was again discussed on 23rd December 1901 but no conclusions were reached. On 21st April 1902 Mr Wingate reported that "a hydrant could be supplied when the main was being laid at about £3, but if laid on afterwards the cost would be about £5".

The Council considered the possibility of a parish fire engine. Had it got the power to incur such an expense? Perhaps there was the possibility "of obtaining help from Leigh". These questions were left in the hands of the Chairman and the Clerk. On 25th July the Chairman reported that he had been asked to attend a meeting of Tonbridge Urban District Council's Fire Brigade. The Council authorised him to repeat the Council's offer of 15th February 1901.

Matters dragged on. Mr Charles Fitch Kemp reported on 5th September 1902 that he and Mr Wingate had attended a meeting with the Urban District Council but that no decision was reached. Questions were raised about the sum that Hildenborough would be required to contribute. Three months later, on 5th December, the Chairman reported that he had heard from the Urban District Council with regard to the Fire Brigade proposals, "enclosing a scale of charges":
- if the Brigade was called out but did not attend the fire   £8-6-3
- attendance at a fire for up to 3 hours   £9-15-0
- attendance at a fire for up to 5 hours   £11-3-9
- for each additional hour   8-7½

The Urban District Council "were not prepared to make any departure from the fees" which were the same for other parishes. Despite this, on 25th March 1903 the Parish Council agreed to seek to discuss with the Urban District Council the possibility of amending the charges. At the same meeting a letter from Leigh Parish Council on behalf of the Leigh's Brigade was considered. The Clerk, Mr G W Johnson, was asked to enquire "the terms on which they would be willing to service Hildenborough in case of need".

A lengthy letter about charges from the Urban District Council was considered by the Council on 22nd April 1903. In the meantime the Parish Council agreed that –
- "hydrants and hose should be provided at suitable places."
- "the services of a sufficient number of men be obtained and paid for by the Council."

Nothing would be done until there had been further consultation with the Urban District Council.

A month later, on 22nd May 1903, the Urban District Council indicated in a letter read to the Council that ...
"... they would be willing to allow their brigade to attend fires within the parish of Hildenborough in consideration of the payment of £50 for the first year and £30 p.a. subsequently."
The letter stated.....
".... that it would be useless to enter into any further discussion with a view to the reduction of the amounts mentioned."

The Parish Council set up a Committee to discuss the matter. Should the terms be accepted or should the Council "provide suitable appliances in the parish at their own expense"? Several members "were of the opinion that the needs of the parish would be met by providing a suitable quantity of hose and a cart together with the hydrants".

On 27th November 1903 the Committee reported to the Council. The Chairman had consulted the Tonbridge Water Works Co. about "placing some hydrants at certain parts of the village" but it was agreed to leave the matter for the time being as the Company stated that "an enlarged main would shortly be placed along the High Road." Any hydrants installed with the present main would shortly therefore have, in all probability, to be replaced. A member suggested that hydrants should be placed in Shipbourne Road (Riding Lane) and Mount Pleasant with 300ft of hose. The Council also faced the problem of housing the "hose and carriage". Members concluded that nothing needed to be done immediately as the matter wasn't "so urgent during the wet season." A year later on 25th November 1904 the matter of "supplying a hose and manual for the village" was again discussed but no decisions made.

In April 1902 the possibility of co-operating with Leigh Parish Council had been considered but on 27th January 1905 a letter from Leigh Fire Brigade was read to the Council. It "would only attend a fire in the parish occurring on premises belonging to the subscriber of 10/- and upwards". The possibility of having hydrants and hoses in Hildenborough was again discussed but for the reasons given on 27th November 1903 it was agreed to do nothing for the time being.

The next discussion was on 7th April 1905 when the Chairman reported on talks with members of the Urban District Council. He hoped that "a satisfactory arrangement would shortly be arrived at". This would be similar to the arrangements made between the Urban District Council and some other parishes – Hildenborough would make "some reasonable payment for the use if required of the Brigade."

On 27th September 1905 the Council again came to no conclusions about fire protection for the village. The meeting was told that a new water main would not now be laid to Hildenborough. Instead, the Water Company was about "to increase the pressure by gravitation from two new reservoirs.... which were now connected with the Hildenborough pipeline". Mr Lees, from the Company, suggested that if Hildenborough wished to install hydrants "it would be well to do so before the winter weather set in". The Council didn't heed this advice. It seems that the Company was slow to increase the water pressure in Hildenborough as Councillors complained at meetings held on 13th November 1905 and 28th March 1906 about the "insufficient pressure of water". Mr Lees, in answer to the complaints, said that "when the new engine was completed the pressure at Hildenborough would be very considerably increased". On 18th April Mr Lees was reported as saying that the new pumping engine had been fixed and that the Company was "anxious to try the hose in front of the Church at an early date". The Clerk reported ...

"... that the pressure of water for the church organ was still at times most unsatisfactory."

The next recorded discussion by the Council about the Fire Brigade was on 11th January 1907 when the Chairman reported that he had received an "informal" offer – the Council should pay £25 p.a. "to secure the services of the Brigade in Hildenborough". He was "authorised to conclude these negotiations but that the limit the Parish should pay should be £20 p.a. Meanwhile, it was agreed that three hydrants....

"... on the High Road would be sufficient for the present – namely, one at the Flying Dutchman, one at Mr Holmwood's corner and one at the Shipbourne Road (now Riding Lane) corner."

On 19th April 1907 the Council was informed that "the Tonbridge Brigade were willing to give their services to the Parish of Hildenborough at a cost of 20 guineas". A sub-committee was set up to consider the scheme and to look at how it would be financed. The

Committee reported on 6th May that –
1. For the sum of £21 p.a. the Urban District Council's Fire Brigade would serve Hildenborough.
2. The Urban District Council would put up four hydrants "free of cost".
3. The Urban District Council hoped that "two or three men might volunteer from Hildenborough to serve in the Tonbridge Fire Brigade". The idea would have the advantage that "some coils of pipe could then be kept at Hildenborough and two men would be on the spot in case of emergency."

The "question of a private fire –call was …. left to Mr Fitch Kemp and Mr Hills to consider" whilst the Council agreed to the proposed scheme.

On 12th March 1908 the Council considered a letter from Captain Bradley of the Tonbridge Fire Brigade. He said that there was nothing in the recent agreement about supplying "hose to be kept in the parish". He said that he would be pleased …

"… to give instruction in hose-drill to two or three local men, and a demonstration with his brigade in Hildenborough."

It was reported that "Messrs A Hodge and R Hitchcock" had agreed to learn the drill and "to hold themselves in readiness in case of emergency". It was resolved to ask Captain Bradley "to give his demonstration between Easter and Whitsun."

On 3rd June 1908 Mr Clarke, a Parish Councillor, reported that he had organised …

"… a supplementary Fire Brigade of four men to drill with the Tonbridge Brigade and that they were attending regularly and working well."

The Council accepted his recommendation that "the following appliances for use at drill and in case of emergency " be purchased:

3 lengths of hose	1 stand pipe
1 nozzle	1 false valve
2 connecting pieces (screw)	1 hose cart

It was also agreed to ask the Tonbridge Fire Brigade to include in the agreement the provision of uniforms for the Hildenborough men. In return for this the Council would agree to increase the annual fee from £21 to £23.

At the Council's meeting on 28th July 1908 the Council agreed to invite tenders for the supply of "four complete uniforms". The lowest tender would be accepted "if the quality was satisfactory". It would seem therefore that the uniforms were to be purchased by the Parish Council rather than by the Tonbridge Fire Brigade. There was concern about the cost of the uniforms and appliances – the meeting was informed that this would be "rather less than one half-penny on the rates".

On 30th September the Council endorsed the sub-committee's acceptance of the lowest tender for the four uniforms submitted by "Shand, Mason & Co." Details of the tenders were given:

Firm	Price
Merryweather & Co	£20-10-4
Hy Simonis & Co	£22–0–0
Shand, Mason & Co	£16-18-0

Messrs Armstrong & Co and Mr Frank East tendered for tunics and trousers only:

Messrs Armstrong & Co	£10-10-0
Mr Frank East	£11-10-0

Tonbridge Burial Board

In the early years the Parish Council frequently discussed the Tonbridge Burial Board. Should the new Hildenborough Parish Council be represented on the Board as it had contributed to the expenses? At the Council meeting of 18th April 1895 the Chairman, Mr Charles Fitch Kemp, explained that the amount contributed was a fixed sum and would cease when the cemetery was paid for and that therefore Hildenborough "had no interest in the matter". However, the meeting on 25th June heard that the Board suggested that Hildenborough should have two representatives on the proposed joint committee of 12 members. Tonbridge Urban District Council would have 6 members and Tonbridge Rural District Council and Southborough Urban District Council two each. On 25th July the Parish Council approved the scheme and on 26th September nominated Mr John Francis and Mr Horace H. Hitchcock as Hildenborough's representatives.

Mr Hitchcock gave a report on the Board's activities to the Council on 31st October 1895. He said that the "Cemetery Loan" was extended for a further six years at the end of which time "the fees would in all probability be sufficient to meet the liabilities". The fees amounted to "£236-19-9 p.a. from which the Vicar of Tonbridge received £60-14-0 and non-conformists £7-8-9". He reported that the cemetery expenses amounted to £180 p.a.. Towards the fees and cemetery expenses Southborough contributed £38 p.a., Hildenborough £60, Tonbridge Rural District Council £55 and the Urban District Council £190.

On 28th July 1896 the Parish Council considered asking for a reduction "in respect of the rate at present levied on account of the cemetery". The matter was referred to Mr J H Johnson of Mountains for his advice. He concluded that Kent County Council "was not at all likely to move in the matter". At the Council's meeting on 21st January 1897 two members proposed –

"That application be made to the Council to separate Hildenborough from the Tonbridge Burial Board area....."

This was rejected by 2 votes in favour but 7 against.

The Council had misgivings about the proportion of the rate payable by the Parish to the Burial Board over a number of years. In 1898 it appeared that the rate would be increased. The Chairman, Mr Charles Fitch Kemp, and Mr Bosanquet expressed the views of the Council at a "special conference" of the Board on 8th November. At the Council meeting on 16th December it was reported that ....

"... it appeared from the local press that the suggestions of Hildenborough Parish Council had been rejected but no official intimation had up to this date been received."

On 21st February 1899 the Clerk read to the Council ...

"... an Order from the County Council directing the payment of £21, being the proportion to be defrayed by Hildenborough Parish Council."

The Hildenborough representatives had not agreed to the amount asked for by the Board which had therefore referred the matter to the County Council to determine. The Council directed the Clerk to ask the County Council why the Parish Council hadn't been consulted before the ruling was given.

The problems of the contribution by the Parish Council to the Board were raised again at the meeting on 2nd November 1900. The Board had levied a precept of £66. Should the rate to be levied be just for "the burial area of Hildenboough (which excluded the Leigh portion of the parish)?" The Auditor had recently ...

"... objected to the rate being paid from the general fund of the Council as it only benefited the burial area of Hildenborough."

He directed that a "special rate" should be levied just on that area. Later that month, on 16th November, the Council was informed that the loan to the Burial Board for which the parish was responsible would be fully paid on 5th January 1901. The Council resolved

– to give notice to the Tonbridge Burial Board that the Council no longer wished to contribute to their funds as the cemetery wasn't used by the Parish.

  – to make application to the County Council "to relieve the Parish from the obligations to pay to the Tonbridge Burial Board".

There was a special meeting of the Council on 4th January 1901 to consider a formal Resolution to be sent to the County Council. It began on a sad note with the news of the death of the Vicar, the Rev. R L G Pidcock the previous month. The Resolution and the supporting letter which it was unanimously agreed to send to the County Council take up two pages of the Minutes book. The Resolution stated that

    - Kent County Council is requested to grant an Order to alter the boundaries of the area under the jurisdiction of the "Tonbridge Joint Burial Committee by withdrawing therefrom the parish of Hildenborough."

The accompanying letter gave reasons in support of the request:

1. Hildenborough, Tonbridge Rural District Council and Southborough Urban Council have 2 members each on the Board and Tonbridge Urban District Council 6. As Southborough members "never attend" power lies in the hands of the Urban District Councillors.

2. Hildenborough has its own churchyard "in which its parishioners both Church people and dissenters can and do bury and we cannot ascertain that any of its inhabitants have ever been buried in Tonbridge cemetery". It is pointed out that there is "sufficient room for a very considerable number of years and when further accommodation is required the Parish will find it".

3. "Tonbridge Cemetery is too far away for Hildenborough people to bury there regularly and to oblige poor people to do so would be a great hardship."

4. Part of the parish (i.e.the Hollanden part which used to be in Leigh Parish) is now outside the Burial Board area.

5. Hildenborough is required to pay a rate to the Board without receiving any benefit.

6. The loan to "the old Burial Board area runs out on 5th January 1901".

7. "Dissenters approve of being buried in the parish churchyard. Proof of this is shewn (sic) by the fact that there are several dissenters on the Council."
(Notice the old spelling of "shewn". Some will recall the notice at railway stations – "All tickets must be shewn"!)

It was reported to the Council on 18th January 1901 that the County Council had raised objections to the request. These objections were considered and responses drafted but no details are given in the Minutes. On 16th April the Council was informed that the County Council had decreed that …

    "… an Enquiry on this matter would be held at the Central Hall, High Street, Tonbridge on Monday the 22nd instant at 11 a.m."

The Council agreed that the Chairman, Mr Charles Fitch Kemp and the Treasurer, Mr Robert Wingate should represent it at the hearing …

    "… with power to employ such legal assistance as they may think desirable."

Messrs Gorham and Warner & Son were employed to assist the Council for a fee of five guineas.

Following the Enquiry the County Council issued a draft Order dated 17th May 1901. This was copied into the Minutes of the Council's meeting of 25th July – three pages of immaculate script. Among the stipulations in the Order:

1. From 24th June 1901 Hildenborough shall be excluded from the area covered by the Tonbridge Joint Burial Committee and shall not be represented on it.

2. Each 31st December the Parish shall pay "in perpetuity" to the Committee the sum of £11 as its contribution towards the upkeep of the old Tonbridge Parish

Churchyard.

3. Each 31st December the Parish shall pay one-sixth of the cost of maintaining the churchyard at St Stephen's Church, Tonbridge.

4. Hildenborough shall pay one-sixth of the existing liabilities of the Joint Committee which …

"… have been incurred in laying out the portion of the Tonbridge Cemetery which has been recently laid out, such total liability to be a sum not exceeding £250 in all."

5. Hildenborough shall pay one-sixth of the compensation payable to the clerk of the Tonbridge Cemetery for loss of fees.

Under Paragraph 4 the Committee was paid £41-13-4 by the Council i.e. one-sixth of £250.

The Council meeting of 23rd December 1901 heard that the "Secretary of State" had made an Order fixing the amount of compensation payable to the Cemetery Clerk at £75-9-9. The Parish's contribution of one-sixth was reported to be £12-11-8. On 21st March 1902 the Council agreed to pay an account rendered by Kent County Council in respect of the Enquiry costs of £2-11-10.

Thus ended the saga of the local churchyards. Records show that payments of £11 p.a. were regularly made by the Council as stipulated in the Order of 1901, despite objections from one or two Councillors. Hildenborough residents now used their own churchyard and were no longer expected to use the cemetery at Tonbridge. The £11 was paid annually well into the 21st Century but in 2016 the Borough Council agreed that no further payments need be made.

Road and Footpaths

The Dust Nuisance

The state of the roads in the Parish was frequently a cause of concern to the Council. The meeting on 18th April 1905 heard a report from the Clerk, Mr G W Johnson, that he had written to the County Surveyor complaining about…

"… the bad condition of the paths at Hildenborough and also the dust nuisance"… on the roads.

The Surveyor, Mr H P Maybury, promised to look into these matters. As far as the dust problem was concerned the Council agreed to ask Mr Maybury "whether he could not use some preparation on the High Road through the village"… as was being "experimentally tried in certain parts of the bye roads by the Rural District Council".

Further complaints led to another letter to the County Surveyor and the Council meeting on 27th September 1905 considered the reply. Addressed to Mr Fitch Kemp as Chairman, it first considered the matter of responsibility for roads:

"Your Parish Council is mistaken in supposing that this is a matter which solely concerns the County Council. So far as the removal of dust is essential to the proper maintenance of the road, it does concern the County Council as road authority, but the abatement of the dust nuisance is a sanitary matter which concerns the sanitary authority – in your case the Tonbridge Rural District Council."

The letter then states:

"In some Urban Districts the tar painting of the road surface has been found to be the only way of dealing with dust and as such treatment is beneficial to the road and has the effect of preserving the surface for which the County Council contributes half the expense. The total cost of tar painting with two coats of good tar should not exceed 1d per square yard."

The County Council wished to see the tar painting treatment used in Rural Districts and …
> "… if the Tonbridge Rural District Council is willing to pay a contribution of one half of the actual cost the County Surveyor is authorised to proceed."

The Surveyor was contacting the Rural District Council and it was hoped that the main road through Hildenborough could be treated "at an early date".

A discussion followed and the matter was referred to Mr Robert Wingate, a Parish Councillor and also the Chairman of the Rural District Council. He said that the Rural District Council was not sure "on whom the cost would fall but it would probably be on the parish". If the parish wanted the road tarred the Parish Council must lodge a request. Members then decided …
> "… that it would be a waste of money for the Parish to tar the roads in their present state."

The Clerk was directed to write again to the County Council deploring the state of the roads.

The Parish Council further considered the state of the roads at its meeting on 28th March 1906. The "High Road" remained in a bad state and "various suggestions as to urging the County Council to do something practical" were put forward.

The dust problem was again reviewed at the Council's next meeting on 18th April when Mr Wingate reported on a discussion which he had had with the County Surveyor, Mr Maybury. The Surveyor had stated that …
> "… the cost for refacing the road with tar would be £30 per mile, assuming the width of the road throughout to be 21 feet."

The County Council would bear the cost of refacing the road with granite which would need to be put down first but the Council would only pay half the cost of "the tar painting". In order to reduce the cost, Mr Wingate had asked Mr Maybury to draw up a scheme …
> "… in which it was proposed to treat only those parts of the High Road passing through the village, or which were adjacent to the houses."

This would reduce the length of road to be treated to two miles. There was a problem: the County Council would not lay down the granite for that part of the road which was due to be dug up shortly "for laying the pipes in connection with the new sewage scheme".

There followed a discussion about the raising of the money to pay for the road improvements but Councillors were unwilling to levy a rate and it was possible that such a levy would not be authorised by the Local Government Board. At this point two Councillors made generous offers:
- the Chairman, Mr Charles Fitch Kemp of Foxbush undertook privately …
> "… to be responsible for the cost of repairing the road from the Station corner down through the village as far as the new drainage scheme would permit."
- the Treasurer, Mr Robert Wingate of Oakhurst (on the corner of Bank Lane and the B245, demolished following planning approval in 2004 for redevelopment) stated that
> "… he was himself going to treat the roadway opposite his house."

At its meeting on 11th January 1907 the members of the Council recorded their deep sense of loss at the news of the death of Mr Wingate.

"Dust laying" was next considered by the Council on 22nd February 1907. The County Surveyor indicated that within Kent a minimum of 100 miles of "high road might be treated with tar during the coming season". The Clerk was asked to enquire if the Council would be granted permission to raise funds for road work through the levy of a rate. The same meeting heard that the Council had the sum of £16-17-11 in the bank. On 4th March the Clerk reported that the County Council Clerk was of the opinion that the cost of "dust laying" could be raised from the rates.

The Council meeting on 19th April 1907 considered the scheme to apply "tar to the high road" at a cost of £30 per mile of which £15 would be payable by the Parish. Members decided to find out first "what could be done by watering the road". Permission to do this would be sought from the County Council.

The problem of the "dust nuisance" was finally resolved at the Council meeting of 6th May 1907, the last to be chaired by Mr Charles Fitch Kemp whose death was recorded with a great sense of loss on 19th December. The idea of watering the "high road" was rejected by the County Council on the grounds that it would cause "a rapid wearing away of the surface". It was agreed to accept the County Council's scheme for applying tar to the road up to a distance of two miles from the Tonbridge boundary. The Clerk was directed to write to the Tonbridge Rural District Council requesting them to enter into an agreement with the County Council in order to raise a special rate to cover the cost. It appears that the work had still not been started by the Spring of 1908 as on 12th March the Council asked the County Council to complete the tarring of the two miles.

The meeting of 3rd June was told that the …

> "…County Surveyor had promised to proceed with the tarring of the main road at once."

Speeding

For decades Councillors have been concerned about speeding traffic with many anxious to see the limit along the B245 (the "high road") through the village reduced from 40 to 30 mph. This was finally achieved in 2016. The Council Minutes of 30th September 1908 include the first reference to the problem. Councillor J T Fellowes Wilson, who lived at Oak Lodge on the corner of the "high road" and Leigh Road, raised the matter of speeding along "the main roads"…

> "… Mr Wilson suggested the erection of notice boards, requesting motorists to drive slowly through the village."

This appears to have been a lone voice as the suggestion wasn't followed up.

By 1908 motor cars were becoming a more common sight. "The Red Flag Act" of 1865 had imposed a 2mph speed limit for steam-driven vehicles in towns with a 4mph maximum in the countryside. Vehicles had to be preceded by a man with a red flag. 1896 saw the first motoring fatality and the first conviction for speeding. Walter Arnold of the Arnold Motor Carriage Co. of East Peckham was fined one shilling by Tonbridge magistrates. He had been speeding through Paddock Wood when he passed the local police constable's house. The P.C. was having his dinner, which he abandoned, and grabbed his helmet and gave chase on his bicycle. After five miles he caught up with the motorist who was clearly travelling at more than the rural speed limit of 4mph. In court it was said that "the carriage was proceeding at about 8mph."

The Red Flag Act was repealed in 1897 and the speed limit everywhere raised to 14mph and then to 20mph in 1903. This was the limit in force when Mr Fellowes Wilson made his suggestion.

Do we need a Scavenger?

At the Parish meeting of 15th April 1897, the Clerk, Mr G W Johnson, reported that the Rev. F A Stewart Savile of Hollanden Park (now the Raphael Centre) in Coldharbour Lane had written to the District Council urging the appointment of "a scavenger" to deal with the problem of "refuse" in the parish. The Clerk to the Rural District Council asked the Parish Council for its opinion, adding that "the cost would be a special expense payable by the Parish". The Council felt that…

> "… such an expense was not necessary for a small parish like Hildenborough."

Mr Charles Fitch Kemp, the Chairman, volunteered…

"... to co-operate with Mr Savile in securing the removal of refuse."

The Rev. Stewart Savile continued to be concerned about the refuse problem and on 10th July 1900 the Council heard that he had suggested the purchase of "a dust cart". The Council did not consider that it had the power to spend money in such a way.

Eventually "scavenging the main roads" became a County Council responsibility but the Parish Council was informed on 12th March 1908 that the County Council...

"... would no longer undertake the scavenging – as distinct from maintaining in repair the main roads in the district, unless instructed to do so by the District Council from whom they would recover the cost."

The Parish Council decided "to take no action".

Footpaths

From time to time the Parish Council considered the question of footpaths. At the meeting on 15th April 1897 the Chairman, Mr Fitch Kemp, referred "to the suggested curbing of the path from Foxbush Corner to the Half Moon" stating that he had offered £25 towards the cost. He understood that the County Council would do the work, bearing half the cost with the Parish Council paying the balance of approximately £45. It was agreed that the Parish Council had no power to spend money in this way. It was suggested that ...

"... the owners abutting on the path should be approached."

The problem of finance must have been resolved as the meeting on 3rd May heard that the County Surveyor, Mr Ruck, had agreed to the planned curbing which would be done shortly.

The April 1897 meeting heard about the Richard Mylls Charity:

"The Clerk read a letter from the Charity Commissioners to the effect that Mylls Charity was by an Order of the Court of Chancery in 1844, devoted to the improvement and maintenance of footpaths to or from the town of Tonbridge and the Chairman stated that Hildenborough consequently had no interest in the Charity."

On 4th January 1898 the Parish Council agreed to send a letter to Kent County Council about the need for footpaths along the "high road" to be repaired. This letter also asked for the construction of a footpath between the Half Moon and the Flying Dutchman. An earlier request for this footpath had been rejected in 1896 when it was reported that...

"the Roads Committee of the County Council did not at present consider that the public demand for such a footpath was such as to justify them in recommending the County Council to incur the necessary expense thereof."

Mr Fitch Kemp, the Chairman reported on 11th March 1898 that he had had a meeting with "Mr Ruck, the County Surveyor and Mr East, the County Councillor for Tonbridge" and that...

"... they had agreed after a considerable conference to advise the County Council to make this footpath on Mr Kemp's undertaking to assist in finding the material."

With regard to footpaths generally the Surveyor undertook "to put them in order". On 21st April it was reported that the Surveyor had placed the matter of the proposed new footpath "before the Roads Committee of the County Council". The meeting of 19th May heard that construction of the footpath was in progress.

The footpath running past Oak Hill to the Flying Dutchman featured in the Minutes of the meeting of the Council on 18th April 1900 when the Council's attention was drawn...

"... to the open drain running down Oak Hill between the hedge and this footpath."

It was agreed to refer the matter to the County Council ...
"... as being a source of danger to pedestrians on dark nights."
Footpaths had been mentioned at the Council's meeting on 30th January 1900 when there was a complaint "as to the cutting up of the footpaths down the High Road by laying down the gas mains". Mains gas finally came to the village the following year. The meeting also considered the question: "should there be a footpath to the station?" The Minutes read:
"The advantages of a footpath from Foxbush corner to the Station were discussed and a letter was read from Mr J H Johnson" of Mountains "stating that he entirely disapproved of the same, and no further action was taken."
The matter of the proposed footpath to the station was raised again at the Council's next meeting on 18th April when Mr Robert Wingate, a member of both the Parish and Rural District Councils, reported that the Rural District Council...
"... were willing to make up the path as they had received an offer of some of the earth required for the purpose."
Some weeks before this meeting Mr J H Johnson had died and, whilst other members agreed that "such a path was desirable", Mr G W Johnson – who was the Clerk to the Council – indicated that he and his family stood by the objections of his late father. At the next Council meeting, on 10th July, the Chairman, Mr Fitch Kemp ...
"... explained that having regard to the feelings expressed by the late Mr Johnson's family with reference to it, his long connection and friendship prevented his doing anything that would annoy or trouble them, and, in addition to that, a considerable portion of the earth he had offered had been used."
Further consideration of the matter was adjourned.
The matter of the footpath to the Station was finally resolved when, at the Council's meeting on 23rd December 1901, the Clerk read a letter which he had written to the Rural District Council on behalf of Mrs Johnson (his mother) of Mountains. She would raise no further objection to the construction of the footpath "on the road waste adjoining her property" but she requested that...
"... it should be neatly finished off in sections at a time and preferably on the right hand side of the road going from the Village to the Station."
At the meeting of 25th November 1904 the Council considered the problem of the poor state of the footpath along part of the "high road" between "Station Corner" and Watts Cross. The Clerk was asked to write to the County Surveyor...
"... drawing his attention to the destruction of this path (more especially apposite the Flat Cottages) caused by the traction engines drawing water from the ponds adjacent to the road at that spot."
(Flat Cottages, part of the Mountains estate, were on the site of what is now a car showroom and a petrol station.)

Mount Pleasant

When the Council first met in December 1894 members were uncertain of the extent of their powers. An example of this is seen in the reference in the Minutes...
"... with respect to roads and sanitary regulations with particular reference to Mount Pleasant where there had been considerable building operations without any proper construction of roads..."
The Clerk, Mr G W Johnson, was asked to consult Mr J H Johnson (of Mountains – his father) for his opinion as to the Council's powers. Mr J H Johnson was a partner in the London firm of solicitors, Messrs J H and J G Johnson of 47 Lincoln's Inn Fields. On 17th January 1895 the Clerk gave details of the advice received – it was for Tonbridge Rural District Council to "compel the owners to make good the roads". The Council agreed to

request the District Council …
> "… to get the roads … leading from the London High Road (now the B245) … to Mount Pleasant, the roads at Mount Pleasant, and the road leading from the Hildenborough and Shipbourne Road (now Riding Lane) to Mount Pleasant to be put in order."

The problems at Mount Pleasant were again considered at the Council meeting of 18th April 1895 when it was reported that repair of the road "was now under the consideration of the District Council". The Chairman, Mr Charles Fitch Kemp was asked to see the Rev. Stewart Savile of Hollanden Park (later known as Hildenborough Hall, then Hardwick House and, in 2016, the Raphael Centre), the landowner, about a suggested new road from "Mount Pleasant to the Shipbourne Road" (now Riding Lane). It was reported that Mr Savile had written complaining about …
> "… the accumulation of rubbish from residences at Mount Pleasant near his plantation into which it was thrown."

Mr Fitch Kemp would also discuss this matter with Mr Savile.

At the Council meeting on 25th June 1895 it was reported that proposals for the new road from Mount Pleasant to the Shipbourne Road were being drawn up. As for the existing roads around Mount Pleasant, the Rural District Council had applied to the Local Government Board to have "the powers of the Private Street Works Act 1892" with regard to "certain private streets in the parish of Hildenborough". A Public Inquiry would be held at "the Working Mens' Institute, Hildenborough" on 2nd July 1895 to hear evidence in the matter. The Chairman was asked to attend, the Council …
> "… agreeing unanimously that such repairs were desirable for the good of the Parish."

Mr Fitch Kemp reported to the Council on 25th July about the Inquiry where some owners of land adjacent to Mount Pleasant, represented by Messrs Gorham and Warner, objected to the application for the roads in the area to be repaired. The Inspector, Mr Codrington, stated that he would recommend to the Local Government Board that "the necessary powers should be granted" except that "the road behind the Half Moon" should be excluded from those requiring repairs.

At the same meeting it was agreed that after Mr Savile had given his formal consent to the construction of the new road from Mount Pleasant to the Shipbourne Road the Clerk should seek the approval of Tonbridge Rural District Council. The road, which would replace the existing footpath would be "not less than 20 feet broad". The Council meeting on 26th September 1895 decided to seek approval for the proposal at a Parish Meeting. The new road should include a footpath. Further progress was delayed at Mr Savile's request, the Council was informed on 31st October.

Early in 1896 the Council again discussed Mount Pleasant. At the meeting of 10th January the Clerk was directed to write to Tonbridge Rural District Council …
> "… drawing their attention to the bad state of the roads at Mount Pleasant, and to the fact that no repairs had yet been effected on the said roads."

The Rural District Council's reply was reported to the meeting of 5th March …
> "… the matter rested with the District Surveyor who was preparing the necessary plans prior to the Clerk serving notices on the frontagers to do the work."

The Minutes of the meeting of 21st April 1896 show that the work on the new road from Mount Pleasant to the Shipbourne Road had started. There was the problem of "storm water from the new roads" but Mr Savile "had given permission for it to be turned into his pit".

As a public footpath was to be diverted, permission had to be obtained and the Minutes for the meeting of 21st May contain the text of Mr Savile's formal request – this runs to two foolscap pages. The Parish Council was asked to approve the planned diversion and to ..

> "... request the Rural District Council for the District of Tonbridge being the Highway Authority for the said District (of which the said parish of Hildenborough forms part) to apply for two Justices of the Peace to view the said public footway so proposed to be stopped up diverted and turned as aforesaid and the said public highway to be substituted in lieu thereof and to do all other acts and things pursuant to the Statutes 5 & 6 William IV cap. 50 section 85, and 56 and 57 Vict. cap. 73 sec 13 or any other Statute enabling you the said Parish Council in that behalf."

At the meeting of the Parish Council on 28th July 1896 the Chairman agreed to write to the Rural District Council to ask if the "elaborate scheme" proposed could be modified and on 26th August he reported that the Rural District Council ...

> "...could not alter the plans as to the curbing and paving of the footpaths as they felt obliged to follow the course adopted as to the paths and roads in other parts of the district especially as the roads repairable by the district were repaired out of the common fund."

Work on the Mount Pleasant roads continued well into 1897 but on 21st January the Chairman reported that "they would shortly be completed". There is a further reference to the "New Road from Mount Pleasant to Shipbourne Road" (now Riding Lane), in the record of the meeting held on 15th February 1901 when ...

> "... the thanks of the Council were due to the Reverend F A Stewart Savile for the improvement he had made in this new road.

Lighting the Village

From time to time the Parish Council discussed the possibility of street lights for Hildenborough. The matter was raised at a meeting held on 27th November 1903 but it was pointed out ...

> "... that no lamps could be erected without the sanction of a Parish Meeting and also that it was doubtful if the necessary sanction for lights in the village would be obtained by people living in other parts of the parish."

It was agreed that nothing could be done but the Chairman, Mr Charles Fitch Kemp pointed out that the Parish would be very grateful...

> "... if any Parishioner would be disposed to place two or three lamps in the village."

Lighting was discussed a year later at the 25th November meeting of the Council. It was suggested that a public meeting should be called for "testing the feeling of parishioners" and to ascertain if they would be willing to subscribe "for the erection and maintenance of such lamps". The question of the "area to be lighted" was considered but the matter was taken no further as...

> "... it was felt that there were very considerable difficulties in the matter..."

The Coronation of Edward VII, 1902

The social event of 1902 was the celebration of Edward VII's Coronation, scheduled for early July. At its meeting on 21st April the Council set up a Coronation Committee to plan the festivities in the village. The same meeting considered a letter from Mr Edwin Hendry, the village postmaster...

> "... requesting the Council to petition the Postmaster General to allow the hours of business at the post office on Coronation Day to be as on Sundays – namely

from 8 am to 10 am for the receipt and despatch of telegrams and from 8am to 10.45am for the despatch of letters."
The Council unanimously agreed to Mr Hendry's request.

Consternation!
The village celebrations were due to be held in early July but at the Council's meeting on 24th June the Chairman, Mr Charles Fitch Kemp made an announcement. The Minutes read:

> "The Chairman referred in appropriate terms to the lamentable illness of His Majesty the King, announced in the afternoon's papers, and stated that under the circumstances he felt it would be impossible to carry out the proposed festivities on Saturday week."

The King, aged 60, underwent an operation for appendicitis, a serious matter at that time for someone of his age. The Council members took the optimistic view that the Coronation would take place after Edward's recovery and resolved...

> "... that a sum not exceeding 2d in the £ on the rateable value of the parish be allowed out of the rates for the purpose of defraying the expenses in connection with the proposed Coronation festivities..."

The Chairman reported that the Local Government Board had authorised such expenditure by Councils. A 2d rate would yield about £140 whilst the estimated cost of the festivities was £120-5-0.

The Council's optimism was justified and a special meeting was held on 25th July to consider when the festivities would be held...

> "... in view of the rapid recovery of His Majesty the King, and a day having now been fixed for the Coronation of His Majesty - namely Saturday August 9th."

It was agreed that the village celebrations should be held on Coronation Day itself.

"This is Hildenborough from A-Z" (revised edition 2006/7 originally published by the Parish Council in 1994) outlines the programme and gives details of some of the items purchased for the celebratory tea whilst the Council Minutes for 5th September 1902 give a breakdown of the cost:

		£	s	d
The Vicar (Rev. J Stone)	Materials for village decoration	1	19	8
E Hendry	Materials for village decoration	3	18	7
W Holmwood	Poles, wire, arch etc.	2	18	2
Mist	Hire of flags	1	10	0
Mist	Decoration of field	5	15	0
Austin	Hire of tents and teas for 710 adults and 347 children	85	7	4
The Vicar	Payments to old people	2	2	6
Powell	Fireworks and torches	21	5	4
The Vicar	Punch & Judy Show	6	3	4
Kennard	Conveyance of band	1	10	0
C H Scott	Maidstone band	10	1	0
A & N Stores	Children's Coronation Mugs	6	17	6
	Total	149	8	5

The Council approved these accounts and agreed to levy a precept for £150 on the Overseers of the Poor. Further accounts were presented for payment at the meeting on 5th December 1902.

Free Press for printing circulars	£1-13-6
Wodderspoon for printing circulars convening meeting	8-6

There is an interesting insight into the financial affairs of the Council in the Minutes for the meeting of 27th November 1903 when the Treasurer, Mr Robert Wingate, reported on the recently completed Audit for the year 1902-03. The payments included:

£11 towards the Tonbridge Joint Burial Committee
£2-3-6 for "Establishment charges"
£10-1-11 for allotments
£151-10-5 for the Coronation celebrations

The total expenditure was £174-15-10 whilst the total receipts, which included £14-4-2 as allotment rents and the balance at the start of the year of £52-1-5 together with the £150 from the Overseers, amounted to £216-5-7, leaving a net balance of £41-9-9.

The Licensing Act, 1904

On 27th January 1905 the Council held a special meeting to consider a letter from the Justices' Clerk at Tonbridge. In accordance with the 1904 Licensing Act the Council was asked to submit any observations about the number of public houses in the Parish and the manner in which they were run. Two councillors, Mr Charles Fitch Kemp and Mr Robert Wingate, did not attend since, as magistrates, they were members of the Licensing Committee of the Justices of the Peace.

After a lengthy discussion the Council drew up a Report which concluded that the current situation was satisfactory. It was noted that there were seven public houses in the Parish.

The New Cock	The Old Cock	The Half Moon
The Flying Dutchman	The Gate Inn	The Grenadier
The Plough		

Four were on "the main high road between Sevenoaks and Tonbridge" but it was considered that in a "parish of over 1,400", seven public houses was not too many. They were well scattered with four …

"… being practically on the borders – namely The Grenadier on the North East, the New Cock on the North West, The Plough on the South and the Flying Dutchman on the East. The Gate Inn is at the Railway Station, and the Half Moon in the centre of the Village."

Commenting on the proximity of the Old Cock and the New Cock "on the high road towards Sevenoaks" it was pointed out that …

"… these are houses more especially used by the heavy road traffic, such as carters and carriers."

The Councillors considered that all the inns are "properly conducted and they are not aware of any complaint against order or morality". Members were "not disposed to suggest any alterations in the existing state of the licenses".

As of 2016, two of the seven inns no longer survive: The New Cock Inn was redeveloped for housing in 2005 whilst the Grenadier in Riding Lane (then Shipbourne Road) was destroyed by a bomb in 1942. The Old Cock is known as The Cock Horse whilst The Gate Inn has become an Indian Bar and Restaurant known as The Cinnamon.

Drainage Problems at Oakhill

Oakhill House, now owned by Fidelity International, was from time to time mentioned in Parish Council Minutes. The home of Sir Richard Nicholson, it was reported on 15th April 1897 that a letter had been received from Tonbridge Rural District Council "in respect of the drainage" of properties at "Oak Hill which flowed into the road drain". The District

Surveyor attended the meeting and the Council agreed to write to Sir Richard...
"... asking him if he could see his way to deal with his own drainage and thus
save the Parish the heavy expense involved in a second drainage system."
Sir Richard's reply was read to the Council on 3rd May 1897. He wrote that the problem
didn't lie with the Parish Council. It was a matter for the Rural District Council ...
"... who were the authority to carry out the work and that he considered all that
was requisite was to pipe and trap the present drain."
The Chairman, Mr Charles Fitch Kemp, had spoken to Sir Richard and it was hoped
that the matter could be resolved "without the necessity of incurring the expense of a new
drainage system".

Clearly the problems at Oakhill were not solved promptly as the Minutes for the
Council meeting on 4th January 1898 show that members were becoming increasingly
concerned about it. Their concerns were heightened by reports of a "case of typhoid at
Oak Lodge" (at the corner of the B245 and Leigh Road). Mr Robert Wingate, a member
of both the Parish and Rural District Councils, explained that the matter was in the hands
of the Local Government Board. This had condemned the drain at Oakhill "as a nuisance
and had suggested three alternative methods of dealing with the sewage":
1. Pumping the sewage from the houses into "the existing Hildenborough
system".
2. Pumping the sewage into "the sewers of Tonbridge Urban District Council".
3. Constructing "a cesspit with an overflow on the land".
Mr Wingate said that the Rural District Council had been asked to employ an expert
to consider the problem and report back to the Board. He said that Sir Richard Nicholson
had been asked if he would separate his water drainage from his sewage drains. The
Parish Council agreed to write to the Rural District Council urging immediate action. On
11th March it was reported that the engineer appointed by the Rural District Council had
recommended that the sewage "should be pumped into the existing system of sewage".

The Local Government Board was due to hold an Inquiry on 30th June but the Clerk
at the Council's meeting the evening before expressed the view that all the Inquiry would
do would be to determine "whether there was a nuisance existing or not". It would not be
looking at remedies. The Chairman commented that there was general agreement that:
− The ditch should be covered
− Proper pipes should be laid down
− Sewage should be taken down to the Medway "and looked after properly there
and kept clear of the Tonbridge water-shed".
On 17th January 1899 the Council heard about "the offensive smell at Oak Hill". The
Sanitary Inspector had been consulted and efforts were being made "to stop the nuisance
as efficiently and speedily as possible".

The Council met on 12th July to consider the Rural District Council's drainage scheme
for Hildenborough. Members were not impressed, agreeing "to oppose such scheme in
toto". No reasons are given in the Minutes but the scheme went ahead as, according to the
record of the meeting held on 30th January 1900...
"... Mr Wingate reported that the District Council had received the sanction of
the Local Government Board to raise a loan of £6,905 to carry out the new
drainage scheme for Hildenborough."
"Disposal of the sewage at Oak Hill" was again discussed by the Council on 23rd December
1901 but no details are recorded. The Minutes for the meeting of 18th April 1906 note
that the Rural District Council had adopted plans for dealing with the problem of sewage
in the whole of the parish and was about to agree a contract for the work to be undertaken.
This wasn't the end of the matter as the record for 19th April 1907 meeting shows that the

Rural District Council had informed the Parish Council that the Local Government Board proposed to hold another "Enquiry" into the Hildenborough sewage scheme. The first Minute book for the period from 1894 until September 1908 doesn't have any report of what happened at the Inquiry or of the conclusions reached by the Inspector.

A "Bathing Place" for the Parish?

From time to time the Parish Council considered the possibility of establishing a place for swimming – either using a pond or even building a swimming pool next to the Institute. The latter idea was ruled out in March 1897 on grounds of expense.

At its very first meeting on 20th December 1894...

"... it was suggested that it would be desirable to furnish a bathing place for the boys of the Parish, and that this might be attained by procuring and cleaning out a pond for that purpose but no resolution was arrived at on the subject."

The idea was next considered at the Council meeting on 26th September 1895 when the Chairman, Mr Charles Fitch Kemp, suggested...

"... that the pit below the school belonging to Lord Derby seemed a suitable site" but it would need to be cleaned out.

The matter was referred to the Allotments Committee and on 21st October the Council heard that two members of the Committee, Mr H H Hitchcock and Mr R Bosanquet had ...

"... inspected the proposed pond and ... had tested the depth and found it about six feet and that they had come to the conclusion that it was not a place they could recommend on account of the expense which would have to be incurred to render it suitable for use."

The suggestion of a "Village Bathing Place" wasn't mentioned again in the Minutes until 22nd April 1903 when ...

"...it was suggested that as it did not seem practicable to use the Council's money, subscriptions should be asked for to provide a suitable pond..."

After some discussion the matter was dropped.

Telephones

In the early twentieth century few people in Hildenborough would have had a telephone but some parishioners were concerned by the increasing number of telephone poles which were appearing in the village. The matter was raised at the Council meeting held on 21st March 1902 when there was ..

"... a long discussion ... as to the telephone posts which were being placed through the village to the station."

The Clerk, Mr G W Johnson, reported receipt of a written objection from a parishioner. He said that he had written to the Kent County Council "in respect to the High Road" (B245) and to the Rural District Council "in respect to the by-road to the station." The County Council had agreed to the erection "of a line of telephone posts" but any proposals from the Parish Council as to siting would be "carefully considered". The Rural District Council had replied that the Council ...

"... had no power to insist on the removal of the telephone posts or that the wires should be laid underground."

The Parish Council concluded that "the power of objection rested more with private individuals than with the Council". The Chairman, Mr Charles Fitch Kemp, undertook "to stipulate that the poles should be painted white".

Powder Mills

The Powder Mills had been in existence since the early 19th Century and in the Minutes for the Council meeting on 28th July 1896 there is the following reference to them:

"Mr Cunliffe suggested that the Parish Council should be represented in any enquiry that might be made before the Magistrates of Tonbridge in reference to the manufacture of cordite and gun cotton at Messrs. Curtis & Harvey's Powder Mills."

Mr Roger Cunliffe of Meopham Bank was the Council's Treasurer. There is no record in the Minutes of what followed the enquiry by the magistrates.

Snippets from the Minutes

The Jubilee Fountain of 1887

On 25th June 1895 the Parish Council agreed to pay the water rate for the Jubilee Fountain amounting to £1 p.a. "as this was an object for the general benefit of the Parish" provided that the Council had the necessary powers to do so.

Lamps

Mr Edwin Hendry, a Councillor, "called attention to the fact that no lights were provided in the National Schools". As they were now required, the Council on 26th September 1895 authorised him "to buy two good lamps". Mr Hendry presented an account for £3-6-9 for the purchase to the Council on 15th November 1895. Payment was approved by the Council – which used to meet at the school.

Tonbridge Gas Co.

The Company wished to make an application to the Board of Trade for "a provisional order" to extend the area for the provision of gas in the parish to include "the houses of Bourne Place, Nizels and Oakhurst". Mr Warner, "agent to the Company, and Mr Donaldson, the Company's Engineer" attended the Council meeting of 16th December 1898. The Engineer said that …

"… gas from the Company's works could probably be supplied in Hildenborough from about 3/9 to 4/- per 1000 cubic feet."

The Council agreed to support the Company's application.

"Sign Post Watts Cross"

It was pointed out at the meeting on 16th December 1898 that it was desirable to have "a direction to Hildenborough Station" painted on the signpost at Watts Cross. The matter was referred to Kent County Council.

The Queen Victoria National Memorial

Mr Charles Fitch Kemp, the Council Chairman, told the Council meeting of 16th April 1901 that he had …

"… received a communication from the Lord Lieutenant of the County enclosing cards for obtaining subscriptions from all classes. The Council resolved to give all assistance in its power."

The Unemployed

At the Council's meeting on 13th November 1905 the Chairman…

"… referred to the gift of the Queen to the unemployed and invited a discussion on the question more particularly as applied to the parish of Hildenborough and arising from this Mr Wingate spoke on the question of underfed children in the Elementary Schools."

The Queen was Queen Alexandra (1844-1925), consort of George V (1865-1935, King 1910-1935).

Water Supply

On 13th November 1905 the Council agreed to contact Tonbridge Water Company …

> "… informing them that the general supply at Hildenborough was not satisfactory, asking them the reason for this and how soon it would be remedied."

The complaint related to "insufficient pressure of water". The Council was told on 28th March 1906 that …

> "… when the new engine was completed the pressure at Hildenborough would be very considerably increased."

On 18th April 1906 the water company reported that the new pumping engine had been fixed and that it was "anxious to try the hose in front of the church at an early date". At that meeting, the Clerk, Mr G W Johnson, reported…

> "… that the pressure of water for the church organ was still at times most unsatisfactory."

Postscript

In the Spring of 1898 the Parish was greatly affected by an accident near Hildenborough railway station in which two platelayers, George Upton and James Goldsmith, were killed. Mr Charles Fitch Kemp, the Parish Council Chairman, and Mr Richard Bosanquet, a Councillor, were both on the subsequent Inquest Jury. It was this jury, which included the Vicar, the Rev'd RLG Pidcock, supported by the Gardening Association, chaired by Mr Bosanquet, which launched an appeal for funds to pay for the memorial to the victims. Until the early 21st century the wording on it was visible and in 2016 Hildenborough History Society decided to launch an appeal to restore the memorial. This appeal was successful.

On 16th July 2016 the memorial, carefully restored by Messrs Burslem of Bells Yew Green, stonemasons since 1880, was re-dedicated by the Vicar, the Rev'd Tim Saiet. Perhaps Burslem had renovated a memorial which they had originally installed in 1898. The memorial was unveiled by Judith Upton, Great granddaughter of George Upton. Earlier, Gareth Owen, Great great grandson of George, had unveiled a commemorative plaque in the booking hall of the station.

The appeal raised sufficient funds to allow a cheque for £600 to be presented to Mr Richard Evans, a trustee of Woking Homes, first opened in 1885 as the London and South Western Railway Servants' Orphanage. Now a care home for the elderly, the majority of the residents are retired railway people or their spouses.

The story of the tragedy of 1st April 1898 was told in the March 2016 edition of the Parish Magazine 'Keys' and, with kind permission, is reprinted here.

"Shocking Railway Accident", 1898

The London train is due. All eyes on Platform 1 at Hildenborough station peer down the line expecting to see the train emerge from round the corner several hundred yards away. Probably none of the waiting passengers realises that near that corner there was a tragic accident resulting in the death of two villagers working as platelayers. The accident occurred on 1st April, 1898 and the details were recounted in the Tonbridge Free Press. Although a local newspaper, this covered international and national as well as local news. Considerable space was devoted to the …

"Shocking Railway Accident, Platelayers killed at Hildenborough"

It was reported that... "A very painful sensation was caused in the village of Hildenborough on Friday morning by a terrible tragedy on the South Eastern Railway near Barleycorn Bridge, situated about half a mile below the station..."

A gang of three platelayers was working on the line that morning. The team was made up of George Goldsmith, the foreman, James Goldsmith, his 19 year old son, and George Upton, aged 30. Around 9.30 each morning, two trains passed each other near the Bridge. The London-bound train was described as a "very heavy one", which travelled up the incline "under a full head of steam" with a deafening roar. The second train, an express which had left Charing Cross at 8.20am, ran through Hildenborough down the incline with steam off, thus creating little noise.

On the morning of the accident the noisy London bound train passed the platelayers, who continued with their work, but George Goldsmith, who was standing between the other two men, looked up to see the train from London rapidly approaching from round the curve 40 yards away at an estimated speed of 45mph. He shouted to the others who had their backs to the approaching train but they failed to hear the warning above the noise of the up train which had just passed. James Goldsmith and George Upton were knocked down and killed outright. The fireman on the express train saw what happened and the train was pulled up. The driver then took it to Tonbridge. There the Station Master called a doctor, Dr Watts, "who proceeded in a brake van to the scene of the catastrophe". The bodies were removed to the Gate Hotel next to Hildenborough station.

The "Free Press" reported that... "The shocking affair has cast quite a gloom over the village where both men were well known, and much sympathy is felt for the bereaved young wife of Upton, and especially for George Goldsmith, whose anguish as he witnessed his son's tragic death can better be imagined than described".

The Inquest

The Inquest was held next day, Saturday 2nd April at the Gate Hotel by the Coroner, Mr Buss and a jury of thirteen. Mr Charles Fitch Kemp of Foxbush, Chairman of the recently established Parish Council, was elected foreman. The other jurors were:

The Vicar, the Rev. R L G Pidcock, Mr R A Bosanquet, a Parish Councillor, of Mardens, Philpots Lane, Mr J H Johnson of Mountains, Noble Tree Road, Mr M C Morris, Headmaster of the local school (*between 1897 and 1913*), Mr A T Heath, Mr W Cheesman, Mr E Ham, Mr W Homewood, Mr E Hodge, Mr G Evans, Mr H Grove and Mr M Biddle.

In attendance were Superintendent Bartlett of Tonbridge Police, Mr W H Harvey, the Station Master at Tonbridge, and Mr Annand, the Hildenborough Station Master.

Having viewed the bodies, the Jury then heard evidence. The first witness was George Goldsmith of Foxbush Cottages, the foreman platelayer and father of James whose health, including sight and hearing, was described as good. (*Foxbush Cottages are a pair of listed cottages, and lie between the Post Office and the Church, although the right hand one has been renamed Beaufort Cottage*). The other platelayer was George Upton, a married man of Kemp's Cottages, Shipbourne Road. (*Shipbourne Road was the original name of Riding Lane and Kemp's Cottages, a row of twelve owned by Mr Fitch Kemp, stood between what is now Thompson's Chemist and the school*). His health was also said to be good.

George Goldsmith described how the platelayers had begun work the previous morning at six o'clock. All went well until about half past nine. The 8.20am express train from London, which did not stop at Hildenborough, was due at the same time as a fast train to London. The trains usually passed at the point where the platelayers were working. The witness stated that they all saw the London bound train coming. Shortly afterwards he called to his colleagues to get out of the way of the approaching express train but they didn't hear him. He couldn't say if the train whistled as it passed Hildenborough station. The curve was so sharp that it blocked the view of the driver who could not see the platelayers. They would not have seen the oncoming train. Had the driver seen the men he would have sounded his whistle but, said Mr Goldsmith, this would not have been heard above the noise of the London-bound train.

Mr Goldsmith, having witnessed the accident, went to Hildenborough station to ask for help from the Station master, Mr Annand, who sent a telegram to the Inspector at Tonbridge. Shortly afterwards, a doctor was sent to the scene but it was clear that George Upton and James Goldsmith had both died instantly. In his view, Mr Goldsmith considered that the driver was not at fault. He was asked by a juryman if he considered that he should have been supplied with a whistle. The Jury considered adding a rider to their verdict recommending that foremen be supplied with whistles but decided against it, as it would have made no difference in this case.

The driver of the express was Joe Dowsey, a man with 21 years' experience who knew the line well. The train was travelling at the regulation speed of 45 to 46 mph when the accident occurred. He stated that had the London bound train not been passing he would have seen the men on the line.

Myles Tully, the fireman, saw one of the men knocked down and the train was brought to a halt within 150 yards of the accident. He was sure the driver had sounded the whistle but did not think that the men could have heard it. He agreed with George Goldsmith that the up train would have obstructed the view of anyone looking out from the express train.

A Tonbridge doctor, Dr H J Manning Watts, arrived on the scene about thirty minutes after the accident. He described to the Jury the injuries suffered by James Goldsmith and George Upton. They would have died instantly.

The Coroner in summing up said that the accident was without doubt due to the up train obstructing the view of the driver of the express from London. The noise of the London-bound train had prevented the deceased from hearing the warning shouted by George Goldsmith. The Jury returned a verdict of "Accidental Death" and expressed the opinion that no-one was to blame for the accident. The Coroner agreed with the remarks of Mr Fitch Kemp, the foreman, who said that they ought to express their sympathy with the families of the two men...

"Both had lived in the parish for a good many years, and bore respectable characters, and the Jury all deeply deplored the accident".

The Gardening Association Meeting

It is clear the whole village was deeply moved by this tragic accident of 1st April, 1898. There is evidence of this in the report of the Gardening Association's meeting at the Institute on Easter Monday. Several jurymen were members of the Association which had been formed two years earlier. Richard Bosanquet, a member of the newly created Parish Council, was the Chairman, whilst Mr A T Heath was the Secretary. Also present were fellow jurymen Mr G Evans, Mr W Cheesman and the Vicar, the Rev. RLG Pidcock. The meeting started with the routine gardening business. It was announced that at the next monthly meeting there would be a prize of 1/6d for the "best Exhibit of salad (three varieties)", and "prizes of 1/6d and 1/- for the best exhibit of two varieties chosen from rhubarb, cabbage and broccoli". The Station master, Mr Annand, had also offered a prize of "a cockerel and pullet, value 15/-, for the best two pound jar of pickled onions, pickled cabbage and mixed pickles, the produce to be grown and prepared by the exhibitors. He had further offered an extra prize of a sitting of black or buff Orpington eggs (a breed of chicken) to the exhibitor of the best eggs in show".

The Chairman then raised the matter of the recent railway accident and invited Mr W Cheesman, one of the jurymen, to make a statement. At the suggestion of the Jury, an appeal for funds to support the bereaved families had been launched. This appeal had been "met with hearty support from all classes of the community". Over 150 donations had been received and no-one had refused to contribute. Mr Cheesman, whose statement was interrupted several times by enthusiastic calls of "hear, hear", said that it was hoped that some of the money raised would pay for a headstone in memory of the two railwaymen.

Mr Cheesman had been asked what the South Eastern Company was going to do for the families. He reported that they were not bound to do anything – "by the Company's rules and regulations the bereaved ones could not claim a penny in compensation". He hoped that they could be induced to offer the families some help. Mr Cheesman pointed out that when the line opened in 1868 no-one wanted to be a foreman of the platelayers for the area of Barleycorn Bridge "owing to the danger incurred by the curve". George Goldsmith was eventually persuaded to take the job and he had worked there for 23 years without encountering an accident... "and now the blow had fallen with such terrible force upon him. What could be worse for a father to see his son smashed to death before his eyes? Surely, in such a case, the Company ought to do something". These words were greeted with sympathetic cries of "hear, hear!" Mr Bosanquet said he was sure that the Jury, through their foreman, Mr Fitch Kemp, a man of influence, would bring pressure to bear on the Company if necessary.

On 7th May, 1898, the Tonbridge Free Press reported that the fund for the railwaymen had reached £71-6s-6d (*today's equivalent would be £7,096*). George Upton and James Goldsmith were buried together in the Village Churchyard. Until recently the wording on their headstone was visible:

To the Glory of God and in Memory of
GEORGE UPTON Aged 30 years
- AND –
JAMES GOLDSMITH Aged 19 years
Two Platelayers in the employment of the SOUTH EASTERN RAILWAY
Who were killed on the 1st April 1898 while engaged in their duty.
"in the midst of life we are in death"
THIS MEMORIAL IS ERECTED BY THE PARISHIONERS

Part 2 – 1909-1924

List of Councillors and Officers

Those who served at various times during the period as Members and/or officials are listed below. The list includes the names of the first two women to serve as Councillors.

Mr Edgar A	Auld
Mr John	Banks
Mr Thomas	Bassett
Mrs Margaret H	Brown (Mrs Tasker Brown)
Mr Albert	Brunger
Mr William	Clark
Mr A W	Cooksey
Mr John T	Fellowes Wilson
Mr Edwin	Francis
Mr Edwin	Hendry
Mr Henry	Hills
Mr Obediah	Jenner
Mr George W	Johnson
Mr Charles	Kemp
Mr James	Killick
Mr William J	King
Mr Sidney U	Lawson
Mr John	Mackney
Mr Charles J	Meade
Mr Mesech C	Morris
Mr Reginald J G	Nevins
Mr Edward L	Panes
Mr Alfred	Smith
Miss Ruth	Turnbull

Chairman	Mr G W Johnson	1907-1937
Clerks	Mr M C Morris	1907-1913
	Mr S U Lawson	1913-1917
	Mr R F Hodder	1917-1921
	Mr F Bampton	1921-1923
	Mr E B Budding	1923-1929

Introduction

The second Minute Book for Hildenborough Parish Council covered the period from 10th March 1909 up to 1st May 1924. Meetings were usually held in the Drill Hall or the adjoining Institute but some early meetings were held across the road at the school. From July 1923 each meeting commenced with prayers. The Minutes for each begin with a list of those present but absences were rarely recorded. In January 1920 the first woman took her seat on the Council, co-opted to fill a casual vacancy. This pioneer was Miss Ruth Turnbull but two years later she wrote…

> "… tendering her resignation from the Parish Council on account of her marriage" to Dr Reginald Langdon Down.

39

There was one other woman member during the period – Mrs Tasker Brown, elected in April 1922.

Only two Councillors served throughout the period. One was Mr J T Fellowes Wilson of Oak Lodge, opposite the "Flying Dutchman". The family is remembered in two roads off the nearby Leigh Road – Fellowes Way which leads to Wilson Close. The other was Mr George W Johnson who served on the Council from its inauguration in 1894 until he retired as Chairman in December 1937. In the early days Mr Johnson, who later became a Justice of the Peace, was the Council's unpaid Clerk and, in 1907, Treasurer. It was in that year that he became Chairman, succeeding the late Mr Charles Fitch Kemp.

Mr M C Morris and Mr S U Lawson were both Honorary Clerks but on 8th November 1917 Mr Lawson, the Clerk from 1913, stated that …

> "… owing to his absence from the parish in connection with war duties he would like the Parish Council to release him from his appointment as Honorary Clerk to the Council."

At the same meeting a letter from Mr R F Hodder, the Headmaster of the local school, was read. He had been appointed an Assistant Overseer on 24th March 1916 at an annual salary of £26 but he was now….

> "… asking for an increase in his salary … on the grounds that, compared with other parishes, he considered his work was underpaid."

The Council, in accepting Mr Lawson's resignation as unpaid Clerk, decided to offer the position to Mr Hodder…

> "… at a salary of £9 per annum, making a total of £35 per annum for the joint appointment of Assistant Overseer and Clerk … to include the duties of Allotments Rent Collector…"

Mr Hodder came to the Council meeting on 12th November 1917 and agreed to accept the joint appointment. Thus, the position of Clerk became salaried and was held by someone who was not on the Council.

The Minutes of the meeting of 24th March 1916 at which Mr Hodder had been appointed Assistant Overseer set out his duties in that capacity:

> "… to make out the rates, the jury lists and the parliamentary voters, to collect the burial rate and the special sanitary rate and post all notices and generally to perform all such duties as appertain to and are incident to the office of Overseers of the Poor and to collect the allotment rents."

Mr Hodder was required to "enter into a Bond for £100."

Each year the Council elected two Overseers from the Parish with the bulk of the work being done by the salaried Assistant Overseer. Mr Hodder replaced Mr E Francis in this post. At the Annual Meeting held on 15th April 1916 Mr Edwin Hendry and Mr E A Auld, both Councillors, were elected as Overseers. Mr Hendry retired from the position that he had held for 33 years in 1921.

Pounds, shillings and pence (£.s.d.)

Each Council meeting was asked to approve accounts for payment and examples are given here.

Conversions: 1/- (one shilling = 12d – pennies) = 5p
2/6 (a half crown) = 12½p   5/- (a crown) = 25p

Month	Year	Item	£	s	d
June	1909	Poor rate	3	3	
		Sanitary Rate			7½

May	1910	Kent County Council – Voters' list		1	1
		Returning Officer – election fees		13	3
July	1914	SE Rail – carriage		1	9
March	1915	Sanitary Rate			5¼
		Hire of School Room for Council Meeting		3	6
January	1917	Gate on allotments		18	4
May	1918	Roneo – printing notices re: seed potatoes		5	0
January	1922	Premium on Clerk's Guarantee Policy		4	0
January	1924	E Stanford Ltd – map for Drill Hall plus carriage	6	11	6

The Clerk to the Council and the Assistant Overseer were required on taking office to "enter into a Bond". In the case of Mr Hodder, Clerk between 1917 and 1921, this was for £100. The Minutes in later years show that a premium of four shillings was paid by the Council to maintain what was, in effect, an insurance policy to protect the Council's funds from misappropriation.

The Coronation of George V, 22nd June 1911

In 1910 George succeeded Edward VII as King and his Coronation took place in the summer of 1911. The Council levied a precept on the Overseers for £200, a sum which would cover "the Coronation Celebrations". That was on 25th April 1911 and the Minutes for the next meeting, on 6th July, give details of the expenditure and some idea of how the parish celebrated the event.

		£	s	d
A W Gamage	Flags etc	6	16	3
H J Bartram	Band	30	0	0
Free Press Ltd	Printing	3	17	7
Hills Bros	Carting & hire	1	14	0
W A Turnbull	Mugs & beakers	5	16	3
The Rev. J Stone (vicar)	Allowance to 23 invalids	2	17	6
Seal Austen & Barnes	Lights	2	7	6
J Woodman	Devices		10	6
S Hitchcock	Labour etc	1	10	0
W Austen	Catering	94	10	0

The Protection of Wild Plants

The Council meeting of 6th July 1911 was given details of a letter from Kent County Council reporting that they had received applications from …
> "… certain parish councils for the making of a Bye Law prohibiting with proper exceptions, the uprooting of wild plants from wayside banks and hedges."

The County Council asked …
> "… if the Parish Council considered the mischief aimed at by the proposed Bye Law arose in their area."

The Council unanimously agreed that "the mischief did arise" and the Clerk (Mr M C Morris) was asked to return the completed application form to the County Council.

The Clerk read a letter from Kent County Council to the Parish Council on 5th March 1912 drawing attention …
> "… to the new bye law prohibiting the uprooting of ferns and other plants growing in or on any wayside bank, hedge, common or other public place, under a penalty not exceeding £5."

The School

There are only a few references to the village school in the Parish Council's second Minute Book covering the years 1909 to 1924. The Headmaster between 1897 and 1913 was Mr M C Morris who was the Honorary Clerk to the Council between 1907 and 1913. Mr R F Hodder, Headmaster from 1914 to 1931, was the Clerk between 1917 and 1921. With a salary of £9 pa, Mr Hodder was the Council's first salaried Clerk.

At a Council meeting held in the school on 10th July 1912 the members considered a letter from Kent Education Committee …

"… which called attention to the desirability of there being at least one lady upon each board of School Managers. It was pointed out by the Chairman that there was already one lady manager for Hildenborough School."

The meeting then re-elected Mr H H Hitchcock as a manager for a further three years.

On 10th November 1915 Mr J T Fellowes Wilson took over as the Council's representative on "the Committee of Management of the Hildenborough Church of England Schools". Records show that he was appointed for a further term on 14th July 1921. On 27th July 1923 the Council was informed that Mr Fellowes Wilson "retires by effluxion of time". He was again re-elected.

The Council provided a representative on the Tonbridge School Attendance Committee and on 8th October 1913 members chose a replacement for the recently resigned Mr R J G Nevins. The Councillor elected in his place was Mr E A Auld.

The Council meeting on 2nd February 1914 was held in the club room of the Drill Hall – hitherto meetings had usually been held in the School. The meeting heard a report from the Clerk, Mr S U Lawson, that a letter had been received from …

"… Mr R F Hodder the schoolmaster, acting under instructions from the School Managers, saying that in future a charge of 1/6 per meeting must be made to the Parish Council for the use of the school room and that they must also make their own arrangements for the preparations and cleaning of the room."

Members unanimously agreed that in future the Council should meet in the Club Room of the Drill Hall at the inclusive charge of 2/6 per meeting.

Housing

Were more houses needed in Hildenborough? From time to time the Parish Council in conjunction with Tonbridge Rural District Council considered the question. On 6th February 1913 the Parish Council considered a letter from the Rural District Council asking if "… there was a need in the Parish for workmen's dwellings." This led to a discussion at the next meeting on 17th February. The Clerk reported that he had received …

"… from the Rural District Council's Surveyor plans and a few particulars of cottages which the Council proposed to build in parishes of the Union where additional houses were required. It was estimated that such houses could be let without loss at weekly rents of from 4/- to 4/9."

Mr George W Johnson, the Chairman, suggested that before considering the plans the Council should consider the question …

"Are additional cottages necessary?"

The Council was told that no applications "had been received from persons desirous of renting cottages". Various points were made in the discussion:

1. Mr W Clark felt that there was a real need for more cottages. He told of a man who could not get a cottage and was sleeping in a barn whilst his family were lodged in an already overcrowded house. Another man, he said, wishing to get

married, had been obliged to rent a house in Tonbridge. It was pointed out however that this man was an employee at the Powder Mills in the Parish of Leigh.

2. Mr J Killick stated that Messrs Curtis and Harvey of the Powder Mills "were arranging for the erection of some new cottages for their employees".

3. It was reported that the Rural District Council "contemplated erecting cottages on the Hilden Park estate".

4. Mr King stated that "there were cottages in the parish not fit for habitation".

5. There was a feeling that ...

"... they were by no means hostile to the erection of cottages for workmen if a need really existed... but there was an objection to doing so for those working outside the parish."

It was agreed to inform the Rural District Council that on the basis of information available there was no need for additional housing but if further evidence came to light the Parish Council would give further consideration to the matter.

On 25th February 1913 housing was again considered by the Parish Council with Mr Frank Harris, Surveyor to the Rural District Council, and Mr H Hills, Hildenborough's representative on the Rural District Council attending by invitation. Also present were "six Parochial Electors" – this is the only record of members of the public attending a Council meeting during the whole of the period of the early Minute books from 1894 up to May 1924.

Mr Harris explained that the Rural District Council's object ...

"... would be to provide cottages only for those workmen who, either because of low wages, say £1 or less, or because of large families, were unable to pay the increasing rents of privately owned cottages."

He pointed out that the Rural District Council's rules "as to letting would probably exclude people working outside the parish...". The Chairman, Mr G W Johnson stated that ...

"... an objection to the District Council's scheme was that there would be absolutely no parochial control."

Mr Harris assured the Parish Council that ...

"... the Rural District Council's sole desire was to supply a need if it existed. They had no wish to advocate anything unnecessary or extravagant."

The Parish Council asked the Rural District Council to publish notices...

"... asking persons having insufficient housing accommodation, or none at all, to communicate with the Clerk."

The Clerk reported to the Parish Council on 15th April 1913 that four applications had been received for "improved housing accommodation". Mr S U Lawson told fellow councillors that...

"... the family of a man working in the parish were obliged to remain in the workhouse because no cottage was available for them."

After lengthy discussion it was agreed to inform the Rural District Council that the number of applications did not justify "a housing scheme" but that "it would be desirable for the Rural District Council to build at least four" cottages "to provide for men earning low wages, say less than £1 per week".

Mr Harris, the Rural District Council's Surveyor attended the Parish Council meeting held on 2nd February 1914 when there was another lengthy discussion. He presented plans for four cottages which the Rural District Council proposed to erect. The Parish Council agreed to support...

"... the scheme for building four cottages with allotments with the option of increasing the number to 12 as required and will give their official support to the Local Government Board enquiry to be held in the parish..."

The Board's Inspector subsequently approved the Rural District Council's plans for the erection of 12 cottages.

The Council meeting on 17th March 1915 was informed that five applications had been received to rent the Rural District Council's four recently constructed cottages. It was agreed to send them to the Rural District Council "to deal with as they thought best".

Shortly after the end of the war the Parish and Rural District Councils again considered housing needs. On 7th January 1919 a letter from the Rural District Council was read asking how many...

"... working men's dwellings it is desirable should be built in this parish and, if needed in a particular part, in what part."

It was agreed to put up posters and deliver a leaflet to all houses:

"Hildenborough Parish Council
Working Men's Dwellings

The Parish Council desires to obtain information as to the necessity for providing additional dwellings for working men in this Parish. Any person desirous of giving such information is requested to communicate on or before 21st January with the Council's Clerk – Mr R F Hodder, The School House."

200 leaflets were to be printed – this gives an idea of the number of houses in the village at this time.

The Council set up a sub-committee to consider the response. It was asked to consider the following points:

1. The number of houses required – if any
2. Locality
3. Any details e.g. provision for old people
4. Are there properties likely to be condemned as uninhabitable?

On 22nd January the sub-committee met to consider the response to the leaflet. Members agreed to hear in person from Mr Alfred Smith of "Meadow Brook" – in April he was to join the Council. He made the following points:

1. "20-25 new cottages" were needed
2. There were cases of "people not marrying on account of lack of houses".
3. Certain unnamed houses should be condemned.

A letter from a farmer was read – he considered that "60 or 70 houses should be built". Definite applications for housing had been received from twelve people. The sub-committee concluded that there was a case for more housing and considered ...

"... that eight cottages would be sufficient for the present ... and recommended that they be erected on the ground already owned by the District Council in the Shipbourne Road" (now Riding Lane)

On 27th January the full Council endorsed the sub-committee's Report which, together with supporting evidence, was then sent to the Rural District Council.

At the next Council meeting on 29th March 1919, one of those held on a Saturday evening (!), the members considered a letter from Kent County Council in which the Parish Council was asked to let the County Council know the details of any ...

"... Ex-service men and women with some capital desirous of taking up cottage holdings."

The County Council asked to be informed of "land for sale or changing hands". The Clerk, Mr Hodder, was asked to put up a notice in the Post Office seeking the information.

On 23rd April 1919 the Council considered a complaint about ...

"... the confusion and inconvenience brought about through there being no system of numbering or naming the houses in the village."
The Clerk was asked to write to Tonbridge Rural District Council to see if that Council had the power to impose a system of identifying properties. On 12th June the reply was considered: the Rural District Council had no power and it was agreed to contact owners where necessary asking them to identify their properties voluntarily.

The Council meeting on 17th September 1919 heard from Mr Henry Hills, Hildenborough's representative on Tonbridge Rural District Council, that all building plots in the village had been approved. He was asked if "huts would be sanctioned" but replied that this would not meet with the approval of the Ministry of Health.

There was concern about the lack of progress in building the proposed cottages and at the Council meeting on 30th September the Clerk was asked to urge the Rural District Council...

"... to push forward with the Building of Cottages and at any rate to make a start with some on the ground owned by the Council in the Shipbourne Road." (Riding Lane)

On 14th July 1921 the Chairman of the Parish Council, Mr G W Johnson read a letter from the Surveyor of Tonbridge Rural District Council giving information about the "New Council Cottages":

	Basic Rent	Total Rent
Powder Mill Road site: 8 houses		
2 Parlour type houses, both let	9/3	15/1
6 Non-Parlour type houses, all let	7/6	12/3
Shipbourne Road Site: 6 houses		
6 Non-Parlour type houses all allotted to tenants		
2 ready for occupation about the 25th inst.	7/-	11/5
Crown Lands: 2 houses		
2 Parlour type houses shortly to be commenced		
Upper Cock: 2 houses		
Abandoned for the present		

A week later the Council was given clarification of the terms "Basic" and "Total" Rent ...

"... Basic Rent meant the net rent exclusive of Rates, Taxes, Water etc.. This is a fixed amount to which the fluctuating amounts of Rates etc. are added to make up the Total Rate."

Apart from considering the need for new houses in the village, the Council was also concerned with the state of existing properties. Following a Parish Meeting on 31st March 1914, at the Council meeting on 22nd April a Resolution was passed requesting action by the Rural District Council ...

"... it is alleged that there exist dwellings in the Parish where the water supply and the sanitary accommodation provided is either inefficient or sanitarily ineffective... "

The Council asks the Rural District Council ...

"... to take the necessary steps to require the owners of such dwellings to put them into a proper sanitary condition in accordance with the requirements and powers vested in the said Rural District Council."

Another Resolution passed at the same meeting asked the Rural District Council ...

"... to immediately undertake the removal and disposal of the refuse from all dwellings requiring it..."

The Council was so concerned about the "sanitary condition of the village" that at the

23rd July meeting a sub-committee was set up to look at the problem and report back to the full Council. It did so on 17th March 1915 but was not unanimous in its conclusions. The sub-committee was asked to reconsider its Report. A unanimous Report was presented to the Council on 26th March which agreed on a Resolution to be sent to Tonbridge Rural District Council...

"... in the opinion of this Council it is desirable to replace all closet apparatuses now hand-flushed with mechanical means, where there is a sufficient water supply and sewer and that all dwelling houses should be provided with proper drain sinks, or other necessary appliance for carrying refuse water from such buildings and be furnished with an adequate water supply."

The Rural District Council was asked to use their powers under the Public Health Amendment Act 1907 "to remedy these defects". It was reported on 21st April that the Rural District Council required detailed information about the properties concerned. It was agreed to leave the matter in the hands of Mr H Hills, then a member of both the Parish and Rural District Councils.

Mr Hills reported to the Parish Council on 10th November that the Rural District Council had not yet adopted the provision of the 1907 Act with regard to "water closets and sinks". He commented on the situation at the Club Cottages stating that...

"... it was impossible in this case to have the flushing system on account of the fear of polluting the stream and the absence of any draining system, ... these cottages were outside the sewage scheme".

Mr Hills also reported that with regard to "scavenging" (i.e. collecting refuse), the Rural District Council would do this monthly instead of fortnightly as hitherto.

"Cesspools" were a problem from time to time. For example, on 12th February 1920 the Councillors considered a complaint about "bad smells near the Council Cottage". The matter was referred to "the man who empties the cesspools". At the next Council meeting, on 22nd March it was reported that "complaints had been made as to a bad smell at Noble Tree Cross". This was probably due to "defective cesspool arrangements" at "Crossways". Miss Turnbull agreed to speak to Mrs Hills about this. A letter from Mrs Hills, one of the family of Mr Charles Fitch Kemp, the Council's first Chairman, was read at the next Council meeting on 22nd April 1920 assuring the Council that "the cesspool arrangements at 'Crossways' were now put right".

The Fire Brigade

One of the Parish Council's constant preoccupations was the Fire Brigade. The Hildenborough group of firemen came under the Tonbridge Brigade but this arrangement was often a cause of conflict.

The first meeting mentioned in the Council's second Minute Book was that held on 30th September 1908 and Mr Clark, one of the councillors, reported on the activities of the Brigade. He had purchased...

"... a thoroughly efficient Fire Manual, which he would be pleased to present to the Council, upon the condition that a suitable building was erected in which to store it."

He pointed out that more fire hydrants were needed in the village and suggested that new ones should be fixed in Mount Pleasant, near the school, with a third at Watts Cross.

The Council thanked Mr Clark for "his generous gift" and decided to set up a Fire Brigade sub-committee "to consider the following matters..."

1. The creation of a building in which to store the fire appliances
2. The purchase of two lengths of suction hose

3. The fixing of additional hydrants
The next Council meeting wasn't held until 14th April 1909 when a Report from the sub-committee was considered. Its three recommendations were approved by the Council:
1. The three hydrants as suggested should be fixed
2. The lowest tender for the purchase of two lengths of hose was accepted. This came from "Messrs Simonis & Co" for £4-15-0
3. A suitable building of "brick or galvanised iron" should be erected...
"... in the Institute garden, at a cost not exceeding £20, to be used as a house for the fire manual, and other appliances belonging to the Council."
The Chairman, Mr G W Johnson, assured the meeting...
"... of the co-operation of the Institute Trustees on the question of the building..."
On 29th June 1909 it was reported to the Council that the hydrants had been ordered and the hose purchased. The Institute Trustees had consented to the erection of the building upon the following terms:
1. The rent would be 5/- p.a.
2. The trustees could require the removal of the building having given three months' notice. Failure to remove it would result in the building becoming the property of the Institute.
The Council did not consider these terms to be acceptable and it was agreed to seek a 14 year lease. It then examined the tenders for the erection of the building from:

Mr W Cooper	£20	
Mr J Killick	Brick £21	iron £18
Mr L Standen	Brick £16-5-0	iron £15-10-0

It was agreed to accept Mr Standen's estimate for a brick building, erection to begin as soon as terms had been agreed with the Institute.
The Council meeting of 25th September heard that the Institute had agreed to a 14 year lease of that part of their garden needed for the Fire Station. The fixing of three fire hydrants ran into difficulties as on 10 February 1910 it was reported that ...
"... it was not within the powers of the Parish Council to incur expenditure for the fixing of hydrants. The Rural District Council however could, and probably would, if requested, obtain the necessary power."
The Council agreed to ask the Rural District Council to apply to the Local Government Board for the necessary power. The same meeting considered if there should be a written agreement with each fireman. No decision on this was taken but it was agreed to ask Tonbridge Urban District Council to amend its agreement with the Parish Council so that the number of local firemen could be increased from four to five. The Urban District Council subsequently gave their consent.
By 31st May 1910 the Fire Station had been erected as at their meeting on that day Councillors agreed to pay Mr Standen 10/- for repairs to the roof. A further sum of £4-9-6 was approved for the purchase of a uniform for the fifth fireman from "Shand Mason & Co." Consent was given for the payment of the £21 retaining fee, payable annually, to the Tonbridge Brigade for their services, an arrangement under which the local brigade was established in Hildenborough.
That there was tension between the Hildenborough and Tonbridge Brigades was clear from a Minute in the Council meeting on 24th November 1910. The local Brigade had attended a fire at the Powder Mills but ...
"... as the premises affected were out of the Parish their action had been adversely commented upon by the Chief Officer of the Tonbridge Brigade who

maintained that the Hildenborough men should attend no fire except with his permission."

The Chairman stated that the matter was to be discussed by the Urban District Council.

A similar problem arose when the Hildenborough Brigade attended a fire at Fairhill as reported to the Council on 7th April 1911. At this meeting there was a lengthy discussion about the local Brigade:

1. The Sub-committee reported receipt of a letter from the local firemen strongly objecting to "the irksome rules imposed upon them" by the Tonbridge Brigade. Resignations were threatened.

2. The Sub-Committee had considered the action of the Chief Officer of the Tonbridge Brigade in respect of the fires at the Powder Mills and Fairhill. Members felt that the local brigade should be at liberty to attend fires just over the Parish boundary on premises "belonging to persons who are ratepayers of the parish."

3. Tonbridge required "a man in uniform to convey alarms" to the brigade there but the Chairman stated that in the agreement with Tonbridge he couldn't find anything about this. Similarly, there was nothing to say that the Chief Officer had any authority to ban the attendance of Hildenborough men at a fire.

4. The Council agreed that "the use of a badged messenger" would be sufficient "to give alarms in Tonbridge". This did not have to be done by a uniformed man. Despite these problems, Hildenborough had no wish to sever the connection between the Tonbridge Fire Brigade and the Hildenborough section.

Later in the year a conference attended by representatives from the Hildenborough Parish and the Tonbridge Urban District Councils "to discuss various points in dispute under the Fire Brigade Agreement" was held. A report of this meeting was presented to the Parish Council on 23rd November 1911. Also considered was a letter from the Urban District Council commenting on the conference discussions. Both Council's agreed that:

1. Hildenborough's honorary firemen would be "treated in the same manner as the Honorary Members of the Tonbridge Brigade". It was confirmed that the Hildenborough men had signed the Roll as members of the Tonbridge Brigade.

2. As members of the Tonbridge Brigade the Hildenborough men must conform to the Brigade rules and ...

"... carry out the instruction of the Chief Officer as to attendance at fires in the District and refusal to attend outside fires."

It was pointed out at the Conference that the Brigade was anxious...

"to attend all fires in the neighbourhood of Hildenborough but they must refuse to attend where the person who requests protection has not entered into the usual agreement to retain the services of the Brigade."

For many months the Fire Brigade didn't feature highly on the Parish Council's agenda but on 22nd July 1913 it was reported ...

"... that it had become necessary to repair the firemen's boots at a cost of 11/3." This expenditure was approved as was the purchase of "three new lengths of hose".

On 12th November 1913 a letter from Sevenoaks Urban District Council was considered. In return for the Sevenoaks Fire Brigade's attendance at any fire in Hildenborough, was the Parish Council prepared to contribute towards the expenses of the Sevenoaks Brigade? "No" was the answer as Hildenborough was bound by the agreement with the Tonbridge Brigade.

In June 1910 it had been agreed that the Brigade should pay an annual rent of 5/- to the Institute for the land on which the fire station was built. Curiously, this wasn't paid for some years but on 23rd July 1914 the Parish Council approved the payment of £1-5-0 to cover the rent for five years.

During the war years the Fire Brigade sub-committee reported periodically on the activities of the village firemen. On 30th September 1919 most of the Council's meeting was spent discussing Brigade matters:

1. The Council agreed to spend £2-15-6 on repairing the "Engine Shed".
2. Should the Council continue paying the annual "Retainer" of £21 to Tonbridge? It was felt that Hildenborough now had an "independent brigade" and had joined the national Fire Brigades Union. The Clerk, Mr R F Hodder, was instructed to write to the Urban District Council to ask if the Tonbridge Brigade would continue to "render assistance in case of emergency" to Hildenborough. If the answer was in the negative would Tonbridge…
    "… render help as before – for a nominal sum – as £21 would not apply to an independent brigade."
3. It was agreed to purchase:
    3 lengths Rob Roy machine made hose @ £8-10-0 each
    3 hydrants for placing at (1) Black Arch, (2) Forge Farm, (3) Leigh Road @ £8-10-0 each
    a mortar £1-17-6
    ½ doz maroons @ 7/6 each
4. "The question of hiring a car for towing the Fire Brigade Engine was left for the Fire Brigade Committee to consider."

On 27th October the Council was told that the Urban District Council "declined to guarantee assistance in emergency". The Clerk had written again and a reply was awaited.

At his request, Mr Bradley, the Captain of the Tonbridge Fire Brigade, attended the Parish Council meeting of 13th January 1920. Amongst the points made:

1. The Parish Council felt that £21 p.a. was too high a figure to pay as "a retainer" to the Urban District Council. Mr Bradley replied that Tonbridge needed an…
    "… additional appliance … on account of the possibility of being called to these outlying districts."
2. Mr Bradley claimed "that a steamer would not be required but for the outlying districts".
3. In answer to a question, Mr Bradley said that Hadlow paid £22 p.a. "but had no Fire Brigade at all and no appliances" whilst Tonbridge Rural District Council paid £10p.a..
4. Mr Bradley said that he did not think the offer of a £10p.a. retainer would be acceptable to the Urban District Council. The Chairman, Mr George Johnson, thought that an offer of £11 would not be unreasonable "seeing that Hadlow pay £22 and do nothing whilst Hildenborough is doing so much".

Mr Bradley said that he would be reporting back to his Fire Brigade Committee.

The next Council Meeting was on 12th February when the Chairman read a letter from Mr Bradley, the Tonbridge Brigade Captain. It contained:

1. An offer from the Urban District Council to continue…
    "… to attend outside the village or outside the working distance of existing hydrants at a retaining fee of £15."
2. For attending fires within the area mentioned above "additional fees would be payable by the owner or occupier of premises".

The Parish Council agreed to these terms.

At the Council Meeting on 22nd March there was a discussion about the efficiency of the village Brigade and the sub-committee was asked to produce a report. The same meeting approved the purchase from Brocks of "seven maroons" for the Brigade at a cost of £2-15-0.

The sub-committee's Report was presented to the Council on 22nd April. The recommendations with some amendments were approved by members "in the event of the formation of a separate brigade":

1. The Brigade to consist of 6 men and a captain. Mr W Clark, a former Councillor and sub-committee member to be an honorary member.
2. Mr George Killick to be asked to be Second Officer, taking charge in the absence of the Captain.
3. The sub-committee would carry out an inspection of all gear and uniforms. An inventory would be made and a report compiled on the condition of each item.
4. The following scale of call-out charges would apply: Captain 6/-, Second Officer 4/6, men 3/6 per hour "the call to count as one hour if not proceeding to the fire".
5. £1 per hour would be charged for use of gear if proceeding to a fire.
6. For "keeping efficient", payments would be made: Captain 30/-, Second Officer £1, men 15/-
7. It had been suggested that a "cast iron mortar" be purchased but this was deemed to be dangerous. A "Brock's Special Steel lined fluted mortar" would be purchased instead at a cost of £3-3-0.
8. Insurance for the men would be considered.

A report from the sub-committee was presented to the Council on 23rd July 1920. It included a list of "requirements":

3 new tunics	3 pairs of trousers	3 drill caps
1 pair of boots	1 new scaling ladder	

The Fire Engine to be repaired.

The following items were "urgently" needed

1 Hurricane lamp	1 Breeching piece	3 canvas hose bandages
½doz rubber washers for use with hose		

The Council agreed to these purchases but tenders would be sought from two firms for the uniforms and boots. At the same meeting the Council authorised the payment of £25-10-0 to the Tonbridge Waterworks Co for "placing 3 hydrants". This payment was delayed for several months because the work was deemed to be "unsatisfactory". Agreement with the Company wasn't reached until the following January when payment was finally made.

On 26th October 1920 the Council unanimously accepted the sub-committee's recommendations for the following purchases with a total cost of £34-0-0.

From Hazell & Co

First Officer's uniform	tunic	£4-17-6	trousers	£2-8-9
	cap	11-0	epaulettes	18-9
Second Officer's uniform	tunic	£4-17-6	trousers	£2-8-9
	cap	8-9		
Fireman's uniform	tunic	£3-10-6	trousers	£1-18-9
	cap	4-9	1 pair boots	£3-5-0

From Sinclair & Co	breeching piece	£4	
From McGregor & Co	6 hose bandages @ 12/6		£3-15-0
	1 doz washers 15/-		

On 30th March 1921 the Council heard that the revised agreement with the Urban District Council had still not been signed....

"... It was pointed out that the local Fire Brigade was to be made a separate unit and the Fire Brigade Retainer reduced."

A letter about this matter to the Urban District Council had gone unanswered and the Clerk, Mr F Bampton, was instructed to write again. The draft Agreement was produced at the meeting of 14th July under the terms of which the Retainer would be reduced from £21 to £15 p.a.. The Agreement was referred to the sub-committee which met on 27th July with Mr R T Woodhams, the "Chief Officer" present. It was agreed to recommend that the Agreement be signed, a recommendation that was accepted by the Council later that same evening. The Hildenborough Brigade became a separate unit on 13th August 1921.

On 25th July 1922 "proficiency payments" were approved for Brigade members:

R Woodhams (Captain) £1-10-0 G Killick (2nd Officer) £1
F G Balcombe, E Quinnell, and F W Hoare (firemen) 15/- each

For "attendance at fire" Mr Killick received 4/6 and Mr Balcombe 3/6. Payments to Brigade members were reviewed as it was felt at the Council meeting on 26th September 1923 that "they were too high at the present time".

Following a Report from the Brigade sub-committee, the payments fixed on 22nd April 1920 were revised by the Council at their meeting on 15th October 1923:

	Up to first 5 hours	After 5 hours
Attendance at fires		
Officer in charge at fire	10/- per hour	7/6 per hour
Firemen	2/6 per hour	1/6 per hour

For turning out: Officer in charge 10/- men 5/-. The fee was to cover time travelling to and from a fire.

At the same meeting the Council agreed to ask the Brigade Captain about the frequency of drills and the inspection of hydrants. Had it been decided "to place the Mortar in Fireman Quinnell's garden?" Mr and Mrs Quinnell ran a sweet shop on the corner of Church Road and Riding Lane, just opposite the Fire Station in the Institute garden in Church Road.

Allotments

By 1909 the Council's allotments were said to be self-supporting but there were problems in maintaining them in good condition. At that time there were two allotments in the village. In 1895 the Council had leased, at £6p.a., land at Great Forge Farm from the Earl of Derby. This bordered the Shipbourne Road (now Riding Lane) and was leased with the consent of the tenant.

Two years later land for more allotments was leased at £3p.a. from Mr O d'Avigdor Goldsmid between Watts Cross and the "Lower Cock Inn" on the "High Road", now the B245. Lord Derby sold his property in 1909 and the Great Forge Farm allotment passed to Mr Charles Barkaway. There is a reference to Mr Barkaway in the Minutes for the Council meeting on 20th April 1910 when it was agreed to ask him to attend to the condition of the hedge.

An Allotments Sub-committee set up by the Council was kept busy submitting reports to the full Council. On 31st May 1910 it reported that "the hedges had been put into repair". The Sub-committee asked that allotment holders should be prohibited from throwing "rubbish into the hedges". Certain "very weedy plots" would be leased to tenants free of charge for six months. The hedge at "the London Road", previously described as the "High Road", should be cut back. The Council accepted these recommendations and approved the payments of £1-8-2 for "Repairing Allotment Hedge" for which no tenant "could fairly be made responsible".

At the Council's meeting on 24th November 1910 the sub-committee reported that at the London Road allotments empty plots had been "cleaned" at a cost of 3/9. Two plots were to be let, rent free for twelve months, as school allotments "in order that they might be cleaned". Rents were paid according to the size of the plots and in the case of Plot 22 it was agreed that it be registered as ...

"... 4 rods instead of 5 rods as about 1 rod was rendered useless ... by the general rubbish heap." (1 rod = 5½yards)

It was reported at the meeting on 7th April 1911 that the allotments had been self-supporting for the year ending 31st March.

Subsequent meetings of the Council heard regular reports from the sub-committee which considered matters such as the state of plots, the need for a new gate at Forge Farm (a Council responsibility) and rubbish heaps. The gate was put in place by the summer of 1912 at a cost of £1-16-6.

The only item on the agenda for the Council meeting of 7th February 1916 was a discussion about allotments. It was pointed out that the lease on the Great Forge Farm allotments was due to expire in September 1916 and the Clerk, Mr S U Lawson, was asked to write to Mr Barkaway about renewing it.

The Council was greatly concerned about the impact of the War on the allotments as many plots were now left uncultivated whilst the tenants were away on active service. The sub-committee suggested ...

"... that soldiers should be employed to find the labour which was necessary" to cultivate the plots.

It was reported that contact had been made with Tonbridge Labour Exchange but that "the military authorities" were unable to help.

It was agreed that the vacant plots must be cultivated and the sub-committee was given authority "to see whether they could get sufficient labour from the civil population in the village" at a reasonable price.

The renewal of the lease on the Great Forge Farm allotments was to cause the Council serious problems. On 13th March members considered Mr Barkaway's response to the Clerk's letter. He ...

"... regretted his inability to renew the lease ... as his tenant refused to keep on the farm unless Mr Barkaway could let him have the ground that was now let for allotments as well."

The Council considered whether powers "under the Allotments Act" should be used but decided to ask Mr Barkaway to reconsider his decision. Had he an alternative "suitable piece of ground" that could be leased? A piece of land was offered, the Council was told on 24th March, but it was agreed that this was too small and was unsuitable. Mr Barkaway would be asked once more to reconsider his original answer.

The meeting held on 15th April 1916 heard of Mr Barkaway's reply.
1. The land had been promised to his tenant, Mr Tester, when the Council's lease had expired.
2. He would ask Mr Tester if he would agree to let the Council have the land for one more year, giving more time to find an alternative allotment site.

The Council decided to write to Mr Tester to ask, if he would be willing to let the allotments to the Council on a 14 year lease. One other matter relating to allotments was discussed – it was agreed ...

"... to purchase sufficient artificial manure to dress 85 rods, more or less" on the Council's lands.

The Council was informed on 5th May that Mr Tester had written to say ...

"... that he was not in a position to let the allotments to the Council for fourteen years."

It was decided to write yet again to Mr Barkaway pointing out that at the recent Annual Parish Meeting...

"... a very decided opinion was expressed that the Council should do their utmost to retain the present allotments."

Mr Barkaway's offer of a one year extension of the lease was unacceptable but the Council stressed that it was anxious to reach an amicable settlement.

On 3rd August it was reported that Mr Barkaway had not replied to letters but that his solicitors, Messrs Gorham Warner & Sons, had written ...

"... requiring possession of the allotments at the termination of the lease on 29th September 1916 and further stating that Mr Barkaway preferred to have no further communication on the matter."

The Council decided –

1. To call a Parish Meeting on 14th August to pass a Resolution if parishioners so desired authorising the Council to place the matter in the hands of Kent County Council.

2. It was hoped that the County Council would secure a fresh lease...

"... for a term of 14 years or at least the retention of the allotments until a year after the conclusion of peace."

Mr S U Lawson, the Clerk, sent the papers relating to the Great Forge Farm allotments to the County Council and a report of their reply was given to the Parish Council on 28th August 1916:

1. "... proceedings must be taken under the Small Holdings and Allotment Act 1908."

2. Before the County Council could hold an Enquiry...

"... the Parish Council must furnish proof that they had instituted enquiries as to what other land was available and the number of Parishioners requiring allotments."

The Chairman, Mr George Johnson, stated that "he was in communication with the Board of Agriculture on the matter and they proposed to make enquiries...." The Council approved the following expenditure:

"Roneo & Co. for typing 12 copies of case re: allotments & correspondence £1"

The Chairman briefed the Council on 13th October about subsequent developments:

1. He had been in touch with the County Council.

2. Following contact with the Board of Agriculture, a Commissioner had been to Hildenborough.

3. Following the Commissioner's visit Mr Barkaway, through his solicitors, had agreed to an extension of the lease to 29th September 1917.

The Council set up a small sub-committee to consider...

"... the requirements of the Parish with regard to allotments and to advise about possible sites."

On a different matter, it was agreed to "leave the selling of the potato crop" in the hands of the Allotments Committee. On 7th January 1917 it was reported that the potatoes had finally been sold "at the rate of £8-10-0 per ton and the chats at £2 per ton".

At that January meeting the Council considered other matters relating to allotments:

1. It was agreed to participate in a scheme run by the Kent War Agricultural Committee to supply seed potatoes to allotment holders and "small cultivators".

2. The Allotments Committee was given the authority to arrange for the cultivation of vacant plots with "labour from the civil population" at the Council's expense.

The Council meeting of 22nd February 1917 was entirely taken up with the discussion about allotments:

1. Orders for seed potatoes had been placed with the Agricultural Committee in Maidstone:

	Cost per ton (20cwts)
50 cwts of "Up –to-dates"	£13
18 cwts of "Arran Chief"	£16
14 cwts of "Dalhousies"	£13

    The potatoes would be delivered to Hildenborough Railway Station and the cost of collection would have to be added to these prices. (a "cwt." was short for "hundred weight")

2. Mr Barkaway, through his solicitors, had offered new terms regarding the lease of the Great Forge Farm allotments ...

    "... the rent to be £8 p.a. from 29th September next, the tenancy being extended to the 25th March of the year following the termination of the War." (A pencil note in the margin of this Minute states "Official termination of war 31 August 1921")

The Council unanimously accepted the revised terms for the extension of the lease.

Perhaps because of the war the full Council didn't meet from April until November 1917 when it met twice – on the 8th and the 12th. At the first meeting the cost of "dealing with allotment hedges" was discussed – "4d per rod for the London Road and 2½d per rod for the Forge Farm allotments", (A rod equals 5½ yards.) Because the landlord had put up the rent by £2 p.a. for the Great Forge Farm allotments tenants would now have to pay an extra 1d per rod. The Council heard a report about potato spraying. 32 parishioners "had made use of spraying materials" for which they paid £10-2-8. A separate Spraying account was being kept by the Council and it showed a credit balance of £1-16-5. Two spraying machines had been purchased at £3 each.

On 12th November the Council heard that a letter had been received from the Kent War Agricultural Committee offering seed potatoes for sale again. This offer would be taken up and subsequently 1 ton of "Arran Chief" and 1 ton of "King Edward VII" potatoes were ordered.

The lease for the Great Forge Farm allotments continued to be a cause for concern and the Chairman reported on 21st January 1918 that ...

"... he had telephoned the Board of Agriculture & Food Production Department regarding the Council's tenure ... and that one of the secretaries had promised to look up the file and write fully on the subject as soon as possible."

Meanwhile, there was a search for alternative allotment sites and land at Crown Lands (the Hilden Park area) was considered. It was reported that applications from 16 men "for about 200 rods of ground" had been received for allotments. The problem with this site was that the land was due to be developed for housing thus making the tenure uncertain,, lasting probably no more than two years. The matter was again discussed at the Council meeting on 26th March. The problem was that land in the Crown Lands area was owned by several different people but it had been agreed...

"... to hire from Mr Sykes of Tunbridge Wells four plots in Hilden Park Road numbered 61,62,63,64 at a rent of one pound (£1) per annum for a period of three years and to continue till the building trade revives..."

Eight plots had been let by Mr F O Streeten but these were outside the Council's control. Mr Streeten would find replacement plots should those be required for development during the next seven years.

On 3rd May 1918 the Chairman reported that there was no progress to report about the Great Forge Farm allotments. Members heard that two tons of seed potatoes had been passed on to "small growers" who had paid a total of £21. Mr Banks had undertaken "to spray small plots at the rate of 9d per hour". He would receive 7/6 for caring for the spraying machine for the year.

The Council meeting on 29th July 1918 heard a detailed report about 'Potato Spraying' which had been carried out in the Parish:

London Road Allotments	30 square rods
Forge Farm Allotments	72 square rods
Crown Land Allotments	17½ square rods
Private gardens	113 square rods

It was agreed to charge private individuals 6d per day for the use of the spraying machine which must "be returned clean and in proper condition".

On 27th January 1919 the Council was told that the County Council would not be undertaking the distribution of seed potatoes during 1919. It was agreed to ask the Gardening Society to undertake the task. If the Society declined, the Council's Allotment Committee would take the matter in hand. The same meeting heard that Mr O E d'Avigdor Goldsmid intended to sell his Hildenborough property, including the London Road allotments. It was confirmed that the Council held these allotments on a yearly basis and that notice to quit could be given by the purchaser.

The next Council meeting, the Annual Meeting, held on 23rd April 1919 considered the possibility of losing both the Great Forge Farm and the London Road allotments:

1. The agreement with Mr Barkaway about the Great Forge Farm allotments would "probably terminate in March 1920, unless Mr Barkaway can be persuaded to alter his mind"

2. The London Road allotments would be offered as a separate lot in the forthcoming sale of Mr d'Avigdor Goldsmid's lands.

3. The Clerk, Mr R F Hodder was instructed to write to the Local Government Board to ask whether Parish Councils are allowed to purchase land, whether money might be borrowed for this purpose and, if so, what would be "the conditions of the loan and method of repayment".

It was reported at the next Council meeting, held on 12th June 1919 that it seemed clear from the "Small Holdings and Allotments Act, 1918" that the Council had the power to purchase the London Road allotment site. A loan could be raised for this purpose. It was agreed to proceed with the purchase, subject to the approval of a Parish Meeting.

A Parish Meeting on 23rd June approved the Council's plans and on 4th July the Chairman, Mr G W Johnson, informed Councillors that he had been told that the London Road allotments could be purchased privately prior to the auction. The owner would be prepared to sell the site to the Council for £100. Mr Johnson had submitted an offer of £70 as he felt that £100 was too high a price. He said that the cost of "conveyance would probably be about £5". The Council resolved to purchase the land "at a figure not exceeding £80".

The London Road allotments were sold to the Council for £80 and on 15th July 1919 the Chairman reported that he had instructed "Messrs Warner & Son" to arrange for the conveyance of the land. The cost for this would be £3 plus two stamps @10/-, total £4. The same meeting heard that Mr Barkaway had stated that he "has no desire to turn out the Allotment Holders" at Great Forge Farm. He gave "his word that no further steps will be taken" to do this. A letter of thanks for this assurance was sent by the Council to Mr Barkaway.

The Council had allotments at three sites:
- London Road (between Watts Cross and the "Lower Cock Inn")
- Great Forge Farm (Shipbourne Road, now Riding Lane)
- Hilden Park. At this site it was hoped to acquire more plots on the former Crown Lands property which were due to become building plots.

With the future of the allotments now settled, the Council decided on 17th September 1919 to adopt recommendations from the Allotments Committee :

1. The London Road allotments
   - Access to the stream to be made easier for tenants
   - Fences to be repaired and ditches cleared
   - Hedges to be cut "at a price not exceeding 6d per rod"
   - "trees and scrub to be cut and cleared on bank adjoining main road."
   - Mr Francis was asked to clear the weeds from vacant ground for the sum of 5/-. This work was regarded as urgent.

2. Great Forge Farm
   - Hedges to be cut in October at 5d per rod
   - Notice board to be repaired
   - Allotments to be measured and numbered

All tenants were required "to sign an agreement as from 29th September".

On 22nd April 1920 the Council heard that the Rural District Council had written to say that certain plots at Hilden Park, formerly on property owned by Crown Lands, would be required shortly for building. The Clerk, Mr Hodder, was instructed to write to the Rural District Council's Surveyor stating...
   - That the Council was not prepared to give up the plots "in fairness to the tenants until the crops had been removed". It "would be necessary to compensate them for unexhausted manure".
   - That the Council considered that building could start on several vacant plots "which stand uncultivated".

At the next Council meeting on 23rd July the Clerk was asked to write to each of six Crown Lands allotment holders "terminating the tenure on 30th September next". The Rural District Council was asked to confirm in writing that they "will give compensation for unexhausted manure on these plots".

At the Council meeting on 29th September a petition was presented to the Council on behalf of "several residents at Crown Lands" asking for more allotments to be provided in that part of the Parish. The Allotments Committee confirmed that there was such a need but that there didn't appear to be any suitable land available. The Clerk was asked to write to Mr F O Streeten, owner of land in the area who had, early in 1918, expressed sympathy with the idea of creating more allotments. Would he be "willing to provide about 1¼ acres of land" for the purpose?

Mr Streeten, it was reported on 20th January 1921, had agreed to lease 1¼ acres of land to the Council for allotments. The Council would pay "Rates and Taxes" and rent to Mr Streeten of £2 per acre per annum. There are examples of the cost of rates and taxes quoted at the same meeting when the following payments were approved:

Rates – Forge Farm Allotments 7/11   Income Tax - London Road 7/11

The lease with Mr Streeten was duly signed and the Council meeting on 30th March 1921 agreed that the rent for the plots on what was to be called "Hilden Allotments" was to be "9d per rod p.a.". Because of the overgrown state of the land no rent would be charged until 30th September. A Resolution was passed thanking Mr Streeten "for his public spirit in so kindly responding to the Council's request for Allotments".

References to the Council's two potato spraying machines occur from time to time in the Minutes. On 9th March 1922 it was agreed that the hire charge should be 1/- per day or part thereof. On various dates a payment of 7/6 to Mr J Banks was approved for "care of spraying machine". It was agreed on 30th May 1923 that the Council "should do their best to sell" the two machines for not less than 30/- each.

Towards the end of the war and beyond there was food rationing and price controls. The Minutes often refer to "potatoes", the production of which was controlled. Breaking the regulations could be costly. In the Old Court House in Cromarty are details of a case: 1919 – John MacLennan guilty of contravention of the Potatoes (Protection) Order through wasting potatoes by not lifting and storing them. He was given 30 days imprisonment or £10 fine.

Roads and Footpaths

The state of the roads and footpaths in the village was often discussed at Council meetings. The first reference in the Minute Book covering the period from March 1909 to May 1924 was on 10th February 1910 when …

> "The condition of the footpaths and roads maintained by the County Council was discussed at length and the Clerk was requested to write a strong letter to the Surveyor calling his attention to their bad state of repair."

A new Council took office at the Annual Meeting on 20th April. After the re-election of the Chairman (Mr G W Johnson), the election of Mr Edwin Hendry as Vice-Chairman, the re-election of Messrs Hendry and M C Morris as Overseers, appointments were made to the Fire Brigade and Allotment Committees. There followed a discussion about the state of hedges at the Great Forge Farm allotments but most of the evening was devoted to discussing complaints from councillors about the state of footpaths and roads:

1. Mr Nevins of Pembroke Lodge complained "of a bad place in the road known as Church Road".
2. Mr Auld referred to the poor state of the footpath "leading across the road opposite the Half Moon Inn".
3. Mr King complained that "a public right of way leading to Tonbridge through Hawden Farm had recently been stopped".
4. Mr Meade drew attention to "the reckless driving of tradesmens' carts round some of the sharp corners in the village". This matter, together with a complaint about "careless cyclists" was referred to the police.
5. Mr Killick stated that he understood "that a new road which was being made on the Building Estate near the 'Flying Dutchman' would be taken over by the District Council as soon as completed". Bearing in mind "the extraordinary traffic to which the road would be subject during the development of the Estate" he felt the action of the Rural District Council to be most unusual. He successfully proposed that the Council should object:

   > "the new road was not one which should properly be repairable at Public expense."

The Clerk, Mr M C Morris, followed up these complaints and on 31st May reported that…

- "the bad places in the roads" were blamed on the Water Company
- With respect to the "New Road" being constructed on the "High Barn Estate" the Rural District Council claimed that it would be beneficial to the Parish especially … "… having regard to the facts that the sewer is to be laid at the owner's expense and that the road will have an extra depth of material which should suffice for 5 to 7 years."

Members were not convinced about the last point but, on the casting vote of the Chairman, decided not to take any further action.

The problem of the blocking of the footpath through Hawden Farm was discussed at Council meetings on 24th November 1910 and 15th March 1911. Discussions had taken place with "Mr Sturgess, Lord d'Lisle's agent" who had offered an alternative path "along the north side of the farm buildings". Subsequently a meeting was held with Mr Sturgess and representatives of the Parish and Urban District Councils. The proposal of an alternative route for the path was welcomed but Mr Sturgess had suggested that when it was completed "an existing path by the orchard might be closed". Mr Peach of the Urban District Council stated that he was collecting evidence about "the status of the footpath".

The issue of footpaths through Hawden Farm dragged on for many months. On 7th April 1911 it was stated that the Tonbridge Free Press had reported that the Urban District Council had approved the proposed new footpath through the farm. On 6th July a sub-committee set up by the Council to handle negotiations with the owner "Lord d'Lisle & Dudley" reported that Mr Sturgess, the Agent, was "not now willing to concede the path proposed by the farm buildings unless the path through the Hop Gardens was closed". Mr Sturgess had been pressed to abide by the earlier agreement and the Urban District Council had agreed to …

"… bear the expense of making the path and of the erection of a fence to protect the adjoining land from trespassers".

Mr Sturgess complained that there "were already two miles of footpaths on the farm" and asked for the "surrender of the path through the hop garden".

Mr Nevins, a sub-committee member, told the Council that "people in the Hawden district were becoming restive about the matter and were planning to send 'a signed memorial' to Mr Sturgess".

The problem at Hawden Farm was still unresolved at the time of the next Council meeting on 23rd November 1911. The Council urged the Urban District Council to find a solution "since parishioners are inconvenienced by the stoppage of the path at the Hildenborough boundary". The disputed stretch of the path was in the Urban District Council's area, not in Hildenborough parish. The matter was being referred by Mr Sturgess, the Agent, to Lord d'Lisle. The Agent considered that "a new path could be granted but not an old path taken away without proper legal proceedings". He was now against the proposed new path "as it would break into a field at present without a footpath".

At the same meeting the Council heard complaints about "The High Road" (now the B245):

1. Attention was drawn …

   "… to the dangerous condition in which the ditch abutting the footpath near the Crown Lands had been left by the workmen of the County Council." There had been …

   "… several complaints from people who had walked into the ditch in the dark and damaged both themselves and their clothes."

2. There was a report …

   "… of the untidy state of the main road on Saturdays and Sundays. The paper and leaves flying about were most unsightly."

The Clerk, Mr M C Morris was asked to refer both matters to the County Surveyor.

Not until the meeting of 10th July 1912 did the Council hear that the matter of the Hawden footpaths had been resolved. The Urban District Council had reached an agreement with Mr Sturgess who, …

"… on behalf of Lord d'Lisle and Dudley was now willing to concede a path between the old and the new orchards fenced on both sides and open at both ends."

The Council considered this to be a satisfactory solution.

The same meeting heard about "the dilapidated condition of several stiles and plank-bridges on the footpath leading from Leigh Road to Hawden Farm". The landowner would be approached about this.

Hawden Farm was mentioned yet again at the next Council meeting which wasn't held until 6 February 1913. The new footpath had been staked out but there was a dispute as to whether a stile at either end of the path was necessary. Mr Burgess would refer the matter to Lord d'Lisle.

At this meeting the problem of blocked paths was raised:

1. Mr Gribble of Great Hollanden Farm "had stopped up a footpath leading from the back of his house to Riding Lane". He had now agreed to allow public use of the path providing …
   "… they did not go through the yard but joined the path by means of the one behind the barn which was an undisputed public footpath."
2. Several footpaths on the Fairhill estate had been closed to the public.

Councillors were informed at their meeting on 22nd July 1913 that the new Hawden Farm footpath "was now open and was a great convenience to residents in the neighbourhood". The meeting also heard …

1. … about the poor condition of the footpath "abutting the London Road". The Water Company was responsible "after laying their new mains. They had cut the land drain pipes crossing the road and had not replaced them".
2. … reports of the poor state of the roads "leading from Foxbush corner to the station and from Watts Cross to Noble Tree".

These complaints were referred to the County Surveyor.

On 23rd July 1914 there was good news for those walking to the station as the footpath from the village "was going to be gravelled as soon as possible". Within a few days war broke out and there are few references to roads and footpaths in the Minutes until 1919.

On 15th April 1916 the Council heard a complaint about "water coming out from the ground on which the 'Flying Dutchman' stands and which was continually running across the footpath by the side of the London Road". The County Surveyor was asked to investigate. At the same meeting there was a complaint about the state of a footpath leading from "Horns Lodge to Tinley Lodge". The Council decided that it "did not recognise any liability to repair this footpath".

At the Council meeting on 23rd April 1919 the Clerk, Mr R F Hodder, was asked to contact the County Surveyor about "the deplorable state of the footpath by the side of the main road between Hildenborough and Tonbridge". Because of the generally poor state of footpaths in the village, the Council, on 12th June, decided to set up a Footpaths Committee. On 1st August the committee reported on a problem "near Meopham Park".

Leigh Parish Council had written to Hildenborough Parish Council about the poor state of a footbridge near Meopham Park suggesting that Leigh would undertake the repair with Hildenborough contributing half the cost. The Footpaths Committee suggested that Leigh Parish Council be informed that Hildenborough had no liability in the matter which was the responsibility of the landowner. The Council accepted this recommendation.

The Footpaths Committee was kept busy in the Autumn of 1919 examining the state of local footpaths. On 17th November it reported to the Council that certain stiles needed repairing. A committee member, Mr A Brunger was…

"... deputed to see some of the owners and ask them if they would attend to these small repairs as they would add greatly to the public convenience".

In other cases the Clerk was instructed to write to the landowners.

The state of the "Main Road" was considered by the Council on 22nd March 1920. The Clerk was instructed to write to the County Surveyor...

"... drawing attention to the disgraceful and dangerous state of the main road between Tonbridge and Sevenoaks."

He was also asked to write to the Tonbridge Water Company,,,

"... drawing attention to a leakage in their systems apposite the church ... which caused a bad patch in the road."

On 23rd July some of the users of the "Main Road" came in for criticism:

"Charabanc Nuisance ... the Clerk was instructed to write to the Chief Constable and lodge a formal complaint and ask that steps be taken to abate the nuisance."

The Clerk, Mr R F Hodder, submitted his resignation to the Council at the meeting of 29th September 1920 and one of his last tasks was to write letters to ...

1. "... the County Surveyor drawing his urgent attention to the dangerous state of the water table at Watts Cross and informing (him) of accidents which had already occurred there."

2. "... Messrs Punnett & Son asking them to cut the hedge" near Crownlands "on the plot of land belonging to them between 'Plaisance' and 'Froxfield'."

At his final meeting as Clerk on 26th October Mr Hodder was asked to write to the County Surveyor drawing his attention to "the deplorable state of the footpath between Flat Cottages and Watts Cross". (These cottages were on the site now occupied by a petrol station and a car showroom.) Clearly not much was done to improve the state of the footpath as on 30th March 1921 the new Clerk, Mr F Bampton was asked to write to the Rural District Council ...

"... respecting the condition of the footpath between Flat Cottages and Watts Cross, and also the path at Hilden Cottage."

A letter from the County Surveyor was read to the Council meeting of 20th April 1921 promising "to see what could be done" about these two footpaths. As nothing was done, at the meeting on 14th July, the Clerk was asked to write again to the County Surveyor.

That same meeting heard a report that "the corner of Eggpie Lane" was dangerous "as it was at the bottom of a sharp hill and was very narrow". The Council agreed that "widening the road would be difficult and expensive and the Clerk was asked ...

"... to see the local AA Inspector to ascertain if it were possible to have a Danger sign erected near that corner."

At the Council meeting on 27th July 1921 a letter from the "Secretary of the A A" was read. The matter had been referred to the "Highway Surveyor" and it was pointed out that the Ministry of Transport ...

"... had issued a circular letter on the standardisation of direction posts and warning signs."

The A A therefore had decided to "let the Highway Authorities deal with these matters."

The Council meeting on 27th July also heard why nothing had been done about the recent complaints about the state of footpaths. The County Surveyor had written to say that ...

"... he had been directed to curtail expenditure on footpaths for financial reasons."

He promised to see if some "minor repairs" could be carried out.

The Council had a further complaint to make: the Clerk was instructed to write about...

"... the dangerous nature of a ditch at the Mill Garage and also about the footpath from the Church downwards, which had been pulled up when cables were placed there and had never been made good."

It was six months before the Council met again but on 23rd January 1922 it was reported that "the ditch by the Mill Garage had been filled in".

At the Council's Annual Meeting on 20th April 1922 it was reported that Mr Hills, the Parish's representative on the Rural District Council ...

"... had used his influence to draw the County Surveyor's attention to the necessity for attending immediately to the main road footpaths from Watts Cross to the Crown Lands. The County Surveyor had promised to gravel and tar the footpaths in question and also to improve the condition of the corner by the Memorial."

However, on 25th July the Council heard that ...

"... the footpaths in the main road, which were so necessary at present, were still unsatisfactory."

On 28th October it was agreed to send a letter of thanks to the County Surveyor for "the very satisfactory manner in which the footpath from Watts Cross to the Memorial had been made". Work on the path ...

"... from the village to Hilden Cottage had not been attended to because the Water Company intended putting new pipes under it."

The Clerk was asked to write to the Company to ask that the work be done as soon as possible. Their response was reported on 13th December 1922:

"... it was proposed to lay a main under the footpath from the Flying Dutchman to Hilden Cottage in the summer of next year."

From time to time the Council considered the dangers on the "main road". For example, on 19th April 1923, it was agreed to propose to "the Automobile Association" that there should be a "Danger" sign about 150 yards either side of the garage at Watts Cross as it was "considered the roadway was very narrow there". On 27th July the Council received a deputation of ...

"... two residents on the London Road complaining of the excessive speed of motor lorries and cars on Oak Hill."

The Council was urged to support their call for "a speed limit of 10 to 12 miles" per hour. Members agreed to forward the proposal to the County Council.

On 22nd April 1924 the Council agreed to a suggestion from Mr E Francis that ...

"... some of the boards put up by the Kent County Council giving the speed of cars through the village at 8mph should be placed on the other side of the road, opposite the Memorial."

The proposal was passed to the County Council whose attention was also drawn "to the bad state of a School Caution sign board on the Shipbourne Road (now Riding Lane) which can hardly be read".

The last major problem covered by the Minute Book for 1909-1924 was that of the obstruction of an alleged right of way on land belonging to the "Princess Christian Farm Colony". On 30th May 1923 the Council heard a complaint that a footpath had "just recently been stopped up", The Superintendent at the Colony had said that she was acting under orders and the Council agreed to send a letter to the "National Society for the Care of Feebleminded" asking for an explanation. In September the Society wrote to say that the matter would be considered by their solicitor but that he was currently "away from town". The Council's response was that "the matter has been held over an unreasonable time" and the Clerk, Mr E B Budding, was asked on 26th September to write again to the Society.

On 13th November a reply from the Society's solicitors "Messrs A F & R W Tweedie" was read to the Council. This said that the closure of the footpath was a matter for the Charity Commissioners "as having statutory Powers to close the right of way under discussion". The Chairman, Mr G W Johnson, undertook to write to the Commissioners on 26th January 1924, with the matter still unresolved. It was agreed to send the correspondence to the Rural District Council "so that immediate action should be taken by them to protect the rights of the public".

The Rural District Council decided to set up a Committee to investigate the problem and on 22nd April 1924 it was reported that this Committee would hold an Inquiry and hear witnesses. This was done on the evening of 1st May and was followed by a Council meeting. The last page in the Minute Book records that the Council agreed that "a Postal order for 5/-" should be sent to Mr George Thorne of Tonbridge, "being out of pocket expenses incurred by him in attending the examination of witnesses" at the Inquiry.

The War

War was declared on 4th August 1914 and on 11th August a "special meeting" of the Council was held at the Institute with several parishioners present. It was called to discuss a request by the Chief Constable to consider the enrolment of Special Constables.

1. There should be special constables in each Parish "employed for the protection of life and property".
2. Unpaid, the constables would be "under the direct orders, control and instructions of the Superintendent of the Police division in which the Parish is situated".
3. The Clerk was required to forward details of volunteers to the Chief Constable as soon as possible.

"In view of this statement" the Council "decided to swear in as many as were willing to serve as Special Constables and several came forward and offered their services". One of those to sign up was Mr J T Fellowes Wilson. He missed the Council meeting on 21st April 1915 "owing to his duty in connection with the special constables".

The next Council meeting, on 31st August, was entirely taken up with matters relating to the emergency. The possibility of holding a meeting to obtain recruits was considered. This would be done following consultations with "Colonel Rathay and Captain Henson".

The only other business at this meeting was consideration of a letter from the Rural District Council with reference to the "National Relief Fund". Did the Council wish to be represented on the Committee that had been formed in Tonbridge…

"… to control, in conjunction with the Prince of Wales' National Committee and the County Committee, such relief as may be required."

It was agreed that the Vicar, the Rev'd James Stone, be appointed as the Parish representative on the committee. To assist him, a sub-committee was set up. The membership included two women, Mrs H Hills and Mrs Scott together with Mr H Hills (a member of both the Parish and the Rural District Councils), the Chairman (Mr G W Johnson) and the Vice-Chairman (Mr Edwin Hendry). The Council heard on 10th November 1915 that …

"… the Committee had £31 in hand which, because there were not so many calls on the fund at the present time, had been placed in the Post Office Savings Department."

There is a reference in the Minutes for the Council meeting held in the Drill Hall on

13th October 1916 to another committee. The Chairman, Mr G W Johnson, reported receipt of a letter "from Lord Harris asking the Council for further help "in the matter of the Kent Prisoners of War Fund. As "he did not think it was necessary he had written to Lord Harris to that effect".

Food Economy
At the Council meeting of 8th November 1917, the Chairman, Mr G W Johnson referred to a letter from "the Food Control Committee of Tonbridge Rural District Council". This committee asked for a "sub-committee representative of all classes" to be elected and the Council agreed to invite the following to serve on it:

Mrs Henry Hills	Mrs Arthur Johnson	Mr Jenner
Mr Wilson	Mr Hodder	Nurse Genese

"and one female representative of the working classes."
    It was reported to the meeting of the Council on 12th November that the following had agreed to serve on the Food Economy Committee:

Mrs H G Hills	Mr A F W Johnson	Mr O Jenner
Mr R F Hodder	Nurse Genese	

Mr E A Auld agreed to serve as the Parish Council's representative. On 21st January 1918 it was reported that ...
    "Mr F Killick and Mrs W Hitchcock had both accepted the invitation to serve on the Food Economy Committee as representatives of the working classes."
Committee meetings had been held together with a well attended "Public Meeting addressed by F O Streeten, Esq. JP".

After the War

Following the Armistice in November 1918 consideration was given to "Peace Celebrations" and a "special meeting of the parishioners" was summoned for 23rd June 1919. This called upon the Council to ...
    "... make arrangements for entertaining the returned soldiers and sailors at supper."
The Council decided at its meeting on 4th July that the supper "should take place in the Drill Hall on Wednesday 23rd July 1919" and that "the catering should be done locally". It was also decided that ...
    "... the Committee arranging the children's entertainment was authorised to spend a sum not exceeding £50 and a further sum not exceeding £15 for presentation mugs."
    At the Council meeting on 15th July the sums made available to the committee organising the children's tea were increased to £80 and to £18 for the mugs. It was explained that the number of children was more than originally thought and that "it was hoped to give parents and friends a cup of tea". The Council also authorised the Chairman "to order fireworks and torches to cost about £20". At the meeting on 1st August it was reported that the cost of the celebrations was well within budget. Approval for the payment of a cheque for £76-15-10 to Captain Duncan was given – he had settled the various accounts on behalf of the committee. Details of these were given and make interesting reading as they give details of prices at the time. Notice how the price of milk varied according to the supplier. Two famous names occur in the accounts – the store "Gamages" and "C T Brock & Co", the supplier of fireworks.

			£	s	D
1	Gamage	Peace mugs £17-2-0 and carriage 6/-	17	8	-
2	W Austin	Inkstand (prize)		2	6

No	Name	Description	£	s	d
3	J Wisbey & Co	Prizes	5	-	-
4	G Castle	Loaves etc	13	4	6
5	Mr Lewis	Milk 2 gallons @ 1/10 3/8			
6	Mr Green	Milk 2 gallons @ 2/- 4/-			
7	Mr Tester	Milk 2 gallons @ 2/- 4/-		11	8
8	SE Railway Co	Carriage on mugs		8	11
9	L Thompsett	Butter etc	4	15	7
10	Band		10	10	-
11	Miss Turnbull's account			10	9½
12	Mrs J T Fellowes Wilson	Tea	1	4	2
13	C T Brock & Co	Fireworks	20	7	-
14	Co-op Stores	Hire of boiler		5	-
15	Mr Gribble	2 gallons of milk @ 2/4		4	8
16	Mr Hendry's account		3	8	7
17	Messrs Hills Bros	Carting		10	-
18	Captain Duncan	Petty cash account		2	6
		TOTAL	78	13	10½

LESS: Cake sold after fete   1 0 0
Tea sold after fete   12 1
Refund from Gamage for
carriage of mugs   6 1

| | | | 1 | 18 | 1 |
| | | | 76 | 15 | 9½ |

(Conversion: 1 shilling (1/-) = 5p   Half a crown (2/6) = 12½p)

There was one account that wasn't settled until 27th October 1919 when a payment of £2 to "R Brown" was approved for "work in connection with peace celebrations".

The final reference to peace celebrations in the Minutes is a reference on 13th January 1920.

> "Dinner to Returned Soldiers and Sailors. It was arranged to entertain the rest of the returned soldiers and sailors on Saturday 7th February … the same committee to make the arrangements and the cost to be met as before by voluntary subscriptions."

In the Minutes for 22nd February 1917 there is a reference to extending the tenancy of the Great Forge Farm allotments to "the 25th March of the year following the termination of the war". The Armistice came into effect on 11th November 1918 and there is a pencil note in the margin:

> "Official termination of War 31 August 1921."

The village War Memorial had been dedicated in October 1920 but in the Council's Minutes there is only one significant reference to it. At the meeting of 20th April 1922 it is recorded that Mr F Burton of "the General Committee of the War Memorial" presented a Resolution to the Council to the effect that …

> "… the upkeep of the grass etc round the cross be handed over to the Parish Council."

The Council agreed "for one year" to the request and it was agreed that …

> "… Mr Banks should take charge of the upkeep and cut the grass for £5 per annum" with effect from 1st April 1922.

This arrangement clearly continued beyond one year as there is a reference to a payment of £5 to Mr Banks in the Minutes for the meeting on 22nd April 1924.

.

Unemployment

In the years following the war unemployment became a serious problem. This was discussed at the Council's meeting on 23rd January 1922 when the Chairman, Mr G W Johnson, reported that he had received "a letter from a man in this Parish asking for employment". Mr Johnson therefore ...

> "... wrote to the Clerk of Tonbridge Rural District Council asking what powers the Parish Council have to provide employment and offering the Council's co-operation if necessary."

The reply stated:

1. That the Parish Council has no power to provide employment
2. That the Guardians and the Rural District Council may provide employment but no work has so far been provided by them.
3. That a limited number of unemployed have received Poor Law Relief.

> At the Council's next meeting on 9th March 1922 the Chairman reported ...
> "... that there were 6 or 8 unemployed in this Parish. These were being provided with work for 2 days per week by local people."

The Council agreed that ..

> "... the system which granted the unemployment benefit if a man did no more than 2 days' work per week was wrong."

On 28th October 1922 the Chairman reported that the Parochial Church Council had asked for the co-operation of the Parish Council with regard to unemployment. It was decided "that the whole Parish Council should form itself into an Unemployment Committee to deal with cases as they arise". On 13th December the Council heard that ...

> "... several prominent residents in the Parish had offered to find work for unemployed men. Two or three men who had applied for work had already been given employment."

Leigh United Charities

From time to time the Leigh Charities were mentioned at Council meetings, usually because the Council nominated a Trustee. It was reported on 21st January 1918 that the Rev'd J Stone's term as a Trustee had expired and that due to the illness of Mr Stone, the Vicar of Hildenborough, a new Trustee was required. Mrs Henry Hills was duly nominated. She was one of the daughters of Mr Charles Fitch Kemp, the Council's first Chairman. Mrs Hills was reappointed on 23rd January 1922 and at the Council's meeting on 13th December 1922 a letter from her was read...

> "... stating that a grant of £3-8-6 will be distributed to 8 applicants who reside in Old Leigh Parish."

Hildenborough incorporated part of the old Parish of Leigh and consequently nominated a Trustee.

Water

Throughout the period of the second Parish Council Minute Book (1909-1924) there are references to problems with water and the Tonbridge Water Company. Sometimes these related to the installation of hydrants for use by the village Fire Brigade but there were also problems with the laying of pipes for mains water. For example, on 23rd October 1922 the Council complained that work on a footpath through the village...

> "... had not been attended to because the Water Company intended putting water pipes under it."

From time to time there were complaints about the charges levied by the company.

The first recorded complaint in the Minute Book was on 31st May 1910 when the Water Company was blamed for "bad places" in the bye-roads but over the years there were several problems with the fountain.

A "water fountain" had been set up to commemorate the Golden Jubilee of Queen Victoria in 1887 at the side of the main road opposite what used to be a newsagent's shop, now a café. The fountain, no longer functioning, was moved to the Village Green in 2005. The Council paid a charge of £1 p.a. to Tonbridge Water Company but the fountain appears to have been out of order quite frequently. The Council meeting on 23rd July 1914 heard that it wasn't functioning properly as a drinking fountain and the Company was asked to "have it seen to". It was reported on 26th March 1918 that the annual charge was due to be paid but ...

"... the Fountain had not been properly supplied with water during the past year." The £1 would not be paid until the fountain had been repaired. Three years later, on 30th March 1921, it was again reported that the fountain "was out of repair".

It was on 1st December 1919 that the Council discussed the charges levied by the "Tonbridge Water Works Company". Members were informed that the company was applying to the Board of Trade "for power to make a temporary increase in their scale of charges". Before taking any action it was agreed to seek "certain details as to the Price of Stock and Rate of Dividends of the Company". A councillor, Mr Alfred Smith, was asked "to interview the Secretary of the Company" and to report back to the Council on 10th December. At that meeting Mr Smith...

"... gave an exhaustive report of his interview with the Secretary. Figures had been given showing how expenditure compared with receipts had increased."

In the circumstances the Council accepted that the increased charge were justified. At the next meeting, on 13th January 1920, the Council heard that the Board of Trade had authorised a temporary increase of 50% in the Company's charges. The same meeting approved the payment of a charge of £1-10-0 for the fountain – hitherto the charge had been £1 p.a..

From time to time the Council reported water supply problems to the Company as on 22nd March 1920 when it was told of "a leakage in their system opposite the Church" causing problems on the road.

On 23rd July 1920 the Council was asked to approve payment of an account for £25-10-0 from the Water Company for "placing 3 hydrants". Approval was withheld and ...

"... the Clerk was instructed to write to the Water Company for certain explanations before their account is settled."

The matter was unresolved by the meeting of 29th September and Mr Woodhams of the village Fire Brigade ...

"... was asked to interview the Secretary of the Tonbridge Water company with regard to the placing of the three hydrants before the Council agree to pay the account."

On 26th October Mr Woodhams reported on an unsatisfactory interview with Mr Thompson of the Company. The Council continued to delay payment and Mr Smith, a councillor, was asked to see Mr Thompson in an attempt to reach a settlement.

The Minutes for the meeting of 20th January 1921 give an indication of the problem of the account for the cost of the installation of the three hydrants, primarily for use by the Fire Brigade. Mr Smith had told Mr Thompson that the hydrant in Leigh Road which "was too deep for a stand pipe to be conveniently used, should be raised". This had been done and the Council now agreed to pay the account. At the same time payment of the charge for the fountain was approved – at the old rate of £1 now that the temporary increase in charges had lapsed.

Snippets from the Minutes

The Annual Accounts for 1911/12
The Parish Council's balance sheet showed an income of £212-15-10 and expenditure of £201-4-7.

Rates on the Allotments
On 25th July 1922 the Council approved the payment of the Rates due on the allotments: "London Road 4/0¾, Hilden 2/8½, Forge Farm 8/1½."

Post Office opening hours
On 23rd September 1909 the Council considered proposals from the Tonbridge Postmaster about reducing Post Office opening hours. It was suggested that the Hildenborough Post Office should close at 2pm on Wednesdays whilst the hours of business on Sunday should be reduced "to one hour viz 8.30-9.30". Mr Edwin Hendry explained the probable effect of these proposals which received unanimous support from the Council.

Poultry lectures
In the early years of the Council members had encouraged the provision of adult education courses in conjunction with Kent Education Committee. These courses continued: on 23rd July 1914 the Council made "an application to the Kent Education Committee for an advanced course of lectures to be held in the Drill Hall" on the subject of poultry.

Telephone cables
On 23rd July 1914 the Clerk was instructed to write "to the Local Contract Manager of the Post Office" stating that the Council considered it very desirable that cables should be laid underground.

Public Recreation Ground
On 12th June 1919 the Council considered in private "the advisability of purchasing a field for General Recreative purposes". It was reported that "the opportunity had arisen of the possible purchase of certain ground under favourable conditions". On 17th September the Council was informed that …

> "… Mr B Lewis had withdrawn his offer to sell the cricket ground for a Recreation Ground but would be willing for the Cricket Club to use it as before."

(Prior to the acquisition of the Recreation Ground in Riding Lane in 1932 matches were played on the Oakhill Cricket Ground at what is now Westwood.)

Pigeons
On 21st January 1918 the Council was asked by the Kent War Agricultural Committee to draw the attention of parishioners for "Simultaneous Pigeon Shooting". On Wednesdays 30th January, 6th and 13th February …

> "… between 2pm and dusk farmers throughout Kent should shoot wild pigeons as so much damage was done to crops last season."

Rats
On 27th October 1919 a circular was read to the Council "from Col Harris re: Rat Order and the formation of a Rat Club". It was agreed to set up a committee of five to organise a Parish rat club. This was set up and on 17th November Mr Alfred Smith was appointed "as official representative of the Council on the Rat Club". On 22nd March 1920 a letter from Col Harris informed the Council that …

"... owing to a modification of the Rat Order no further grant would be paid to the Rat Club by the Rural District Council."

Notice Boards

On 13th January 1920 the possibility of providing a large notice board outside the Drill Hall was raised but no conclusion reached. At the next meeting, on 12th February, it was reported that discussions with Mr Hendry had led to his offer to have a small board placed "on each side of his small shop window". It was agreed to purchase "two boards 24" x 18" glazed etc. for £3" (ie 2ft by 1½ft). On 20th January 1921 it was pointed out to the Council ...

"... that the two Notice Boards outside Mr Hendry's shop were chocolate colour while the shop itself had been painted green."

The Council decided that the boards "should be painted green to harmonise with the shop".

The Notice Boards were again considered on 30th March 1921. On whose authority had the words "Women's Institute" been painted on one of the boards? The Council had not given its consent and it was agreed that the offending words...

"... should be painted out and that the letters 'H.P.C.' should be painted at the top of each board and the words 'Parish Notices' at the bottom."

This work was duly done at a cost of five shillings.

Rural Industries

On 14th July 1921 the Council considered a letter from the Rural Industries Sub-Committee of the Kent Agricultural Committee asking about rural industry and social life in the village. The survey was completed and the Chairman, Mr G W Johnson remarked,,,

"... that the village was very much alive, especially with regard to its social life."

A seat at Watts Cross?

On 27th July 1921 the Council was informed of the offer of "a garden seat to be placed at Watts Cross for the convenience of Autocar passengers". It was pointed out that before the Council could accept the offer ...

"... the matter must be approved by the County Council and also by the owner of the ground on which it was proposed to place the seat."

The Hildenborough Institute

The Chairman reported to the Council on 25th July 1922 that "the Deed of Trust" for the Institute had expired and that it was necessary to form a new Trust which would include one member elected by the Parish Council. Mr Alfred Smith was elected as "a Manager of the Hildenborough Institute and Drill Hall Trust".

Beating the Bounds

In 1923 the custom of Beating the Bounds (boundaries) was revived. This took place over two weekends in November and on 13th November the Council received a Report on the event. There had been problems, including the weather and some hostility from landowners. It was agreed to send a letter to ,,,

"... Mr David Rogers of Hawden Farm, Tonbridge, in consequence of the hostile reception which the party received from him whilst passing through his property."

There is an account of the event by a Councillor, Mr Edwin Francis, in "This is Hildenborough from A-Z" published by the Parish Council originally in 1994 and in a revised edition in 2007.

Part 3 – A Selection of Historic Photographs

Mount Pleasant looking towards the junctions with Half Moon Lane and Church Road.

Mount Pleasant. The Village Green is on the right.

"The Poplars", now
"The Cottage", Watts Cross

Mr John Francis (1838-1908)
and his wife outside their home
"The Poplars" (now
"The Cottage"), Watts Cross.
Mr Francis was a member of
the inaugural Parish Council.
For many years their son
Edwin (Ted) was also a
Parish Councillor.

The Jubilee Fountain. Marking Queen Victoria's Golden Jubilee, 1887, it was originally sited on the B245 opposite what is now "Café 1809".

The Jubilee Fountain, no longer in working order, was moved to the Village Green in 2005.

71

The junction of Coldharbour Lane and the B245. The Cottage no longer exists.

The Post Office, now "One Stop", with Foxbush Cottages on the left.

An early photograph of the "Half Moon" and the corner of Half Moon Lane. "Posts and wires in 1942 were considered by the Council to be a danger to the public especially during the 'Black Outs'. The Rural District Council was asked to have them removed from the front of the "Half Moon".

Mr M C Morris, Headmaster of the village school 1897-1913 and Honorary Clerk to the Council 1907-1913.

The Memorial in the Parish Chuch to Charles Fitch Kemp, J.P., D.L. of Foxbush. He was Chairman of the Parish Council from its inauguration in 1894 until his death in 1907.

The Rev'd R L G Pidcock, Vicar of Hildenborough 1894-1900.

74

The Rev'd James Stone, Vicar of Hildenborough 1901-1918

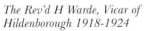

The Rev'd H Warde, Vicar of Hildenborough 1918-1924

The War Memorial. Designed by Mr H P Burke Downing F.S.A., F.R.I.B.A. (1865-1947), the Memorial was unveiled on 5th October 1920. It was the only War Memorial designed by this architect. On it were engraved the names of 37 First World War casualties. The names of the 16 Second World War fallen were added in due course.

Noble Tree Corner

The Peace Celebrations – the Tug of War on a wet day in July 1919.

The Peace Celebration procession passes what in 1927 became the Village Green, July 1919.

William Castle's bakery was at 170 Tonbridge Road, now a hairdressing salon. These photographs show two different delivery vans.

Watts Cross. The windmill, dating from 1812, was dismantled in 1961.

Webber's Garage and the junction of the B245 and Half Moon Lane.

Mrs Kingswood in front of the
Institute, now the site of the
Village Hall. She was
appointed Caretaker in 1897
and lived "rent free" in the
adjoining cottage.
She was paid "2/- (10p) per
week" for extra work in the
Institute.

*Edwin Hendry, (1861-1953). A member of the inaugural Parish Council of 1894, Mr Hendry
bought the Post Office and neighbouring cottages from the Estate of the late Mr C Fitch Kemp in
1912. The store bore his name until it was bought in 1996 and became "One Stop".*

Flat Cottages, demolished in 1935. Built as homes for labourers on the Mountains Estate of the Johnson family, the site is now a garage and a car showroom beside the B245 between the War Memorial and Watts Cross.

The "Flying Dutchman"

Mr Walter J King, a Councillor for thirty years, with his son, D W King. The 1936 photograph shows him harvesting potatoes on his land at Hubble's Field, opposite the Riding Lane allotments.

Shipbourne Road, (now Riding Lane) opposite the entrance to the Recreation Ground.

The Recreation Ground. The land was purchased by the Parish Council in 1931.

The Recreation Ground Pavilion. This was officially opened on 4th June 1932.

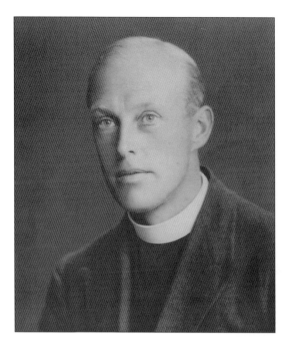

*The Rev'd L G Chamberlen, M.C.,
Vicar of Hildenborough 1924-1934,
Parish Councillor 1927-1932.*

*The Rev'd W H Bass,
Vicar of Hildenborough 1935-39.
A Parish Councillor for some
years.*

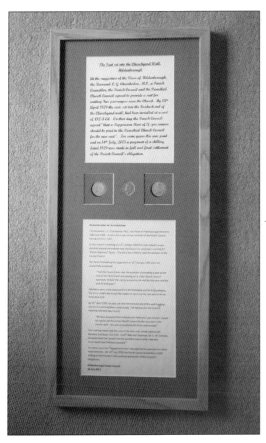

The 1929 shilling, as the final payment from the Parish Council for the seat built into the Church Wall in 1929. The display case can be seen in the Church Centre.

The Parish Council Chairman, Mr Mike Dobson hands over a 1929 shilling to the Vicar, the Rev'd Tim Saiet, at the seat set into the Churchyard wall. This was a final payment to the Parochial Church Council as rent for the use of a section of the wall, 14th July 2015. The seat dates from 1929 and was installed for the benefit of waiting passengers at what was then the 'bus stop. The Vicar, the Rev'd L G Chamberlen M.C., led the campaign for the seat.

Rev'd E H Wade, Vicar of Hildenborough 1934-1935. He was the father of Virginia Wade, Ladies' Champion at Wimbledon 1977.

Masters' Tea House. One of a series of cafés along the B245 which catered for the cars and coaches using the road before the by-pass was opened. Demolished in 1973, it is now the site of Weald Court, opposite the Half Moon.

The Green Rabbit Guest House and Café, demolished in 1975 to make way for the Orchard Lea group of houses.

The Cemetery for Dogs and Cats at "The Boiling Kettle" Café (now the BP Garage). The café survived until 1956. Memorials to animals killed on the road can still be seen at the back of the BP Garage.

The Village Fire Brigade.
Hilenborough Volunteer Fire Brigade, 1938.
Back row– David Seal, William Woodgate, Fred Stroud
Front row – George Smith, Reg Woodhams (Hon. Chief Officer), Fred Balcombe (Chief Officer),
Alix Upton (Second Officer), Harry Haffenden.

Home Guard - in 1944

Back row - C.E. Clarke, R.G. Paine, J.S. McFarland, S. Dann, F. Benbow, W.H. Peacock, W. Smith.

Second row - A. Seal, unknown, W.H. Martin, F. Stewart, J. Horton, A. Butt and S. Wickenden (cadets).

Third row - J. Playfoot, unknown, R. Wenban, J. Fuller, C. Wheatley, C. Giles, R. Corp, N. Seale.

Front row - G.M. Parrott, G.F. Green, W.L. Pritchard, A.W. Challen, P. Andrews, J. Savage, A.E. Cowell.

Photo: Allwork

Inspection of the Special Constables
From right to left in line: Mr Wickenden, Fred Goad, Mr Steed, Mr Tompsett, Mr Radcliffe, Owen
?, ?, George Neil.

> Correspondence.
>
> Correspondence was read from the T.R.D Council dated 20th Nov 1942 in reference to the Posts and Wire at the Fore-court of the Half Moon. Whilst this matter was under discussion the alert was given, and in view of the fact the most of the members were A.R.P. workers, it was proposed by Mr Gwyther, seconded by Mr Francis and carried that the meeting be adjourned.
>
> 10th Feby 1943.
>
> The meeting was continued on Wednesday 10th Feby 1943 at 7.30 pm with Mr F. Burton in the chair, the above mentioned were present with the exception of Mr Webber who sent an apology for his absence.

Extract from the Minute book for the Meeting on 18th January 1943. This had to be adjourned because the Councillors who were members of the Air Raid Precaution Committee were called out on an alarm.

The Rev'd E W E Fraser,
Vicar of Hildenborough 1939-1951,
Chairman of the Parish Council
1946-1950.

The Drill Hall and Institute on the corner of Riding Lane and Church Road.

The Ball Room, The Old Barn Tea House, Stocks Green Road, Hildenborough.

The Old Barn Interior.

The Car Park, The Old Barn Tea House.

SOME PETS AT THE OLD BARN TEA HOUSE

Some pets – and the stocks – at The Old Barn Tea House, Stocks Green Road.

93

Mr Frank Burton (left), Parish Council Chairman 1938-1946, as Gardeners' Society Chairman, presents a cup to Mr Ted (Edwin) Francis, for many years a Parish Councillor.
Photo: Kent Messenger

Mr F G Balcombe, Clerk to the Parish Council 1929-1964, seen in his role as the School's "Lollipop Man".
Photo: Kent & Sussex Courier

Mr A G T Oakley with his children Robin and Jennifer, V.E. Day, 8th May 1945. The photograph was taken at their home, Oldhouse Farm, Philpots Lane. Gerald Oakley was chairman of Hildenborough Parish Council between 1950 and 1955. His son, Robin, wrote a paper "Memories of Living in Hildenborough in the 1940s and 1950s" in 2016. Illustrated with numerous photographs, it is an important contribution to the history of Hildenborough and is in the archives of the Hildenborough History Society (www.hildenboroughhistorysociety.weebly.com)

This sketch of the family home is by Pamela Oakley, wife of Gerald and mother of Robin, Jennifer, Sally and David.

Hildenborough Station, 1875. The photograph shows a team of platelayers. Perhaps one was George Goldsmith. He started work as a foreman in that year, a job he was still doing when his son, James, and George Upton were killed in the railway accident of 1st April 1898.

Hildenborough Station, 1947. Railway gangers and officials. Sid Huggett is receiving an award on behalf of the team for the best kept length of line in the area. The man in the bowler hat is Archie Cooper, killed a year later in an accident, whilst two of the other men are named as "Woodgate and Upton". The "Upton" is William George Upton, (in cap and black jacket) elder son of George, killed in the 1898 accident.

The Gate Hotel, next to Hildenborough Station, dates from 1868. On 2nd April 1898 the Inquest into the two platelayers killed the day before was held at the Hotel, now known as The Cinnamon (2016).

In Memory of

GEORGE UPTON and JAMES GOLDSMITH
Aged 30 years   Aged 19 years

Two Platelayers in the employment of the
SOUTH EASTERN RAILWAY

Who were killed on the 1st April 1898
whilst working on the track near Hildenborough Station

HILDENBOROUGH HISTORY SOCIETY
2016

The plaque commemorating the accident on 1st April 1898 which killed two villagers, George Upton and James Goldsmith, both platelayers. It was unveiled at Hildenborough Station on 16th July, 2016.

"London Jack" was a dog who collected money for the Southern Railway Servants' Orphanage in Woking. At the ceremony to dedicate the refurbished memorial to the two platelayers, George Upton and James Goldsmith, killed on 1st April 1898, Hildenborough History Society presented Woking Homes, as it is now known, with a cheque for £600 (16th July 2016). The memorial is in the Bluebell Railway's Museum as is, with the help of a taxidermist, "London Jack".

The renovated memorial unveiled on 16th July 2016, which marks the grave of George Upton and James Goldsmith, platelayers killed in a railway accident on 1st April 1898.

The family of Judith Upton, Great Granddaughter of George Upton and Granddaughter of Alix Upton, younger son of George, born in 1898 after the death of his father in the 1st April 1898 railway accident. Alix can be seen in the 1938 photograph of the village Fire Brigade as second officer.

The family is shown at Hildenborough Station on 16th July 2016 when Gareth Owen, Great Great Grandson of George Upton, unveiled the memorial plaque. This commemorates the accident which killed George together with James Goldsmith.

From left: Wayne Owen, Jose Dominguez, Alun Owen, Finley Sale, Gareth Owen, Jan Owen, Isabelle Sale, Hannah Sale, Harrison Owen, Judith Upton, Paul Sale, Trevor Upton, Jo Upton.

Part 4 – 1924-1938

List of Councillors and Officials

Those who served the Council as members or officials are listed below. Nine councillors were elected to serve for three years at Parish Meetings and 23 parishioners were Council members at one time or another.

Councillors:
Mr J Banks
Mr J G Barns
The Rev'd W H Bass, Vicar 1935-1939
Mr A Brunger
Mr F Burton
Mr F H Buss
The Rev'd L G Chamberlen, MC Vicar 1924-1934
Major C E W Charrington
Mr J T Fellowes Wilson
Mr E Francis
Dr D B Fraser
Mr P Gallon
Mrs L Houghton
Mr G W Johnson
Mr C Kemp
Mr W J King
Mr J Mackney
Mr E T Maidment
Mr A B McIvor
Mr A Smith
Mr E Tasker Brown
Mrs M Tasker Brown
Mr W J Webber

Chairmen:
| Mr G W Johnson | 1907-1937 |
| Mr F Burton | 1938-1946 |

Clerk
| Mr E B Budding | 1923-1929 |
| Mr F G Balcombe | 1929-1964 |

Councillors and Clerks

Between 1924 and 1938 23 parishioners served on the Parish Council. Amongst their number were only two women, Mrs Margaret Tasker Brown and Mrs Louisa Houghton. Miss Ruth Turnbull had been the first woman member of the Council. Co-opted in December 1919, she had resigned in 1922 on becoming Mrs Langdon Down. In that year Mrs Tasker Brown became the first elected woman councillor. In 1928 she was joined on the Council by her husband. Mrs Houghton joined the Council in the same year.

During this period two Vicars of Hildenborough served as councillors, the Reverend L G Chamberlen and the Reverend W H Bass. Mr Chamberlen, holder of the Military Cross, was Vicar from 1924 to 1934 and joined the Council in 1927. He was particularly active as a councillor and was a driving force behind the purchase of land for the Recreation Ground. At the Council meeting on 19th March 1934 the Minutes record that –

"The Chairman proposed a hearty vote of thanks to the retiring Council and especially mentioned the Reverend Chamberlen for the work he had done in connection with the Recreation Ground."

The Council had only two Chairmen during the years 1924 and 1938. The first was Mr George W Johnson whose service to the Council is unequalled. He was a member of the inaugural Council in 1894, serving as Councillor and Clerk until 1907 when he briefly held office as Treasurer, relinquishing that post when he became Chairman. He remained Chairman until the end of 1937. Thus he was Chairman for 30 years and for many years he never missed a meeting. It is sad to see in the Minute Book a reflection in later years of his declining health. Missed meetings invariably led to messages sent by the Council wishing him well and his return was greeted with a warm welcome. Nevertheless, he was clearly becoming increasingly frail as his signatures verifying the Minutes indicate.

Mr Johnson finally resigned on 9th December 1937 but he was not present to hear the tributes paid to him as the councillors accepted his resignation "with regret". His resignation letter stated...

"... that he had served on the Council ever since it was formed in 1894 and owing to his recent illness he felt he could no longer carry on with the work. He concluded by thanking the Members for the courtesy they had always shewn (sic) to him as Chairman."

It was agreed that the vacancy should not be filled until the next Annual Parish Meeting. This was held on 20th April 1938 when the Vice Chairman, Mr Frank Burton, was elected Chairman. In his absence, the Vicar, the Reverend W H Bass was elected Vice Chairman. Mr Bass, who had joined the Council in 1937, was Vicar of Hildenborough between 1935 and 1939. Mr Burton, elected to the Council in 1931, remained as Chairman until 1946.

Two Clerks served the Council in the period covered by the 1924-1938 Minute Book. Mr E B Budding held office from 1923 until his death in 1929. The Minutes of the Council meeting of 15th December 1924 reveal that as with previous Clerks, insurance was taken out by the Council against the misappropriation of funds by the Clerk. The Council agreed to pay an annual premium of 4/- so, presumably, the risk was regarded as very low! Mr Budding's salary was £10 p.a., payable quarterly. In addition to this sum, the Minutes for 15th November 1926 show that Mr Budding received £26 p.a. as "Assistant Overseer" of the Poor. The Council paid for his "National Health Insurance" and "Unemployment Insurance" of 9/9 and 8/8 per quarter respectively according to the Minutes of 1st November 1927. Occasionally the Clerk was paid an additional sum for extra duties. Mr Budding was paid 15/- on 15th October 1928 for "Work getting out Notices re: Fires".

A Parish Meeting was held on 13th November 1928 to discuss street lighting. This involved considerable extra work for Mr Budding and he received additional payments:

Arranging for 500 Notices of the meeting to be
printed and distributed	15-0d
For acting as Poll Clerk at the meeting	1-5-0d
"Getting out forms for Poll"	1-0-0d

Mr Budding was unable to attend the Council's meeting on 6th May 1929 and the Minutes were written up by one of the Councillors, Mr Alfred Smith, in the finest handwriting of any in the entire Minute Book. At the next meeting, on 4th June, the Chairman, Mr G W Johnson...

"... said that they had to meet under rather sad circumstances owing to the sudden death from pneumonia of the Clerk, Mr E B Budding."

The Council stood in silence "as a token of sympathy".

Clearly, it was necessary to appoint a new clerk as soon as possible and it was agreed that the Chairman and Vice Chairman (Mr F H Buss) should draft an advertisement for the position. The full Council would meet to consider the applications with the appointment to run from 1st July. The Chairman commented that …

"… the work had enormously increased in recent years and the post was under paid at £10 a year. It was agreed that the salary be increased to £20 per annum."

The special meeting of the Council to appoint a new Clerk was held on 28th June 1929. It was reported that …

"The following advertisement was inserted in 'The Courier' of June 14th: Wanted: Clerk to the Parish Council of Hildenborough. Salary £20 per annum. Usual duties, which include recording Minutes of the Council and of their Committees, collecting allotment rents, keeping the accounts and preparing the balance sheet, and such other duties as appertain to the office of Clerk to a Parish Council – Applications in writing to be sent to the Chairman, Mr G W Johnson, Noble Tree Cross, Hildenborough stating age and qualifications by Saturday 22nd June next."

14 applications were received in response to the advertisement – which cost the Council 9/3d – and Mr Johnson and Mr Buss drew up a shortlist of three for interview by the Parish Council. After the interviews a vote was taken and Mr Fred Balcombe was appointed.

Mr Smith, who had acted as Clerk for the past weeks offered to assist Mr Balcombe as far as possible. It was reported that …

"… the clerical work was considerably in arrears … It was decided Mr Balcombe should be paid for additional work when it was completed."

Mr Balcombe gave outstanding service to the Council and to the village holding the post of Clerk until 1964. At the time of his appointment he was Chief Officer of the Village Fire Brigade. "This is Hildenborough from A-Z" records that he was "Hildenborough's first lollipop man" – there is a fine photograph of him fulfilling this role.

With effect from 1st July 1935 Mr Balcombe's salary was increased from £20 to £30 per annum. As in the past, this was paid quarterly.

There is a sad entry in the Council Minutes for 19th October 1936 recording the resignation of Dr D B Fraser as a councillor:

"The Clerk was instructed to write to Dr Fraser and thank him for all he had done in connection with Parish affairs, particularly the Recreation Ground and the Silver Jubilee. The Council expressed their regret that the Doctor was forced to go abroad and they hoped the change would restore his daughter to health."

Elections to the Council were held every three years by a show of hands at the Parish Meeting. Until 1947 when the number was increased to the current level of eleven, there were nine seats on the Council and it wasn't until 1st April 1948 that elections took place by secret ballot. At these Parish Meetings to elect the Council the number present was sometimes low. In March 1931 63 parishioners met to elect 9 candidates from 13 nominations. For conducting the election, as Returning Officer, Mr B Lee of Tonbridge Rural District Council was paid a fee of 11/9d.

Most Council meetings were held at the Drill Hall with some at the adjoining Institute in Riding Lane. A few took place across the road at the school whilst the meeting on 15th July 1935 was held in the Pavilion at the Recreation Ground. Most meetings took place on Monday evenings but they could be held on other days. A few were held on Saturdays.

In April 1928 the Council decided to hold meetings at fixed intervals. Regular meetings would be held on the third Monday in January, April, July and October with additional meetings as required. Committees would report to these meetings. In that year there were Finance, Fire Brigade, Allotments and Footpaths Committees. In later years Lighting and Recreation Ground Committees were established whilst the work of the Footpaths Committee was expanded to include 'Health and General Purposes'.

Throughout the period of the Minute Book 1924-1938 Council meetings began with prayers. Meanwhile, at the 20th April 1928 meeting the Council considered the suggestion that smoking be permitted at meetings. Mr Buss, seconded by the Vicar, the Reverend L G Chamberlen, MC, proposed that smoking be allowed...

> "... but one Member said he did not think it was quite the thing to do whilst discussing the affairs of the parish."

That view didn't prevail and the Council voted to permit smoking at meetings.

The period 1924-1938 marked years of political tension covering episodes like the General Strike of 1926, the rise of the Labour Party, the problems following the Wall Street Crash of 1929, the formation of the National Government in 1931 and the Abdication Crisis of 1936 to mention just a few. However, at no time did party politics enter the Parish Council. Only once did the Council discuss something that related to one of the controversial national issues of the day when the Chairman, Mr G W Johnson, read a letter at the meeting of 21st January 1929 from ...

> "... the Honorary Secretary of the Tonbridge appeal, Miners' Relief Fund and it was decided that as the Women's Institute were arranging for a house to house collection in Hildenborough, the matter be laid on the table."

A name that features in the Council Minutes quite frequently is that of Col. F Harris, Tonbridge Rural District Council's Surveyor. Sometimes he attended Parish Council meetings but the Council regularly consulted him about problems in Hildenborough. The Colonel had a remarkable record of service to the community and at the Council meeting of 12th February 1935...

> "Councillors and ex-councillors were invited to subscribe to a fund organised by the Clerk to Pembury Parish Council for a presentation to Col. Harris as a token of appreciation for his services at District Surveyor for 46 years."

On 18th March 1935 the Council agreed that "Mr Mackney and Mr Francis should represent the Parish Council at the luncheon to be given in honour of Col. Harris". The Minutes for 9th September record that "Mr W N Miller" attended the meeting as successor to Col. Harris when "A hearty vote of thanks was passed to the Surveyor for his attendance and explanations".... about "the Town Planning Acts and the Zoning of the Parish etc.".

For some years Hildenborough was represented on the Rural District Council by Mr Horace Hills and the Minutes for 6th May 1929 record that "it was an honour to Hildenborough that he was Chairman of the Rural District Council". At the Council meeting of 11th April 1930 it was noted that ...

> "Mr Horace Hills' resignation from the Tonbridge Rural District Council had caused a vacancy for a representative from the Parish of Hildenborough on the Tonbridge Rural District Council. The Council pledged themselves to support Mr John Mackney, with one exception."

Mr Mackney was the Parish Council's Vice Chairman. There is no indication of the outcome of the election but he appears to have won as there is a reference in the Minutes for 18th January 1937 when he was asked to report to the Rural District Council about the provision of Council houses.

Pounds, Shillings and Pence (£ s. d.)

The present decimal currency dates from 1971 and it is perhaps helpful to give examples of conversions from the old pounds, shillings and pence:

6d (sixpence)	= 2½p	1/- (one shilling)	=	5p
2/6 (half a crown)	= 12½p	5/- (five shillings, a crown)	=	25p
One guinea (one pound and one shilling) = £1.05p				

At each Council meeting approval had to be given for various payments to be made. These examples give some idea of monetary values at the time.

Dec. 1924	Tonbridge Water Co.	Supplying water for fountain for the year	£1
July 1925	Tonbridge Joint Burial Board	Annual payment	£11
Feb 1926	Guarantee premium	The Clerk - for one year	4/-
	Mr Balcombe	Fireman's boots	£3
Nov. 1926	Mr C Barkaway	Rent – Forge Farm allotments – one year	£8
	Hobson & Sons	Fireman's helmet	£2/6/4
April 1927	Merryweather & Sons	Fireman's uniform	£4/7/6
	Mr H C Skinner	Work on War Memorial	£2/10/-
July 1927	Mr R Woodhams	Repairing fountain	7/6
Jan. 1928	Mr A Skinner	Work on allotments	£5/10/6
Mar. 1928	Mr G B Budding – Clerk	Postage for the year	12/8
	Mr G W Johnson	Rent – Fire station	£1
	Mr G W Johnson	Hire of meeting rooms 14@2/6	£1/15/-
July 1928	Mr W J Webber	Repair to mowing machine	12/6
July 1929	Tonbridge Rural District Council	Rates – 6mths	10/9
Oct. 1929	Tonbridge Free Press	Advertisement for new clerk	6/6
	Brock & Co	Maroons and carriage	£2/9/-
July 1930	Mr A Skinner	Work on Village Green	£1/7/-
Oct. 1930	Parochial Church Council	Rent for seat set into churchyard wall	1/-
	Mr E Towle	3mths salary – work on Village Green	10/-
Jan. 1931	Mrs Slattery	Cleaning after meetings	2/-
April 1931	Mr B Lee	Returning Officer for election	11/9
	Clerk's Insurance Bond	Renewal for one year	5/-
Oct. 1931	National Fire Brigade	Affiliation fee for one year	£1/10/-
	Shelter insurance	Village Green	2/6
Nov. 1931	Merryweathers	New fire hose	£8/15/8
	Tonbridge U.D. Council	Use of motor roller	£1/10/-
Jan. 1932	B K Smith	Battery for fire lamp	10/-
	T Nutting	Work on cricket pitch	£6/10/-
Mar 1932	T Nutting	Extra for rolling	5/-
April 1932	R Woodhams	Removing fire maroon box	3/9
July 1932	B Goodale	Flagpole – Recreation Ground	4/-
Oct. 1932	A Huggett	Spiles and rails for Forge Farm allotments	£2/0/6
	Smith (Brasted Ltd)	Stone	£2/14/0
	B Goodale	Repairs to Village Green seat	11/-
July 1933	Searle Austen & Barnes	Drinking cup for fountain	5/-

Oct. 1933	J Sturgess	Queen Anne's Bounty	3/10
	M Ponsford	Material and repairs to footbridge	£2/10/9
April 1934	J Sturgess	Tithe	3/10
	R Woodhams & Son	Repairs at Pavilion	7/9
July 1934	C Bishop	Repairs to mower	12/-
Jan. 1935	G Baker	Bridge repairs	£9/2/6
	Merryweather	Fire hose 1x50ft	£2/19/8
Mar, 1935	Warner, Son & Brydone	Re: tithe	£2/2/-
April 1935	Postmaster General	Fire telephone	£2/18/5
July 1935	Farrants	Recreation Ground roller	£6/8/3
	R Woodhams	Painting Pavilion	£15/10/-
	Reliant Fencing Co.	Fencing – Recreation Ground	£5/12/-
Sept. 1935	Brock	Maroons for fire calls	£2/5/9
	Tonbridge U.D. Council	Purchase of fire tender	£10/-/-
April 1936	Parish Clerk	Postage – one year 1935/36	11/3
Oct 1936	Webber's Garage	Rent for tender etc.	£2/8/3
Jan 1937	Southern Railway	Carriage – hose couplings	11d
	Woodman, Tonbridge	Copper wire for hose binding	5/-
July 1938	W Pratt	Concrete round swings etc	£21/8/-
	Parker	Repairs to 3 pairs of firemen's boots	7/-
	Fermor	Sand for children's pit	15/-

Finance

Each year the Council appointed a Finance Committee which made recommendations to the full Council about the raising of revenue through the precept levied on the Tonbridge Rating Authority. The Council, under the Rating and Valuation Act, 1925, elected two "Local Government Electors" to serve on the Authority's Rating and Valuation Committee. The first nominees, chosen on 20th April 1927 to serve for one year were Parish Councillors Mr J Mackney (of Limes, Mill Lane) and Mr J T Fellowes Wilson (of Oak Lodge, on the corner of Tonbridge Road and Leigh Road – remembered nowadays by Fellowes Way and Wilson Close). The Committee also recommended accounts for payment by the Council. The Committee Minutes were recorded in a separate book, no longer in existence, with the exception of the meeting of 25th May 1925 which are in the Minute Book for Council meetings. At that meeting Mr F H Buss made a complaint, regularly made whilst he was on the Council, asking ...

> "... why the Council should have to pay £11 per annum to the Tonbridge Joint Burial Board"

He felt that as Hildenborough had its own burial ground this payment, first made in 1900, should no longer be paid. It was still being paid in 2015, but Tonbridge & Malling Borough Council has now agreed that it should no longer be paid. Mr Buss, at the same meeting suggested that the Council maintained "an inventory of all the Parish Council's property", now standard practice.

The Minutes for the Council meeting on 17th February 1927 give an indication of the Parish Council's finances. A letter had been received from Tonbridge Rural District Council asking for an estimate of expenditure and income for the year to 31st March 1928. The Clerk considered that expenditure would total £159, income £19 making "a nett requirement of £140". The same meeting "decided to issue a precept upon the overseers for £164 to purchase the new ground and for work to be done thereon". This referred to the purchase of the land for the Village Green.

On 28th June 1929 a report was given to the Council about the new rating assessments for the village:

"Their penny rate had dropped under the De-rating Act from £99 to £64 and the Council would be compelled to economise in their expenditure on village improvement."

The Clerk, Mr F G Balcombe, reported to the Council on 20th March 1930 about ...

"... an interview with the Clerk to the Rating Authority regarding the estimate of money required by the Council for the Financial Year ending March 31st 1931. £222 had been asked for and as the Council had exceeded their estimate for the previous year it was hoped they would not exceed £160 if possible in 1930-1931."

The Annual Meeting of the Parish Council on 11th April 1930 approved the accounts for the year ending 31st March:

Total receipts £216-2-10d	Expenditure £175-14-9½d
Balance at Bank as per pass book	£36-4-4d
Cash in hand with Clerk	£4-3-8½d

Payments to the "Tonbridge Burial Joint Committee" were made by the Parish each year although Hildenborough no longer used Tonbridge Cemetery for burials. On 19th January 1931 the Council received a demand from the Committee...

"... for the sum of £7-4-6d being one sixth of the sum expended on St Stephen's Churchyard. The Clerk was instructed to obtain a statement as to how the money was spent before paying the amount".

The sum was duly paid.

Mr F H Buss lodged his annual protest against the payments made to the Tonbridge Burial Board on 23rd November 1937. There was some sympathy for Mr Buss's view as the Minutes show:

"Mr Mackney agreed it was obsolete and ought not to be continued."

Mr Mackney had recently retired as Vice Chairman of the Council.

The Village Fire Brigade

The Parish Council had been established in 1894 and one of the powers conferred on it was the power to maintain a Village Fire Brigade. For a few years the Council took no action but in November 1900 Tonbridge Urban District Council proposed a scheme whereby it took over the management of the existing Tonbridge Fire Brigade for the benefit of Tonbridge and the neighbouring parishes. Following lengthy negotiations it was agreed in 1907 that the Urban District Council's Brigade would serve Hildenborough for a fee of £21 p.a.. In 1908 the Council heard that a "supplementary Fire Brigade of four men to drill with the Tonbridge Brigade" had been set up.

The period of the Minute Book from 18th July 1924 to 19th July 1938 shows that the Parish Council devoted much time to the activities of the Village Fire Brigade. Eventually, under the 1938 Fire Brigade Act, Tonbridge Rural District Council took over responsibility for parish brigades with effect from 29th January 1939 and the village's volunteer brigade was disbanded.

At the first meeting of the Council covered by the Minute Book on 18th July 1924 a report on the Village Brigade was given by "Chief Officer Woodhams" about hydrants. The Clerk, Mr E B Budding, was "instructed to order a pair of fireman's boots and cap for Fireman Quinnell". Estimates for "6 lengths" of "fire hose" were to be obtained. It was agreed...

"... that as soon as the Chief Officer's report of a fire is received, payment should be made to the men...".

It was also agreed that the Council would pay an annual subscription to the National Fire Brigade Union on behalf of the firemen. The Council would pay for insurance to cover the firemen in case of ...

"... accidents or illness that may occur from doing their duty at drills or attendance at fires."

Rules for the Brigade were to be drawn up for consideration by the Council's Fire Brigade Committee. The Clerk was asked to get particulars about "either a 'Pyrena' or a 'Minimax Fire Extinguisher'". He was instructed to purchase an "Electric Hand Lamp" for use by the Chief Officer when attending fires.

Finally, the same Council meeting approved a payment of £15 to Tonbridge Urban District Council for the services of the Brigade for one year. It was agreed to pay Tonbridge Waterworks £1-7-4 for repairs to a hydrant.

The Minute Book doesn't usually have a record of Committee meetings but details of a meeting of the Fire Brigade Committee on 21st October 1924 are included:

1. The Clerk was asked to order "6 lengths of hose, each 50 feet of 'Rose' brand" at once as they were urgently required.
2. It was proposed that each fireman should be insured for £300 with insurance of £500 for the captain.
3. When the Minimax Fire Extinguisher came to hand "it should be either put up in the Institute passage or Mrs Sparrowhawk be asked to have it in her home."
4. The Captain reported that "the Members of the Brigade are compelled to have 12 hourly drills in the year."

Meanwhile, on 22nd September 1924 the Council approved proficiency payments for the firemen: R Woodhams, Captain £1-10-0d, George Killick, Second Officer, £1, Firemen E Quinnell, F W Hoare and F Balcombe 15/- each. Also approved was a payment of 4/- to Hobson & Son for a "Fireman's cap" whilst boots for Mr Balcombe cost £3.

On 17th April 1925 the Council considered the set of Rules for Brigade members:

1. The Brigade is under the sole control of the Parish Council.
2. The Captain is responsible to the Council for the control of the Brigade.
3. The pay shall be 15/- for each fireman which shall be paid at the end of each year.
4. The Brigade shall consist of Captain, 2nd Officer and four men.
5. The men shall be paid for fires within one month at least of the fire, before if possible.
6. The pay for attendance at a fire to be as follows:
   Call and first two hours   7/6
   After the first two hours   2/- per hour
7. All members of the Brigade must attend fire calls and drills unless able to give the Captain a satisfactory reason for absence.
8. Any member attending a fire or drill when under the influence of drink, he may be suspended by the Captain and reported to the Council.
9. There shall be 12 drills each year.

With the exception of No.8 the Council adopted the Rules. At the same meeting the Council considered a report from the Captain about the conduct of one of the men. It was decided to ask the Captain to seek the man's resignation. Steps would be taken to fill the vacancy. This decision was subsequently rescinded and the offender given "a second chance" at the Council's meeting on 25th September 1925.

The meeting on 17th April 1925 authorised the payment of £27-18-9d to "Messrs Rose Hose Co. Ltd – lengths of hose, couplings and leather straps."

The Council approved the payment of the annual retainer for the firemen on 25th September 1925 at the same rate as hitherto. Payment of the annual subscription of £1-10-0d to the "National Fire Brigade Association" was agreed. It transpired that in the past this subscription had been paid "out of his own pocket" by the Captain, Mr R Woodhams. A vote of thanks to him was passed.

Unfortunately, details of the Fire Brigade Committee's Reports to the Council are not recorded in the Minutes but some information about the Brigade's activities can be gleaned when Council decisions are minuted. The Minutes for 15th February 1926 record approval for the following payments:

Hobson & Son Ltd.	Firemen's uniforms	£10-7-6d
Seal Austin & Barnes	Hydrant Plates	£2-2-0d
F Balcombe	Fireman's Boots	£3-0-0d

A "special Meeting" of the Council ten days later agreed that the annual rent for the Fire Station should be £1. The Station was situated at the Riding Lane end of Church Road where the Village Hall kitchen is today.

A change of Fire Brigade Captain was recorded on 19th April 1926. Mr Woodhams had resigned and "Mr A W Tomlinson" was appointed Captain in his place. At the Council's meeting on 15th November 1926 payments of £2-6-4 to Hobson & Sons for a fireman's helmet and £4-18-9 for the annual pay for the firemen were approved. The pay had been increased this year:

Second officer   £1-3-9d (increased from £1)

Firemen: F Balcombe, E Quinnell, A Upton and F W Hoare
                                        18-9d each (increased from 15-0d)

There was no mention of a payment to the Captain.

The Council meeting of 27th January 1927 heard from the Chairman, Mr G W Johnson, that …

"… the Tonbridge Fire Brigade's engine was temporarily out of use and that he had asked Captain Tomlinson to ask the Sevenoaks Fire Brigade to stand by to help our Fire Brigade in the event of a fire taking place in this Parish."

Fires were apparently rare but the Council on 20th April heard of one when a letter from Mr W W Horsburgh of "Shirley Dene" was read in which …

"… he expressed his appreciation for the great help of the Fire Brigade in helping to extinguish his motor car which caught alight in his garage."

At that meeting:

"The question was raised as to the advisability of having a number at the Telephone Exchange of the Fire Brigade, but nothing was decided, as, in the event of a fire, anyone calling up the exchange would only call 'Fire' and the exchange would ring up Mr Tomlinson."

Amongst the accounts approved for payment that evening was one for £4-7-6d to Merryweather & Sons for a fireman's uniform.

The Fire Brigade Committee frequently discussed the provision of hydrants in the Parish and on 19th July 1927 the Committee recommended to the Council …

"… that 2 new hydrants be put in the Stocks Green Road and the Clerk was instructed to write to the Tonbridge Water Co. to have these put in as soon as possible, one opposite the Old Barn Tea House and one near Barley Corn Cottages."

The "Tea House" was owned by Commander A W Tomlinson, the Fire Brigade Captain. The same meeting approved…

"Firemen's Pay for turning out to fire at Mr Cazalet's Farm on 4th May - £1-5-0d"

In addition to the annual retainer fee, the fireman were paid for each fire attended. The owner of the property or their insurers would be sent a bill for the Brigade's services.

At the Council meeting on 1st November 1927 the annual payments to the firemen were approved:

Firemen's pay plus 4 wet drills each

2nd Officer Balcombe	£1-15-0
Fireman Quinnell	£1-10-0
Fireman Upton	£1-10-0
Fireman Killick	£1-10-0
Fireman Hoare	£1-10-0

As in the previous year there is no record of a payment to the Captain, Cdr A W Tomlinson who, apparently, gave his services free.

On 12th January 1928 the Council heard that the two hydrants ordered the previous July for Stocks Green Road had not been installed. Tonbridge Water Co. stated that they would be "installed as soon as they got delivery of same". That meeting went on to consider long service medals for eligible firemen. The matter would be taken up with the National Fire Brigades Association. It was felt that four firemen qualified together with "Mr W Clark as late Captain of the Brigade".

The Council considered a letter received ...

"... from the Tunbridge Wells & District Steam Fire Brigade in which they asked the Council to give them financial support."

It was unanimously agreed "that the letter be laid on the table".

"Fireman Hoare's boots" were discussed by the Council on 8th March 1928 and it was agreed that new ones should be purchased for him. The Minutes for 16th July show that the Council passed for payment an account of £3-2-6d for the boots. The same meeting agreed to pay "Hobson & Son" £6-5-5d for a fireman's uniform. Perhaps this was for a new recruit as there is reference to a payment of 16/3d to "Seal" in the list of annual payments approved that evening.

From time to time the Council considered the state of the Fire Station and on 20th April 1928 the question of "repairing the roof and painting the door" was brought up. The Fire Brigade Committee was authorised to get the work done.

The Council meeting of 16th July 1928 heard from Mr F H Buss of the Fire Brigade Committee that consideration was being given to reviewing the agreement with Tonbridge Urban District Council and their Fire Brigade. Hildenborough paid an annual retainer of £15 to the Urban District Council for the services of the town's Brigade. It had been agreed that there should be a meeting between Commander Tomlinson, Hildenborough's Captain, and Captain Bradley from Tonbridge to draw up suggestions for a new agreement. The Parish Council considered that the retainer fee "should be reduced considerably".

On 15th October 1928 the Council received a Report from the Fire Brigade Committee but few details are given in the Minutes except that ...

"It was suggested that this Council sever their connection with the Tonbridge Fire Brigade."

The meeting authorised payments to the firemen for their attendance at a fire at Forge Farm:

Captain Tomlinson   £1

Firemen Balcombe, Upton, Killick and Quinnell   12/6 each

It was reported that the Brigade had attended a fire at Hilden Farm on 22nd July but the firemen hadn't been paid as the sum of £15-3-0d had not been received from the Insurance Company. Mr Buss, of the Fire Brigade Committee...
> "... pointed out that this payment to the Firemen was the Council's liability and should therefore be paid".

Payments were approved for the Brigade members:
"Second Officer Balcombe	£2-11-6
Fireman Seal	£1-7-6
Fireman Quinnell	£2-5-6
Fireman Upton	£2-13-6
Fireman Killick	£1-2-6"

This discussion was followed by the presentation of long service medals:
Silver Medal	20 years	George Killick
Bronze Medals	10 years	2nd Officer Balcolmbe; Fireman Hoare

Was the former Captain, Mr R Woodhams, eligible for a medal? The meeting heard that part of his service had been with the Sevenoaks Brigade who would be contacted about Mr Woodhams' service with them. He was presented with a silver long service medal at the Council meeting on 15th April 1929. It was confirmed that he had 25 years' service with the Sevenoaks and Hildenborough Brigades and "was still carrying on as Hon. Officer".

At the April 1929 meeting it was reported that "a rate payer" in the Parish had paid a "Retaining Fee to the Leigh Brigade". She wished to know if, should there be a fire at her home, she should call the Leigh Brigade. Would Leigh be permitted to use Hildenborough's hydrants? The question was referred to the Fire Brigade Committee. The same meeting approved the payment of £12-16-0 to Tonbridge Water Company for hydrants. On 6th May 1929 it was reported "that the Leigh Fire Brigade could not possibly be permitted to use Hildenborough's hydrants".

The Council agreed on 15th July 1929 that a new type of hydrant "of the modern screw down type at a cost of £6-10-0" should be fixed outside the Parish Church. Authority was given for the payment of £15 to cover the retaining fee to the Urban District Council. £6-16-6 as "Firemen's pay for three fires was agreed" and a total of £7-15-0 for "Fireman's Drill Pay" for one year was also approved.

The Minutes for the Council meeting on 20th March 1930 recorded the resignation of George Killick "as a fireman after over twenty years through illness." At the same meeting it was agreed ....
> "... that a Fire Bell extension for night calls be added to the telephone at Mr Quinnell's at an additional rent of one shilling and six pence per quarter."

Fireman Quinnell lived at No. 8 Riding Lane and fired the maroon to summon the firemen to the Fire Station in Church Road nearby.

The Brigade vacancy was filled by the Council on 11th April 1930 when Mr W Woodgate was appointed. A uniform would be ordered for him whilst it was agreed...
> "...that owing to Mr Killick having served the Brigade over 20 years he should be presented with his uniform and equipment."

Sadly, George Killick died within months of his retirement and at their meeting on 27th May 1930 councillors agreed to send a letter of sympathy to his parents.

The meeting on 11th April also considered the need for "new hose" and agreed that two hydrants "be fixed, one at or near the Black Arch, the other near the Lower Cock Inn".

The Brigade Captain, Mr Tomlinson, reported to the Council on 21st July 1930 that firemen had been called ...
> "... to the residence of Mr S Constable. The Clerk reported that he had

111

rendered an account for thirty shillings and had received a cheque from Mr Constable for that amount."

The Council agreed at this meeting to pay to Hobson & Son the sum of £9-12-0 for the equipment for Fireman W Woodgate, the replacement for the late George Killick.

For the next few months the Council was preoccupied with the purchase of the land for the Recreation Ground but on 15th April 1931 the Clerk, Mr F G Balcombe reported that …

"… the Fire Brigade received a call to 'Hildacot' on 8th March and an account for £2-5-0 had been sent to the owner of the property."

Mr Balcombe told the Council on 20th July that a new hydrant had been installed outside the Church and that "the KCC had promised to repair the hydrant at the corner of Mount Pleasant Road".

On 26th October 1931 the Council adopted proposals from the Fire Brigade Committee:

1. Two 50ft lengths of hose would be purchased at once and then "one length per annum".
2. The telephone be moved from Mr Quinnell's house to that of the Clerk (opposite the Village Green).
3. The "maroon box would be installed on the Village Green."
4. The Clerk, who was the Brigade's Chief Officer would "fire the maroon on receiving a fire call".

An account for two lengths of hose for £8-15-8 from Merryweather's was approved for payment by the Council at the meeting of 30th November 1931. The same meeting agreed to the payment of £13-1-0 to Tonbridge Water Works for hydrants.

The firing of the maroon on the Village Green led to a complaint…

"…signed by 19 rate payers in reference to the fire maroon being used between 10pm and 6am."

This was considered by the Council on 18th January 1932 and it was agreed that the Chief Officer should decide if the firing of the maroon between those hours was really necessary. The same meeting agreed to "purchase leggings for the firemen."

From time to time the Council received reports of fires in the village. For instance on 21st March 1932 the meeting heard that …

"The Fire Brigade received a call to Woodfield Avenue on 2nd March 1932. The account had been forwarded to Messrs Brooks & Son, Bradford Street, Tonbridge."

Councillor Major C E W Charrington was not present at the Council meeting of 20th April 1933 when the Clerk reported that the Fire Brigade had been called to his house, Vines, on "Saturday April 1st at 9.20pm." A letter from Major Charrington was read asking…

"… that it should be made known that he was more than delighted at the very prompt way in which the Fire Brigade turned out."

The Clerk reported that an account had been sent to the Major "for Fire Brigade services for £3-8-6". At the Council's meeting on 17th July 1933 the Clerk reported that following a chimney fire on 15th June a cheque for £1-17-6 had been received for the services of the Brigade.

On 16th July 1934 the Council discussed the testing of fire extinguishers and private hydrants. Details were left to the Fire Brigade Committee but the Council agreed that …

"… Hydrant covers be painted white. The paint had been given and the members of the Brigade were willing to do the painting."

The Council authorised the purchase of "three new 50ft lengths of hose" at the meeting of 21st January 1935 together with repairs to twelve lengths of hose. The Minutes show that "Merryweather" charged £2-19-8 per 50ft length of hose. The Council agreed that the Fire Brigade Committee...

"... should be given power to act regarding the purchase of a motor tender which Tonbridge Urban District Council had for disposal for a price of about £10. The Committee were authorised to dispose of the manual."

The Trustees of the Institute had considered an architect's report on the Fire Station but they "regretted that they could do nothing to improve the condition." The Brigade rented the land on Church Road for the Fire Station at the back of the Institute. The Council paid the rent of £1 p.a. according to the Minutes for the meeting of 26th October 1931. In addition rates were paid – a payment of 9/7d was approved on 22nd October 1934.

The Clerk reported on 12th February 1935 that the Council's offer of £10 for the "motor tender" for sale by the Urban District Council had been accepted. This led the Chief Officer, Commander Tomlinson of the Old Barn, to offer to buy the manual tender for "two guineas". His offer was accepted. The Fire Brigade Committee was asked to investigate possible locations for housing the motor tender. The Committee would also "obtain quotations for third party insurance". At the next Council meeting, on 18th March 1935, the Village Green was mentioned as a possible site for housing the tender.

Was the Village Green a suitable site for housing the tender? The Fire Brigade Committee recommended it to the Council on 15th April 1935 but did the Deeds allow building on the Green? The matter was referred to the Council's legal advisors for an opinion. Meanwhile, the Council continued to maintain the Brigade, paying accounts as they were presented. At this April meeting approval was given for payments to...

"Merryweather	New hose	£10-7-2
Tonbridge Urban District Council	Fire Brigade Retainer	£15
Postmaster General	Fire 'phone	£2-18-5"

On 15th July 1935 the Fire Brigade Committee reported that the Council's solicitors...

"... Messrs Warner, Son & Brydone had perused the deeds relating to the Village Green and they found that there was no restriction to prevent the Council from building on that portion of the green obtained from Mrs Elizabeth Baker."

It was agreed that the newly acquired tender should for the time being be housed at Mr Webber's garage next to the 'Half Moon'. The Committee also reported on changes of personnel within the Brigade. The Council accepted the resignation of Cmdr. Tomlinson as Chief Officer and appointed Mr Fred Balcombe (Clerk to the Council) as his successor. The Committee was given the authority to appoint – and equip – two additional members of the Brigade. The list of accounts for payment show that Third Party insurance for the "Motor Tender" had been arranged with Municipal Insurance for a premium of £5-10-0. Firemen's "Annual Drill Pay" totalling £7-15-0 was approved.

The Chief Officer reported to the Council on 9th September 1935 that the Brigade had been called out to Meopham Bank on 8th August. An account for the Brigade's services of £5-0-6 had been sent to Mrs MacFadyen. Several of the accounts approved for payment at that meeting relate to the Brigade:

Hobson & Sons	Fire Brigade clothing	£14-19-8
Brock	Maroons for fire calls	£2-5-9
Members of the Brigade	Services at Meopham Bank fire	£3-0-0
Tonbridge Urban District Council	Purchase of Fire Tender	£10-0-0

Second Officer Upton was the latest member of the Brigade to be awarded a long service medal. On 20th January 1936 the Council agreed that he should receive a bronze medal for ten years' service.

Later that year, on 19th October, it was reported to the Council that the Brigade had attended a fire at Forge Farm in Riding Lane on 29th September. This must have been a

major incident since the account, paid in full, which was sent to the insurers Law Fire and Insurance, totalled £17-6-0. Accounts subsequently approved for payment include:
"Wages for Fire Brigade at Fire including messenger   £12-17-6
Six breakfasts – Firemen at recent fire   3-0
An account for £2-8-3 for "Rent for Tender etc." submitted by Webber's Garage was approved.

At that October 1936 meeting the Council adopted recommendations by the Fire Brigade Committee …

"… that appliances etc. for the use of the Fire Brigade be obtained as soon as possible for a sum not exceeding forty pounds. Firms supplying goods with a discount for cash paid within one month to be paid within that period subject to the Committee's approval of such goods obtained."

On 18th January 1937 the Clerk reported that the Brigade had been called to "Hawden Farm by Mrs Hamlyn on 17th December 1936". An account for £15-18-6 had been sent to the insurers. The list of payments approved at that meeting show that the wages for the firemen at "Hamlyn's fire Dec. 17th – 18th " totalled £11-11-0. The Council also approved numerous other payments for the Brigade including:

Southern Railway	Carriage – hose couplings	11d
Tonbridge Rural District Council	Rates – fire station	10-6
Pocock Bros	New boots for Fireman Stroud	1-16-8
Pyrene Fire Extinguisher Co.	Brigade equipment	11-17-6
Hobson & Sons	New leggings for firemen	1-2-6
S Dixon & Sons	Fire Brigade equipment	3-15-3
Cayless Bros	Fire Brigade equipment	6-4-4
Corfe & Son	Fire Brigade first aid box	13-8
AKWA Hose Coy	Fire Brigade equipment	4-14-2
Seibe Gorman & Co	Fire Brigade equipment	15-6
Woodman, Tonbridge	Copper wire for hose binding	5-0
Kent Wallpaper Co.	Paint, varnish, brushes for fire ladder etc.	12-7
Municipal Mutual Insurance	Fire Brigade and 2 casual workers	2-3-2
Webber's Garage	Housing tender etc	2-6-0
National Fire Brigade Association	Subscription	1-10-0
Hobson & Sons	Hat for Fire Brigade 2nd officer	8-0

It was agreed that Webber's Garage "should fix safety glass to the windscreen of the Fire Tender as soon as possible". This was done and on 5th April 1937 an account for £8-18-7 to cover "garage of tender and safety glass etc." was submitted by Webber's Garage and approved for payment. At the same meeting the annual retainer fee of £15 payable to the Urban District Council was also approved for payment. From the numbers of accounts relating to the Brigade that were paid by the Council it is clear that a significant proportion of the Council's expenditure related to the Village Fire Service.

Fireman Quinnell's resignation from the Brigade was submitted to the Council on 19th July 1937 on grounds of ill health. He was thanked for his services over the previous eleven years. The Council asked the Fire Brigade Committee "to engage another Fireman and to have him properly clothed and equipped". The Committee was also asked to "prepare a scheme for building a Fire Station to house the tender".

Significant matters relating to the future of the Brigade were considered at the Council meeting on 18th October 1937.

1. Three firemen were paid a total of 15/- for attending a fire on 2nd September
2. The annual purchase of a 50ft length of hose was reported.
3. Matters relating to "Air Raid Precautions" were considered.

4. It was agreed to pay Hobson & Son £2-19-1 for "Fireman Haffenden's clothing" and White 5/6 for his hat.
5. It was agreed to bring before the Rural District Council the possibility of that Council...

> "... taking over the Fire Brigades in Rural Parishes as had recently been done by Sevenoaks Rural District Council concerning Leigh".

Parish Councillor Mr J Mackney would raise the matter in his capacity as a member of Tonbridge Rural District Council.

The next Council meeting on 23rd November 1937 heard that there was "no immediate likelihood of the Fire Brigades in the Tonbridge Rural District Council area being taken over". It was reported that the Brigade had been called to a chimney fire on Sunday 14th November at "the residence of Mr Martin of Russettings" who had been sent an account for £2-10-0 for the services of the Brigade. Southern Railway "had just settled an account for 15/- for the services of three firemen who were called to a fire in September".

There was so much business for the Council to consider at their meeting on 20th April 1938 that, after 2½ hours, it was adjourned until 28th April. Brigade matters were discussed then. Permission was given for the "Chief Officer of the Fire Brigade to erect a Rescue Platform for Drill purposes, also to fix a dummy hydrant, both at the Recreation Ground". It was agreed that Fireman David Seal should be awarded a bronze long service medal for ten years' Brigade membership. The Council's meeting of 19th July 1938 is the final one recorded in the Minute Book for the period from July 1924 and shows that the medal cost the Council 11/1d. The last entry in the Book refers to a "fire call":

> "The Chief Officer reported attending a fire with one fireman on 20th June 1938 at Post Office Cottages and an account for £1-7-6 had been sent to the insurance companies concerned. Full report appears in the Fire Brigade book."

Unfortunately, the book does not seem to have survived.

Allotments

The Parish Council was established in 1894 and from the start allotments were a matter that was frequently under discussion. The earliest allotments, originally leased from the Earl of Derby, were at Great Forge Farm in what is now Riding Lane whilst land was later to be acquired for additional plots beyond Watts Cross towards the Lower Cock Inn. These new Bourne Place allotments were leased by the Council in 1897 from Mr O d'Avigdor Goldsmid. In 1919 these London Road (now the B245) allotments were purchased by the Council. Further allotments were leased from Mr F O Streeten at Hilden Park but after the First World War the land was gradually released for building. The Minutes show that Mr Streeten was paid rent of £2-10-0 p.a. whilst Mr Charles Barkaway received £8 p.a. for the Great Forge Farm allotments.

The Council had an Allotments Committee which reported regularly to the full Council. For example, on 17th April 1925 it was reported ...

> "... that it would be necessary to have a ditch dug in the Hilden Allotments to help the surface water as it lay so wet during the Winter months, this would probably cost 30/-"

The Committee was authorised to spend up to £2 on this work. It was reported that...

> "... as this particular allotment was paying its way so well, the rent in future for 10 rods should be 5/- per year instead of 7/6, commencing 1st April 1925"

This was agreed. (A rod equals 5½ yards.)

Unfortunately the Minutes of the Allotments Committee apparently no longer exist and there are only occasional references to allotments in the Council Minutes. By 1928 there appeared to be a falling demand for plots as on 16th July 1928 the Council agreed ...

"... that some bills should be printed stating that there were 'allotments to let' and put up on the notice boards in the allotment grounds. It was decided to have 50 bills printed..."

The Council regularly employed men to undertake maintenance work at the allotments e.g. hedge cutting, ditch clearing, maintaining fences, installing marker posts, keeping empty plots in a reasonable state. On 16th July 1928 payments were authorised by the Council:

"J Springate   work on Forge Farm Allotments   £1-16-0
E Ledger   work on Hilden Allotments   £1-10-0

A payment of £2-8-4 to "E Goldsmith" for allotment work was approved on 21st January 1929. It was reported to the meeting that ...

"... one of the allotment holders had refused to pay his Allotment Rent of 5/-"

It was agreed that the Chairman, Mr G W Johnson, should write to the defaulter.

The decline in the demand for allotments was confirmed when on 15th July 1929 the Allotments Committee reported...

"... that the top half of Hilden Park Allotments were not in use and recommended that half should be surrendered."

It was pointed out that houses were being built nearby and that consequently the vacant plots might be needed. It was agreed to leave the matter for now but that "desirable" plots should be offered rent free for one year.

The Council held a special meeting on 25th November 1929. One item on the agenda was the Hilden Park allotments. Through his solicitors, Mr F O Streeten had asked if the Council ...

"... would be willing to permit Mr Streeten to retake possession of so much land as he will require on the Hilden Park Allotments."

It was known that there were plans to build houses in the area and it was agreed to call a meeting of allotment holders to discuss the situation.

A special meeting of the Council was called for 12 December 1929 when the following Resolution was carried by five votes to four –

"That this Council having fully considered the letter received from Messrs Warner, Son and Brydone on behalf of Mr Streeten, agrees to waive their rights under the Agreement for Allotments at Hilden Park, and give them up as from 30th June next, subject to Mr Streeten agreeing to compensate the Allotment Holders in the sum of £25 with an additional £5 to cover any cost the Council be put to in regard to any rearrangement of fencing etc.."

The Clerk, Mr F G Balcombe, "was instructed to give the Allotment Holders the necessary notice" providing that Mr Streeten agreed to pay the compensation.

On 20th January 1930 it was reported that Mr Streeten's solicitors were asking for "earlier possession of the allotments". It was agreed that the Allotments Committee should meet the plot holders to discuss this. On 20th March it was agreed that 3 months' notice was insufficient. It should be "6 months, or 3 months and reasonable compensation."

At the Council's meeting on 11th April 1930 it was reported that Mr Streeten's solicitors had paid £30 to the Council in accordance with the proposals of 12th December 1929. For the land which would remain as allotments, Mr Streeten would be paid £1 p.a. in rent. On 27th May 1930 the Council heard that compensation had been paid to those affected by the loss of their plots. The remaining plots had been fenced off at a cost of £3-1-0. On 21st July there was confirmation that there were still vacant plots at Hilden Park and at Forge Farm when it was agreed that "the grass should be cut on the pathway and vacant plots".

A year later, on 20th July 1931, the Council heard of the derelict allotments at Hilden Park and it was agreed that Mr Streeten should be asked "to release the Council of their tenancy at Hilden Allotments, and if willing give tenants notice to quit". The end for the Hilden Park allotments was recorded in the Council Minutes for the meeting on 26th October 1931:

> "The Clerk reported that the Allotment holders had been given six months' notice to quit … from 30th September 1931, Mr Streeten having released the Council of their tenure."

At the same time it was agreed to seek a new agreement with Mr G Barkaway regarding the Forge Farm allotments in Riding Lane. The same meeting agreed a payment of £4-7-9 to W Fry for work done on the London Road and Forge Farm allotments.

A letter from Mr G Barkaway was read to the Council meeting on 25th July 1932 "giving the Council one year's notice to terminate their tenancy on 24th June 1933" at Great Forge Farm. A meeting of the allotment holders was called for 12th September 1932 when it was reported that Mr Barkaway had agreed that the termination would be put off until 30th September 1933. The meeting heard that "35 men were willing to continue to cultivate the old allotments". A Resolution was passed asserting that "there is no other ground suitable" for allotments "within reasonable distance".

In view of the demand for allotments the Council decided to take a firm line over the Forge Farm site. On 17th October 1932 the following Resolution was passed unanimously:

> "That Mr Barkaway be asked to let the Parish Council have two acres or thereabouts of the present Allotments on a 21 year lease; if he, Mr Barkaway, would not agree the Council would forward a resolution to Kent County Council asking" for "a compulsory hiring order." (sic)

On 7th December the Chairman, Mr G W Johnson, told the Council that he had met Mr Barkaway "hoping to come to a settlement regarding the Allotments". As Mr Barkaway continued to insist that he required the land the Council instructed the Clerk to contact other landowners in the hope of identifying alternative sites. The meeting of 16th January 1933 heard the results of these enquiries:

> "Messrs Fox & Manwaring had replied stating that Foxbush Estate had no land suitable for allotments. Mr C Barkaway Senr. wanted £4 per foot frontage in Riding Lane and £3 per foot frontage in Church Road but would consider an offer."

Mr A Barker, representing the Kent Agricultural Committee, attended the Council's meeting on 20th April 1933 and reported on an unsuccessful interview with Mr G Barkaway. In the search for a suitable 2¼ acre site it was agreed that the Allotment Committee should…

> "… approach Mr Calvert of Bourne Place with the possibility of getting a plot adjoining the existing Allotments on the London Road …"

Were this approach to be successful, a meeting of allotment holders would be called in order to ascertain the number willing to use the land.

The Council decided in May 1933 that the provision of new allotments could be taken no further. A decisive meeting was held on the 10th with councillors and eleven allotment holders present.

A piece of land adjoining the London Road allotments was offered as an alternative to the Forge Farm site but no-one was prepared to take plots there. No doubt this was because they were some way from the centre of the village. Four allotment holders were prepared to take plots on the Village Green but the Council considered that the demand was insufficient to justify the Council spending money preparing the Green as an allotment site. The Chairman, Mr G W Johnson, closed the meeting saying that the allotment

holders appeared unwilling to move to the new site and that ...
"... as far as the Parish Council was concerned they were unable to do anything more in the matter."
The Council did however continue the search for suitable sites for allotments as is shown in the Minutes of the meeting of 16th July 1934 when it was agreed ...
"... that Tonbridge Rural District Council be asked to let the land at the rear of the new council houses to the Parish Council for allotments."
If so, "what would be the rental?" The Council meeting on 22nd October was read a letter from the Rural District Council "re Allotments at the Housing site in Riding Lane" but no details are given. "This is Hildenborough from A-Z" tells us that between 1940 and 1960 there were allotments on the site of what is now Mount Pleasant Court.

In the remaining years covered by the Minute Book 1924-1938 there are very few further references to Allotments. The Allotments Committee continued to report to the Council but no details of these Reports are given with the exception of one presented to the Council on 19th July 1938. It was agreed to have work done on the London Road allotments by the Reliant Fencing Co. for £11-6-0 and it was reported that "Mr Foy had cleaned out the brook and cleared 2 plots". For this he was paid 15/-.

The Jubilee Fountain

To commemorate Queen Victoria's Golden Jubilee in 1887 a drinking fountain had been erected beside the main road through the village. The site was opposite what is now Dame Kelly Holmes' "1809 Café". Long disused, it was moved to the Village Green in 2005. Maintenance of the fountain became the responsibility of the Parish Council when it was established in 1894 as shown in the Minutes for the meeting of the Council on 30th July 1925 when –
"The Clerk was asked to get an estimate from Mr Woodhams for the cleaning of the fountain."
At the next meeting, on 25th September 1925, Mr Woodhams' estimate of £1-10-0d was accepted. Early in 1926 more work was required as there had been some damage to the stonework of the fountain. On 25th February an estimate from "Messrs Morley Bros" of £2 "for cleaning, repairing the Fountain and painting the railings at the back" was accepted. This wasn't the end of problems with the fountain as the meeting of the Council on 19th April heard that it was leaking badly. The Clerk, Mr E B Budding was instructed to ask the Tonbridge Water Co. to deal with the problem.
The Parish Council spent another 7/6 on 19th July 1927 for more repair work carried out by Mr Woodhams.
On 20th April 1933 the Council instructed the Clerk to "report to the Waterworks that the supply of water at the Fountain was insufficient". It was noted that the drinking cup was missing. At the next meeting, on 17th July, the Council approved the payment of 5/- to "Searle Austin & Barnes" for a replacement. On 16th October it was agreed to pay "Tonbridge Water Works" £1 for one year's upkeep of the fountain.
On 18th October 1937 the Footpaths Committee was asked to look at a suggestion "that the drinking fountain should be moved to the other side of the road". The Minutes Book doesn't record any conclusions reached by the Committee.

The War Memorial

The village War Memorial was set up on land given by Mrs Henry Hills, daughter of Mr Charles Fitch Kemp, the first Chairman of the Parish Council. Designed by Mr H Burke Downing, it was dedicated on 5th October 1920. It belongs to a charity with the County

Council acting as Trustee whilst the surround is maintained by the Parish Council. On 17th April 1925 the Council agreed …
> "… that Mr J Banks be appointed to look after the ground round the War Memorial on the same terms as before, viz £5 per annum".

It was reported that the stone work of the Memorial was "getting very dirty". The problem would be taken up with the County Council following an inspection by three parish councillors. No action was taken as the Council heard on 30th July 1925 that poor weather had been responsible for the state of the Memorial.

The War Memorial was discussed by the Council on 19th April 1926 when the Chairman, Mr G W Johnson, …
> "… read a letter which he had received from Mrs H G Hills asking if the chains, not the posts, round the Memorial could be painted white."

The Clerk, Mr E B Budding was asked to write to the County Council asking that the chains should be painted white. The County Council was also informed that …
> "… a piece of the stone on the platform at the base of the Cross has become flaked and required replacement."

The Memorial is next mentioned in the Council Minutes for 15th November 1926 when it was reported that the kerbstones, newly laid along one side of the Memorial, bordered an area where "the ground was below the kerb". It was agreed that …
> "… the turf should carefully be taken off and the ground raised so that when the turf is put down again it will be level with the kerb."

By April 1927 the Council Minutes show that care of the War Memorial was in the hands of Mr H Skinner who was paid wages of £2-10-0 every six months. A year later the Council instructed the Clerk …
> "… to write to Kent County Council calling their attention to the desirability of painting the chains round the War memorial white as before."

In January 1934 the Minutes record that …
> "… Mrs H Hills requested the Parish Council to apply to the Kent County Council asking for the chains to be repainted at the War Memorial. The Clerk was instructed to write to the Surveyor."

There are various other references to the War Memorial in the Council Minutes for the period. For example, in March 1930 …
> "… Mr Barns proposed, Mrs Houghton seconded that the Footpaths Committee should meet and decide the question of cleaning the War Memorial. All were in favour with the exception of one."

On 27th May 1930 Mrs Tasker Brown reported to the Council on the Footpath Committee's meeting …
> "… which was held at the War Memorial on the 6th inst.. An estimate had been received from Messrs Burslem & Son for renovations to the Memorial, the estimate was £2-5-0d and had been forwarded to Kent County Council. It was agreed that the Clerk should write to Kent County Council and ask them to instruct Messrs Burslem to proceed with the work as soon as possible, and advise the Surveyor to have the oak posts brushed only and not oil dressed as previously mentioned."

In July 1930 the Clerk, Mr F G Balcombe, was instructed to ask the County Council for a statement of accounts concerning the War Memorial. In the following January the Clerk was asked to write to Mrs Hills to…
> "… acknowledge receipt of the Deeds of the War Memorial site."

In March 1935 a new caretaker, Mr J Seal, was appointed to look after the surrounds of the Memorial. Mr Seal's name appears regularly in the record of payments by the Council as he also worked on the allotments and, for 3/6 per week, caring for the Recreation Ground. He received £5 p.a. for looking after the Memorial.

In the early 21st Century the County Council continues to act as the Trustee with financial responsibility for the charity set up after World War One to establish the Memorial whilst care of the surrounds is still undertaken by the Parish Council. At the suggestion of the Council it was granted a Grade II listing by Historic England in 2016.

Seats at Bus Stops

The Vicar of Hildenborough between 1924 and 1934 was the Rev'd L G Chamberlen, MC and in 1927 he joined the Parish Council. He was clearly a very active member and one of his interests was the provision of seats for waiting 'bus passengers. Following his suggestion, at the Council meeting on 20th April 1927 it was agreed to ask Kent County Council for permission to install seats at the "principal stopping places of Auto Cars and Red Cars". Both companies would be asked if they would provide the seats.

On 19th July 1927 responses to the Council's enquiries were reported ...

1. The Auto Car Co. "would be pleased to go further into this matter when the views of the KCC are at hand".
2. The "Redcar Services" regretted that they couldn't provide seats.
3. The KCC gave a favourable reply. Seats could be permitted along the "main road" where no obstruction would occur. The Surveyor would discuss suitable sites with the Council.

The Council agreed that "simple" seats should be erected at Watts Cross, the Church, Coldharbour Lane and Crownlands (near what is now the B P Garage). Estimates were to be obtained...

"... from the Redleaf Mills and Baltic Saw Mills for oak posts and boards, 9ft by 9ins and 2ins thick. Each seat was not to exceed £1".

The Council was to hear on 15th July 1929 that "Auto Car Services" declined "to make a grant towards the cost of the seats on the London Road".

On 12th January 1928 the Council considered a report from the Footpaths Committee which had been given responsibility for the seats. It recommended that an estimate from Mr Huggett of £3-7-6 "for supplying the wood and erecting... three seats" be accepted. This was agreed.

At the Council's meeting on 15th October 1928 the Vicar asked if a seat could be placed somewhere near the Church for passengers waiting for "Motor Autocars" 'buses. The Clerk was asked to seek the sanction of the County Council.

The Vicar, the Rev'd L G Chamberlen followed up his suggestion of a seat near the Church on 21st January 1929 when he successfully proposed...

"That this Council take over the question of providing a seat at the end of the church wall and paying for it, if the Church Council approves, to bear the cost of preparing the wall for this seat and the plot of land given."

Estimates were to be obtained from Mr B Goodale and Mr R Woodhams. The Vicar undertook to put the matter in hand but the cost was to be no more than £20.

By 15th April, 1929 the seat, set into the Foxbush end of the wall, had been constructed. On that day the Council agreed "that a Peppercorn Rent of 1/- per annum should be paid to the Parochial Church Council for the new seat". The Minutes show that this rent was paid for some years but a question at a 2015 Council Meeting revealed that it was not currently being paid. It was later agreed that a final payment of 1/- should be handed over by the Council to the Church in a short ceremony. A shilling dated 1929 was obtained for this purpose.

At a little ceremony on 14th July 2015 the Parish Council duly handed over the 1929 shilling to the Church. The Council Chairman, Mr Mike Dobson presented it to the Vicar, the Rev'd Tim Saiet. Together with the story of the Church wall seat, the shilling can be seen in a display case in the Church Centre.

That Council meeting in April 1929 heard that the cost of the new seat, constructed by Mr Goodale, had been £12-3-0d. At the next meeting, on 6th May, the Chairman, Mr G W Johnson "congratulated the Council on the excellent way in which the new Churchyard seat had been erected".

There seems to have been some dissatisfaction with the Church wall seat as on 20th July 1931 the Clerk was asked to write to the County Council...

> "... and ask them to raise the seat ... if the KCC would not carry out the work, it was to be done at the expense of the Council".

In a letter dated 24th July the KCC Surveyor said that he would give instructions for the seat to be raised but, as the work had not been done by the Council meeting of 26th October 1931, the Clerk was asked to write again to the Surveyor.

The Church wall seat was mentioned in the Minutes of the Council's meeting on 16th January 1933 when ...

> "The Clerk was instructed to see Mr Goodale and ask if something could be done to prevent rain water from settling on the Church Seat."

At their meeting on 15th April 1937 councillors agreed...

> "... that a seat be erected opposite the Boiling Kettle. After consideration it was recommended by the Vicar that the London Passenger Transport Board be approached on the matter".

The Vicar at this time was the Rev'd W H Bass, a member of the Council. The 'Boiling Kettle' café survived until 1956. The site is now the BP Garage.

Telegraph Poles

From time to time the Council discussed the matter of telegraph poles. It was reported on 12th January 1928 that the Chairman, Mr G W Johnson, had written to the County Council following a request from several parishioners. They wanted the telegraph wires along the main road to be laid underground. A recent storm had caused eight poles to be blown down, prompting the suggestion. Mr Johnson had heard from the County Council to the effect that ...

> "... this matter entirely concerns the Postmaster General and the County Council has no voice in it".

Mr Johnson said that he would write to the Postmaster General but pointed out that "the new poles were at the Railway Station". It was hoped that the Postmaster General "would be able to suspend operations" unless it had been decided already that "the underground arrangement cannot be adopted". The Council passed the following Resolution unanimously...

> "... that the Postmaster General be requested to arrange for the telegraph lines passing through the Village to be placed underground owing to the great danger of overhead wires as shewn (sic) in the recent storm, and also to their unsightliness".

In "This is Hildenborough from A-Z" there are two photographs showing telegraph wires in the village, one showing how heavy snow brought them down during Christmas 1927.

On 8th March 1928 the Chairman reported at length on developments following the Council's last meeting. Apart from correspondence with the "General P.O." he had had

talks with the "Assistant Sectional Engineer" who had said that there were "serious technical reasons against having wires placed underground through the village". He went on –
> "The route carries long distance circuits including Continental wires, and this would have a detrimental effect on transmission, and in the public interest it is essential that a proportion of long distance circuits should follow overland routes as these are more efficient than underground".

The Engineer promised that "the single poles which had stood on the footway" would be removed and that the wires would be erected on double poles on the opposite side of the road. There would be no obstruction to pedestrians or traffic and, against a background of trees, would be less conspicuous. The Clerk was instructed to write to Mr Barnet Lewis ...
> "... thanking him on behalf of the Council and the inhabitants for consenting to allow the P.O. to erect the double poles on his side of the road adjoining his property".

The Village Green

A special Parish Meeting was held on 3rd December 1926. Lighting in the village was discussed and parishioners also considered the suggestion that land in Mount Pleasant should be purchased "for a playing field for the children of the village". The Vicar, the Reverend L G Chamberlen, MC, had told the meeting that he had received an offer from...
> "... Mrs Baker of Tonbridge of a piece of land situated in Mount Pleasant for £100 and another smaller piece adjoining belonging to Mr William Williams of Sevenoaks for £75".

The Vicar proposed a Resolution asking the Parish Council to purchase the two pieces of land. There was unanimous agreement.

On 16th December the Parish Council considered the Resolution passed at the Parish Meeting and it was agreed unanimously that ...
> "... steps should be taken to acquire the two pieces of land forming the village green in Mount Pleasant at a cost of £175".

It was agreed to ask "Messrs Knocker & Thompson" to act for the Council. On 27th January 1927 letters from the solicitors were read and the Council decided that as soon as the land became the property of the Council "the grass should be made respectable".

Arrangements to complete the purchase of the land were made at the Council meeting on 17th February when ...
> "The Conveyances from Mr Williams and Mrs Baker's Trustees were produced and the Chairman and Messrs Alfred Smith and Edwin Francis were authorised to execute the Conveyances on behalf of the Council."

The meeting agreed unanimously that the documents be signed.

The Vicar, who had become a co-opted member of the Council the previous month, reported on what now needed to be done. The ...
> "... first thing to be done to the new ground was the removal of the thorn hedge and opening the ground to put down drains".

He proposed...
> "...that J Springate be employed at £2 per week together with F E Smith at 30/- per week, starting on Monday 21st February".

Clearly the Council was determined to move quickly as it was proposed that work should begin only four days later. With one dissentient, the Council agreed to Mr Chamberlen's proposition and the Footpaths Committee ...
> "... were authorised not to exceed an expenditure up to £30 to the end of March for work on the new ground."

The Vicar reported at the next Council meeting on 20th April 1927...
> "... that 1,000 land drain pipes had been put in the new ground in Mount Pleasant, also that 20 tons of Breeze had been put on it. The only thing at present, he said, was the question of keeping the grass down".

The matter of the grass was passed to the Footpaths Committee. (Breeze – small cinders.) There was one other problem: it had been proposed that the road on the west side of the new ground should be widened but the Rural District Council Surveyor had stated that a plan was not yet available. The Surveyor was Colonel F Harris (who held office for 46 years until 1936) and it was agreed that ...
> "... the Footpaths Committee should arrange to meet with Col. Harris to ascertain the amount of ground which would be required for widening".

Col. Harris was mentioned at the Council meeting on 19th July 1927 when it was reported that he had promised to send some sand to be put on the green. He proposed to put a kerb on the south side "as he wished to widen the road there".

The next meeting of the Council wasn't held until 1st November 1927 when it was reported that Col. Harris....
> "... had sent another load of earth to be spread on the Green. He also suggested that a few shrubs be purchased. This he was instructed to do".

At that meeting the Council agreed to deposit various documents for safe keeping with Lloyds Bank in Tonbridge including ...
> "... Deeds and Conveyance of Land in Mount Pleasant from Exors Baker to Parish Council, Deeds etc. re: Land in Mount Pleasant from Mr Williams to Council".

It seems that the "kerbing" promised by Col. Harris had not been done by April 1928 as the Council meeting on 20th instructed the Clerk, Mr Budding, to see the Colonel about his promise. That Autumn the Council, on 15th October, agreed to the Vicar's suggestion that ...
> "... any planting of shrubs on the Village Green should be done now... and that the Footpath Committee should go into this and ... spend up to £20".

The Vicar, the Reverend L G Chamberlen, was a very active member of the Council and the Village Green remained one of his great interests. At the Council's Annual Meeting on 15th April 1929 he made more suggestions about the Green. He suggested that ...
> "... an ornamental shelter be put up, also a few more seats be got".

It was agreed to leave the matter to the Health & General Purposes Committee. The Council's Vice Chairman, Mr F H Buss promised to draw up plans for a shelter for the Committee to consider. Mr John Mackney suggested that ...
> "... two small shelters should be erected and that one corner should be fenced off and thickly planted with shrubs".

Much of the Council's meeting on 6th May 1929 was taken up with a discussion about the Village Green. Mr Buss's plan for a shelter was approved:
> "It would have an open front, be ten feet by seven feet, with a thatched roof".

It was felt that the ground should be levelled and made more attractive before the shelter was erected. There was a suggestion that "an additional strip of land adjacent, with several trees should be acquired" but the idea was not pursued. The Council accepted an estimate from Mr R Woodhams of £18-10-0d for the thatching. Estimates would be sought...
> "... for heather work, twelve inches thick"

Mr Buss was appointed to superintend the work. It was also agreed that "two plank seats should be erected near the fence".

At the next Council meeting on 4th June 1929 the idea of a thatched roof for the Village Green shelter was dropped. It was pointed out that it was difficult to obtain heather. Furthermore there was "a risk of heather being moved by wind". There was also the danger of fire. Mr Woodhams was therefore instructed ...

> "... to tile with old tiles so that it would not be too conspicuous. The expense would be less and the cost of upkeep practically nil".

The concrete floor had been laid and it was thought that the building would be finished in about a week. The Council agreed that "when the grass had finished growing to any extent" it should be scythed.

In the Minutes for the Council meeting of 15th July 1929 there is a reference to "Hildenborough Women's Institute." The Institute had written to the Council requesting that a "Litter Basket" should be placed on the Village Green. The Council agreed and the Clerk "was instructed to obtain a wire cage" for the Green. The same meeting heard that seats ordered three months before for the Green had not yet been delivered. It was agreed that unless the seats within a week had been installed by "Mr Huggett", the order would be cancelled and handed to "Mr Goodale". Mr Tasker Brown then asked about the new shelter – why had it been ....

> "... boarded higher at the front than was previously agreed upon. It was pointed out to him that it was to prevent the wind and rain from entering and all were in favour that the additional boarding was an improvement".

At the Council's meeting on 21st October 1929 it was agreed that:

1. The Village Green shelter should be insured by the Municipal Insurance Co. for £50. The Minutes for 20th October 1930 show that the premium for the year was 2/6.
2. It was agreed unanimously that two trees and two shrubs on the Green which had died should be replaced. The Minutes for the meeting of 25th November show that payment of £1-17-6d was made to "Hollamby's Nurseries".

Should rates be paid on the Village Green? This question was raised at the October 1929 meeting and it was agreed that the matter should be investigated before any payment was made.

The Minutes of the Council's meeting on 25th November 1929 reveal the cost of building the shelter:

> "R Woodhams   shelter   £34-0-8"

The matter of the payment of rates on the Village Green was still unresolved by the Council's meeting on 20th January 1930. It was pointed out that payment was overdue and it was agreed that the Clerk should seek a meeting with the rating authorities. The Clerk reported back to the Council on 20th March, 1930. He referred to a report...

> "... from the 'Tonbridge Rural District Council rating authority dated 14th March 1930 stating 'that the present assessment is fair and reasonable'."

It was agreed that payment of the rate should be resisted and that the Clerk should write to the rating authority referring to an opinion given in a letter from "The Playing Fields Association".

On 11th April 1930 the Council heard that the matter of rates and the Village Green had been resolved:

> "A letter was read from the Rating Authority dated 25th March 1930 saying that the Assessment of the Recreation Ground (sic) had been taken out of the valuation list and the amount of 5/5 paid for the half year ended September 30th last will be refunded."

The Minute refers to the "Recreation Ground" but the heading in the margin reads "Village Green Rates". The Council didn't acquire the Recreation Ground until 1931. At the meeting on 11th April 1930 it was agreed that ...

> "... the grass be cut soon on the Village Green and that it should be cut twice a

year".

At the next Council meeting, on 27th May 1930, it was reported that Mr J Coomber had offered to erect swings on the Village Green "if the Council found the materials". His offer was rejected "as they might constitute a danger". The "question of hard cricket balls" was then discussed with the Footpaths Committee asked "to draw up rules". There was a cricket ball factory in Mount Pleasant, opposite the Green.

Rules for the Village Green were drawn up by the Footpaths Committee and agreed by the Council on 21st July 1930. A notice board was to be erected and …

> "Estimates were received for painting and erecting a notice board from Mr Woodhams £1-2-6, B Goodale 11/6. Mr Goodale's estimate was accepted…"

The Minutes for 20th October show that ultimately Mr Goodale was only paid 10/6! At the July meeting the Clerk …

> "… was instructed to ask Mr Fowle if he would keep the shelter clean inside and pick up rubbish from the Green for the sum of £2 per annum, to be paid quarterly, 10/- per quarter."

Mr Fowle agreed to take on the task, a job that he did until January 1936.

Traditionally, Hildenborough has marked 5th November with a bonfire. Until 2015 the Scouts organised a bonfire and fireworks evening on the Recreation Ground but originally a bonfire was lit on the Village Green. The Council, on 20th October 1930 agreed …

> "… that a bonfire be permitted on the Village Green for 5th November; it was decided that the Bonfire should not be prepared prior to November 1st"

At the same meeting it was reported that a number of the shrubs on the Green had died – it was agreed to replace them.

The Council meeting on 20th July 1931 was read a letter from Mr Walter complaining about "the nuisance on the Village Green". No details are recorded but it was agreed that "if the trouble continued" the Footpaths, Health and General Purposes Committee should investigate. The same meeting agreed "that new tiles be put on the shelter where necessary". For cutting the grass on the Green a payment of £1-4-0d to Mr T Nutting was approved.

In the years following there are fewer references to the Village Green in the Minutes as the Council's attention become focused on the purchase of a "playing field". There is a mention of the Green in the record of the Council meeting of 16th July 1934:

> "A letter was read from Mr C Barkaway Jun'r offering to cut and clear the grass on the Green each year, the cost to be outset (sic) by the crop"

It was agreed that the matter should be considered at the Council's meeting in January 1935 but there is no mention of any decision taken at that meeting.

The Annual Parish Meeting on 20th April 1938 had such a lengthy agenda that at "9.55pm", it was adjourned until 28th April. The last item for discussion related to a proposed site for "a Memorial Cottage to the late Mrs Henry Hills". The following resolution was agreed unanimously:

> "That a frontage of 60 feet to the required depth West to East, on the Village Green in Mount Pleasant be handed over at a nominal charge of one guinea to the Trustees of the Mrs H Hills memorial as a site for the proposed erection of a Parish Nurse's House, clinic and garage. In handing over the land the Trustees of the Memorial Fund will be responsible for all and any legal charges appertaining to the conveyance of the land."

It was agreed that the Resolution should be put before a Parish Meeting. This was held on 12th May under the chairmanship of Mr F Burton. Strong objections were raised against any building on either the Green or the Recreation Ground and the scheme was rejected by 23 votes to nil.

In 2013 the Parish Council obtained the official registration of the land as a Village Green, giving it added protection from possible development e.g. for housing – or a car park. There is no shelter nowadays on the Green – when did that disappear? – and in the same year the Parish Council began work turning the Green into a meadow.

The Recreation Ground

From time to time the Parish Council, established in 1894, discussed the possibility of acquiring land as a "playing field" or recreation ground but it was not until the 1930s that the current Recreation Ground was established. Land for the Village Green had been purchased in 1927 but a larger recreational area was needed. In the Minutes for the Council meeting of 1st November of that year there is the following entry:

> "Mr Buss proposed and Mr Kemp seconded that the Council endorse the action of the Chairman in electing (sic) Col. Henson to act for the Council in making an application for a Grant from the Carnegie Fund through the National Playing Fields Association towards purchasing a field for sports etc. in this village."

A "special meeting" of the Council was called for 31st July 1930 to discuss a report by Mr J Mackney, the Vice Chairman. Before the report was given the "Council went into Committee". Mr Mackney then stated that...

> "... he had heard officially that the Foxbush Estate had been re-sold, and as certain portions of that Estate were offered for sale, would the Council think it advisable to move in (the) matter of the Cricket Field and possibly a small part of the wood if the same could be obtained at a reasonable sum."

The "Cricket Field" was the open space that is now Westwood. On the proposal of Mr Mackney it was agreed to investigate the possibility of purchasing...

> "... at reasonable cost the Cricket Field and about one acre of wood adjoining"

A sub-committee was set up to approach the Vendors. This reported to a special Council meeting on 30th Sept 1930 with the recommendation that as "the price asked is excessive" the Council do not proceed with the purchase. The Council agreed and the Clerk was instructed to convey the decision to "Messrs Fox and Mainwaring", the Agent.

That "special" Council meeting heard a report from the Vicar, The Reverend L G Chamberlen about an "interview" that he had had with Mr G Barkaway ...

> "... re the field 'School Meadow'. Mr Barkaway had offered to sell to the Parish the School Meadow and shaw bounding the field with a frontage of about 1,200 feet for the sum of £1,250"

Mr F Buss felt that the price was too high and stated that there was land for sale between "the Club Houses and the Match Box" further down Shipbourne Road (Riding Lane). He suggested that the "Agent or owner" should be approached and the prices of the pieces of land compared. The owner was Mr John Mackney, the Council's Vice Chairman, and he declared that the ground was "far from suitable, furthermore (he) was not prepared to discuss the matter".

Mr Buss suggested that the Council's allotments "near the Lower Cock" could be put up for sale in order to raise funds. The Vicar than proposed that Mr Barkaway's offer should be placed before a Parish Meeting. This was agreed unanimously with Mr Alfred Smith reminding the Council ...

> "... they ought to try to visualize twenty years ahead."

It was decided to adjourn the meeting so that Col. F Harris, the Rural District Council's Surveyor, and Col. J Henson, Secretary of the local branch of the National Playing Fields Association, could be present to offer their advice.

The meeting reconvened on 6th October 1930. Whilst Col. Henson was unable to be present, Col. Harris attended and gave his opinion...

"... the piece of land ... was a very suitable site and he would do his best to have that position placed on the map as a scheduled open space."

The Council agreed to call a Parish Meeting for 30th October to discuss the matter.

Meanwhile the Council heard from Messrs Fox & Mainwaring about the Cricket Field, known as the Oakhill Cricket Ground. In a letter dated 16th October the Agent asked the Council to reconsider their decision not to purchase the land. At their meeting on 20th October the Council instructed the Clerk to reply that ...

"The Council's decision not to purchase was final."

The Parish Council met in the school on 27th October 1930 for another discussion about "the proposed purchase of the Recreation Ground" and the forthcoming Parish Meeting. The Vicar reported that ...

"... the following grants had been promised

Kent Playing Fields	£150
National Playing Fields	£40
Carnegie Trustees	£120"

Three days later over 90 parishioners attended the "special Parish Meeting". On the proposition of the Vicar, the Reverend L G Chamberlen, the meeting unanimously approved the purchase of ...

"... the field and shaw adjacent to the National Schools owned by Mr Barkaway ..."

The cost was not to exceed £1,250 and the money would be raised in part by a loan and by grants. It was agreed that the allotments near the Lower Cock Inn on "the Sevenoaks Road" could be sold.

Following the Parish Meeting, the Council met on 10th November when a letter from Dr D B Fraser was read stating that ...

"... he was prepared to make an offer of a loan of £1,100 at four per cent per annum, redeemable by a fixed ... payment at the rate of £60 per year, and a final payment in 1963 of £40-12-2d, and any unexpected income could be paid at the end of any one year for the redemption of capital outstanding on the above loan."

Dr Fraser laid down a proviso about the cost of the upkeep of the Recreation Ground: not more than one quarter of the annual cost should be payable out of the rates with the rest recoverable from "the clubs hiring the ground". The Council agreed to write to Dr Fraser accepting his offer but without the restriction of the proviso.

The Council agreed that "Messrs Warner, Son and Brydone," solicitors, should act for the Council. Mr Barkaway would be informed that his offer of the land for £1,250 was accepted...

"... subject to the consent of the Public Authorities to purchase."

An "Executive Committee" was appointed to oversee the purchase.

Col. C E Warner, as solicitor to the Council, attended the Council meeting held on 19th January 1931. A report from the District Valuer was accepted and Col. Warner explained the agreement between the vendor, Mr G Barkaway, and the Council. The purchase ...

"... was conditional to the Ministry and the Kent County Council granting permission for the loan."

The agreement to purchase was then signed by the Chairman, Mr G W Johnson, and the Clerk, Mr F G Balcombe, following the unanimous approval of the Council.

On 12th February 1931 the Vicar, the Reverend L G Chamberlen successfully proposed a Resolution ...

"That for the purpose of Purchasing the land referred to in the Resolution passed at a Parish Meeting on 30th October 1930, this Council do forthwith take the necessary steps to apply for sanction to purchase the land and to borrow on loan the necessary amount required."

The Council unanimously agreed to accept the offer of the grants mentioned at the meeting of the Council the previous October.

The Annual Parish Meeting on 15th April 1931 heard that ...

"... Mr Barkaway was now prepared to sell the land for £1,150. Mr Barkaway stipulates that his costs are paid so that he gets the full purchase money, and the Council's solicitor agreed to this."

Col. Warner reported to the Council on 20th July 1931 that ...

"... the question of the loan was still going on. The Board meet on the 24th inst. when the matter would be considered ... The rate of interest had dropped from 4¾% to 4½%."

The offer of a loan by Dr Fraser, now a member of the Council, had clearly been replaced by an application to the Board of Public Loan Commissioners. On 26th October 1931 the Council unanimously passed this Resolution:

"The Council having approved the form of the Mortgage Deed for £1,100 at 4½% interest to be given to the Public Loan Commissioners towards the purchase of the Playing Fields and Recreation Ground in Shipbourne Road. It is hereby resolved that the Chairman and two members of the Council be authorised and are hereby required to execute the said Mortgage Deed and the Authority to the Secretary, Public Works Loan Commissioners for the delivery of the Certificate for payment to Mr S W Burgess, Treasurer of the Council."

The Deed was signed by Mr G W Johnson, Chairman, Mr John Mackney, Vice Chairman, and Mr Edwin Francis. The Treasurer was the Manager of Lloyd's Bank, Tonbridge. Cheques for £40 and £120 were handed over to the Council by Col. Warner. These represented the grants by the National Playing Fields Association and the Carnegie Trust respectively.

Col. Harris, the Surveyor to the Rural District Council then submitted plans relating to a pavilion for the "Playing Field". It was agreed that the pavilion should be erected at the top of the field. Once the accounts for the purchase of the land had been received, the Council could then turn to the cost of the pavilion. Col. Harris ...

"... anticipated getting a number of unemployed men who could work on the ground and no payment would have to be made to them. The Council would however have to find a suitable man to supervise the work and pay him and would also have to find tools."

The meeting then turned to the question of charges to clubs for use of the playing field. It was agreed that the football and cricket clubs should each pay £2 per season with the stipulation that each club "shall do their own work on their respective grounds". It was agreed to permit "Mr Barkaway to turn sheep into the playing field".

Having approved the provisional lay out of the ground, the Council then agreed ...

"... to get a man to lay a hedge near the ponds. Dr Fraser offered to give poles to help make a fence if necessary."

Plans for the Pavilion were considered by the Council on 18th January 1932 when it was agreed that six builders should be invited to tender for the work of building it. On 11th February details of the tenders received were given:

Mr Woodhams	£275	Mr Killick	£287
Mr Hyder	£350	Mr Punnett	£368
Mr Goodale	£403	Mr Baker	£420

Dr Fraser, Chairman of the Advisory Committee, reported to the Council on an interview with Mr Woodhams and the architect. It was found…
"… that by slight alterations the cost of building a pavilion could be reduced to a price of £259-12-6."
The Council then accepted Mr Woodhams' revised estimate.

Work on the pavilion now proceeded with Dr Fraser and the Advisory Committee supervising it. It was agreed by the Council on 21st March 1932 that "the ground in future shall be called the Recreation Ground". At the same meeting it was agreed:
"That this Council will gratefully accept seats for the Recreation Ground and equipment for the children's ground."
The Vicar, the Rev'd L G Chamberlen reported to the Council on 20th April 1932 that …
"… he had been successful in obtaining seats, equipment and a sand pit."
That meeting agreed that the pavilion should be insured for £250 with an additional sum for the contents. The Council authorised a "Part payment for pavilion" of £200 to Mr R Woodhams. At the following meeting on 25th July 1932, payment of the balance of £51-17-5d was approved whilst it was agreed to pay Mr B Goodale 4/- for a flagpole for the Recreation Ground. The Pavilion had meanwhile been officially opened on 4th June 1932, a fact recognised 80 years later by a plaque unveiled on 4th June 2012 during the celebrations for Queen Elizabeth II's Diamond Jubilee.

Various matters relating to the Recreation Ground were dealt with at the Council's meeting on 17th October:
1. A letter from the solicitors, Messrs Warner, Son & Brydon about "tithe apportionment" was read. It was agreed that the Council should "make a voluntary redemption in the neighbourhood of £4". A further payment of £6-2-11d was authorised by the Council on 19th March 1934.
2. It was reported that "Third party insurance had been effected".
3. There were funds left over in the "seat fund (given by the public)".
4. The Football Club asked for lighting in the pavilion. It was agreed to have oil lamps with the club paying for their maintenance.
5. Using surplus funds from the seat fund, it was proposed to provide "a drinking tap".
6. It was agreed to provide a stile "at the road entrance of the cinder path" and a gate between the Glebe Field and the Recreation Ground.

The difficult question of "Sunday games" on the Recreation Ground was raised at the Council meeting of 17th July 1933 when the Vicar, the Rev'd L G Chamberlen, a councillor proposed that …
"The Council disapproves of games being played on Sunday".
Dr Fraser proposed an amendment which was carried unanimously:
"The Council has considered the question of allowing Sunday games on the Recreation Ground and strongly recommends that they should not be played until the matter has been placed before the Annual Parish Meeting."
This meeting was held on 19th March 1934 when the following Resolution was defeated by 34 votes to 21:
"That the Recreation Ground be open on Sundays for games to be played only by parishioners."
The Council meeting on 17th July 1933 also dealt with a less controversial matter. It heard of an offer by Col. Harris, the Rural District Council's Surveyor of a roundabout for the Recreation Ground, an offer which was accepted with thanks.

Problems with the cricket pitch were discussed at the Council meeting on 16th October

1933. The Vicar reported that it was in a dangerous condition and that it was essential that it should be re-laid at a cost of about £35. It was agreed that the Cricket Club should attempt to raise sufficient funds but that the Council would contribute £10 towards the cost. At the 15th January 1934 Council meeting the Vicar reported that the work had been carried out. Private subscriptions plus the Council's donation had covered the cost. The meeting agreed to the clearing out of the ditches at the Recreation Ground.

The Reverend L G Chamberlen, MC, was Vicar of Hildenborough from 1924 to 1934 and served as a parish councillor from 1927 until March 1934. The Minutes for 19th March record a special vote of thanks to him "for the work he had done in connection with the Recreation Ground".

At the Council's meeting on 21st January 1935, Dr D B Fraser reported to the Council on behalf of the Recreation Ground Committee. Mr Mackney, the Council's Vice Chairman, was thanked for having the ground rolled with a heavy roller. The Committee's request for authority "to have 40-50 yards of new fencing erected" was granted. The Clerk was instructed to write to Mr Barkaway asking him…

"… to desist in his practice of getting through the hedge between the Recreation Ground and the Glebe Field."

The Committee was given authority to arrange "for the re-painting of the pavilion and seats."

The main part of the Recreation Ground Committee's report dealt with the question of "a whole or part-time groundsman or caretaker". It had been suggested that a caretaker's "cottage or bungalow" should be erected close to the pavilion. Dr Fraser presented a plan from Col. Harris, the Surveyor to the Rural District Council, with an estimated cost of £400. The Council agreed to leave the matter for future discussion.

Estimates for the painting of the pavilion were considered at the Council's Annual Meeting on 15th April 1935, "one from Goodale £19-10-0d and one from Woodhams £15-10-0d." The latter was accepted. It was reported that a length of fencing was required "from the sand pit to the pond" and authority to proceed with this and other tasks was given. The Football Club asked for permission to "close the ground on the 20th inst." but the Council felt that they had no authority "within the meaning of the Act" to grant permission.

It was at this meeting that the Council gave "permission for the ground to be prepared for the tree planting ceremony". To commemorate the Silver Jubilee of King George V and Queen Mary a tree was planted at the entrance to the Recreation Ground by the Council Chairman, Mr G W Johnson. In 2015 a replacement commemorative plaque was put up by the Parish Council.

On 22nd April 1936 the Council heard that various maintenance jobs had been carried out at the Recreation Ground. It had been harrowed and rolled whilst the greasing of the swings was in hand It was felt that there was, for now, sufficient sand in the pit. The Recreation Ground Committee was reviewing the charges made for the use by clubs of the grounds and the pavilion.

A report on the income and expenditure by the Recreation Ground Committee was presented by Dr Fraser to the Council on 20th July 1936. It was agreed to print the report for circulation to all concerned prior to a further discussion at the Council's meeting on 19th October. Dr Fraser was not present at that meeting and he had submitted a letter of resignation from the Council. This was accepted with great regret and the Clerk was instructed to write to him…

"… to thank him for all he had done in connection with Parish affairs particularly the Recreation Ground and the Silver Jubilee."

From time to time the possibility of creating another playing field was considered. The Council heard on 5th April 1937 that the Parish Meeting of 15th March had asked that "a piece of land at Crown Lands" be zoned for playing fields. This referred to land near what is now the BP Garage. Mr McIvor, a member, reported to the Council on 19th July 1937 that a survey that he done had shown that …

> "… there were 230 children living in an area adjacent to the suggested site for the playing field."

The March Parish Meeting had also asked that the Council should investigate the drainage problems at the Recreation Ground. At the July Council meeting the Recreation Ground Committee was asked to do this …

> "… with a view to preparing a scheme for draining the ground and get the ground prepared without any increase to the rates; this could be done over a period of years."

The Committee would co-opt representatives of the various organisations which used the ground for a meeting in September.

The Minute Book does not convey the degree of anger expressed at the Parish Meeting of 15th March. Stuck in the Book is a lengthy report from 'The Tonbridge Free Press' with the headline:

Recreation Ground at Hildenborough
Council Concerned Over Its Bad Condition
Unable to be Used

It was reported that the Cricket Club had had to hire a ground elsewhere. The club paid £10 p.a. for use of their pitch - in the circumstances this was reduced to £2. Likewise, the Football Club found their pitch unplayable and had gone elsewhere. Mr F Burton, the Vice Chairman of the Council, declared the situation to be a "horrible scandal" whilst Mr F Buss reminded fellow councillors that much had been promised when the land was bought…

> "… there would be tennis courts and all sorts of things."

It was not fair that the ground should be left in the condition it was. He declared that…

> "It would be difficult to find a recreation ground with a better outlook even in the County of Kent."

The Recreation Ground Committee reported to the Council on 18th October 1937…

> "The Committee were still waiting for an expert from the County Council to come and view the ground for his advice on draining. One drain had already been opened up…"

On 23rd November 1937 the Committee reported that there had been a meeting with…

> "… the expert on drainage … and he had recommended a herring bone system of drainage. Mr Miller, the Rural District Council Surveyor, was going to let the Parish Council have an estimate of the cost of the scheme."

On 17th January 1938 the Recreation Ground Committee recommended to the Council a scheme submitted by the "KCC expert". Work should commence in the Autumn at a cost of around £400. There was a difference of opinion on the Council with some feeling that the plans were incomplete and too expensive. It was finally agreed that…

> "… the Council instead of adopting the report should accept it."

The scheme would be put before a meeting of the Committee and representatives of the interested organisations.

Meanwhile, the Council considered other matters relating to the Recreation Ground. The January 1938 meeting heard that there was a small sum over from the Coronation festivities and it was agreed that this should go towards…

"… the cost of having something done to the ground at the swings etc…"
Estimates would be sought.

The Annual Parish Council meeting on 20th April 1938 was exceptionally long and had to be adjourned until 28th April. There was a lengthy discussion about the memorial to the late Mrs Henry Hills. A letter was read…

"from the Secretary of the District Nursing Association regarding a site at the Recreation Ground for building a cottage for the nurse."

The Chairman, Mr Frank Burton, explained that a Committee had been formed to …

"… provide a Nurse with Cottage and to be a suitable memorial to the late Mrs Henry Hills."

Mr F H Buss spoke in favour of something "which would keep the memory green of the late Mrs Hills". He asked that consideration be given …

"… for a Fire Station to adjoin the cottage, also an ARP (Air Raid Precaution) depot for storage if the cottage scheme went through."

Mr W J Webber reminded the meeting that there was a plan for "A cottage for a caretaker at the Recreation Ground".

At the adjourned meeting on 28th April the Council voted unanimously that the Village Green was a more suitable site for the "Memorial Cottage". That meeting also discussed various matters relating to the Recreation Ground:

- The sand pit
- Fencing at the pond
- The boys' cricket pitch
- "concreting the swings etc. and for the chains to be painted and all woodwork to be done with creosote"

It was agreed to invite tenders from Mr Pratt, Mr Goodale and Mr Woodhams. The Committee was empowered to accept the best offer. Permission was given to the Fire Brigade…

"… to erect a Rescue Platform for Drill purposes, also to fix a dummy hydrant, both at the Recreation Ground."

The Clerk was authorised "to purchase 4 telegraph poles and a quantity of timber etc. for this purpose". Finally, Mr Buss "offered to paint the flag pole if it were lowered by somebody".

The next Council meeting was held on 19th July 1938 when it was agreed to purchase "2 yards of sand for the sand pit from Fermor Bros @ 9/- per yard". Meanwhile "Woodhams" was undertaking work "to screen the lady's lavatory … as per estimate £3-17-0d" whilst "Goodale" would carry out minor repairs "on the instruction of the Clerk". The problem of drainage was then discussed. A report had been received from Mr Seal of Garlands, the Recreation Ground caretaker, which stated that the number of pipes necessary would be as follows:

"2inch – 16,266   3inch - 900   4 inch – 916"

Mr Seal was charging 16/- for his services. The Council referred the scheme back to the Recreation Ground Committee for further consideration. It was empowered to seek estimates.

In the list of payments approved at the July meeting it is recorded that "W Pratt" was paid £21-8-0d for "concrete round swings etc.".

As a footnote to the story of the Recreation Ground, it is worth noting that the Council secured the registration of both the Recreation Ground and Westwood as Village Greens in 2015 as it had done with the Green in Mount Pleasant in 2013. This gave all three open spaces significant protection from development. It was not until 1982 that the Council purchased the land at Westwood.

Footpaths

During the fourteen years covered by the Minutes Book from 1924 footpaths were frequently mentioned at Council meetings. Often there were problems about blocked or ploughed up footpaths. For instance, on 22nd September 1924 the Council heard that "the footpath ... from Powder Mills Road to the Black Arch on the Leigh Road" having been ploughed up, would be reinstated. Meanwhile a dispute with the "Princess Christian Farm Colony" had been settled. Obstructions on a "Public Right of Way" had been removed...

> "... by the Farm Colony people thus showing that they acknowledge the right of the Public to use the footpath that exists through their grounds."

At the Council's Annual Meeting a Footpath Committee was appointed. This reported regularly to the full Council. Frequently there were references to broken stiles, overgrown hedges and damaged footbridges e.g. at Selby's and Collins' farms, sometimes because the landowner refused to put right the problem. There was a long-standing dispute over a damaged bridge at Collins' Farm which the Council was told on 25th September 1925 had been inspected by the Committee. There had been a discussion about who should pay for the repairs. The Council heard on 15th February 1926 that "Mr Williams" had "said that he would not do anything towards repairing the footbridge" whilst "Mr Burr, on behalf of the Hon. J Hope Morley, said he was quite willing to do his share".

The damaged footbridges at Collins' Farm and at Selby's Farm had still not been repaired by the Council's meeting on 19th April 1926 and the matter was referred to Tonbridge Rural District Council "asking them to approach the owners with the object of making them do the necessary repairs". The Council didn't meet again until 15th November when a letter from the Rural District Council was read stating that the repairs were a matter for the owners, not the Council. It was agreed to ask the Rural District Council to put pressure on the owners but, should this fail, the Rural District Council should undertake the repairs. At their meeting on 16th December 1926 Parish Councillors reluctantly agreed to get estimates from "Mr R Woodhams and Mr Killick" for the repairs to the two bridges.

The saga of the footbridges dragged on and the Council agreed on 27th January 1927 to seek an estimate for the immediate repair of the Selby's Farm footbridge from Mr Huggett. The same meeting discussed the state of the footpath from Watts Cross to Hilden Park Road along the main London Road. The Clerk was asked to draw the County Council's attention to its "deplorable condition ... caused by the sinking of the ground after having been opened to lay electric cable".

The problem of the footbridges was raised again at the Council's meeting on 17th February when Mr Huggett's Estimate of £1-18-0d for repairing the Selby's Farm footbridge was accepted. It was reported that "the Hon. Hope Morley" would be approached to see if he would agree to pay half of the cost of repairing the footbridge at Collins' Farm.

On 20th April 1927 the Council heard that "the Hon. G Hope Morley ... refused to have anything done" about repairing the Collins' Farm footbridge. Members decided to accept an estimate of £3-18-6d from Mr Huggett who would undertake the work "at once".

On 15th July 1929 the Council heard about the encroachments on a bridle path, whereabouts unspecified. It was claimed that ...

> "... existing ditches on either side ... prove that it is a Bridle Path and not merely a Right of Way."

The Rural District Council would be informed about these encroachments which included "a Dairy, Garage and Fence".

was often called upon by the Council to undertake various maintenance jobs.

The Annual Meeting of the Council on 20th April 1928 heard complaints about poor drainage allowing rain water to collect...

"... on the corner of the Underriver Road where it joins the main road just beyond the Mill Garage and forms a deep and wide pond extending halfway across the road."

It was also reported that ...

"The ditches on both sides of the Shipbourne Road just beyond the council houses at Garlands are in a very bad condition and require cleaning out."

There were also "complaints of a very bad smell rising from the drains ... at Garlands". These matters were referred to the Rural District Council.

The unresolved problem of the "bad smells" at Garlands was mentioned at the next meeting on 16th July and the Clerk was asked to write to the Rural District Council about this and about smells from the "septic tank at the Mill House". The topic of refuse collection was discussed at the same meeting when the Clerk was asked to write to the Rural District Council ...

"... asking if it would be possible to have this collection quarterly, particularly from houses in the Shipbourne Road as far as Vines also up the London Road beyond Watts Cross."

On 15th October the Council instructed the Clerk to ask the Rural District Council what decision had been made about refuse collections. He was also asked ...

"... to obtain a copy of the By-Laws on Sanitary matters and Buildings."

As the problems of refuse collection and "bad smells" at Garlands were still unresolved, the Council agreed on 15th April 1929 to send a delegation to the Rural District Council. Three matters were to be raised:

1. The collection of refuse "above Watts Cross".
2. The overflow from cesspools "at the council houses at Garlands".
3. The ditch near Garlands which "was considered to be a danger to the public".

The Council meeting on 6th May 1929 heard that Col. F Harris, the Rural District Council's Surveyor had stated that "the house refuse at Watts Cross would be collected in future".

"Bad smells" were again discussed at the Council's meeting on 4th June 1929...

"Mr Tasker Brown reported on an objectionable odour from a culvert near Watts Cross and Mrs Houghton commented on the smells in Shipbourne Road (Riding Lane). Mr Buss explained the sewage system in use at the council cottages in Shipbourne Road and contended that no smell should come from these. The septic tank was perfectly sealed, if designed rightly, and the overflow was completely purified."

Mrs Tasker Brown suggested that "a list of the sources of odours" in the village should be made and Col. Harris, the Rural District Council Surveyor invited to inspect them. This was agreed.

At the end of the month, on 28th June councillors were still complaining about bad odours from "a culvert at Watts Cross" and "the mysterious smell near the Council Cottages at Garlands". It was reported that Col. Harris "had the matter in hand". On 15th July the Council heard that "new breeze was being put down at the septic tank in Shipbourne Road".

Should sewers be assessed for rates? This question came before the 15th July meeting when a letter from Pembury Parish Council was read. This asked for support "in protesting against the Assessment of Sewers for Rateable Purposes". It was agreed to support Pembury's letter to the "Tonbridge and District Assessment Committee".

There is a curious entry in the Minutes for the meeting of 21st October 1929:

"Sanitary Officer's Report: a report was read from Mr E Poole re the bedding of Maggie Nye. The report was adopted as being satisfactory."

Later in the Minutes there is a further reference to Mr Poole "re the disinfecting" of a cottage in Mill Lane "after the death of a T B case" asking why "disinfecting was not carried out by the Sanitary Authority".

The matter was raised again on 25th November 1929 when Mr and Mrs Tasker Brown, both councillors, successfully proposed …

"… that a letter be sent to Mr Poole asking who was responsible for notifying the Sanitary Inspector when the necessity arose for a house to be disinfected."

From time to time the matter of lavatories was raised at Council Meetings. For instance, a complaint was received by the Council at its meeting on 20th July 1931 about "the unsanitary condition of the convenience at the 'Flying Dutchman'". A report by the Rural District Council was requested. The same meeting asked the Sanitary Officer to investigate a claim "that the convenience for men at the Half Moon was inadequate". On 5th April 1937 the Council discussed the need for a "Lavatory for Workmen at the Kent County Council yard". This was at Crown Lands near what is now the B P Garage. Not until 20th April 1938 did the Council hear that the County Council had agreed to provide a lavatory at their yard.

Plans for a drainage scheme at Watts Cross were discussed by the Council on 7th December 1932. This had been drawn up following an Inquiry held at the Rural District Council offices. Col. Harris heard the Council reject the plan "unless the £250 be paid by those who originally promised it".

Col. Harris was also present at the next Council meeting to report that "£125 had now been promised" toward the cost of the scheme. Following a lengthy discussion it was agreed that –

"This Council now approve the Drainage Scheme as outlined to serve the Main Road to Watts Cross, (and) recommends that it be proceeded with."

That was on 16th January 1933, and Col. Harris was present yet again at the Council's meeting on 17th July 1933, this time to explain a "Drainage Scheme for the Vines Area". The Council agreed:

"That with the explanation of the scheme as outlined by Col. F Harris and provided reasonable offers towards the cost are forthcoming and subject to contributions from Tonbridge Rural District Council and the Kent County Council totalling 50%, the Parish Council Approves the scheme."

As Surveyor to the Rural District Council Col. Harris clearly worked very closely with the Parish Council and yet again, on 16th October 1933, he attended a Parish Council meeting. The Vines Area Drainage Scheme was once more on the agenda. Whilst present, the Colonel was tackled on another problem:

"Mr Kemp drew Col. Harris' attention to the odour which came from the manhole opposite the Vicarage."

Col. Harris promised "to look into the matter".

Protests against the rating of sewers had been agreed in July 1929 and on 16th July 1934 the matter was raised again when a letter from Sevenoaks Urban District Council was read. This called for support for "the de-rating of sewers". The letter was "laid on the table in view of the fact that the Tonbridge Rural District Council had supported it".

On 20th January 1936 the Council heard that …

"… since new drains had been put in, the flooding in Riding Lane had been worse, particularly at the lower entrance of the Recreation Ground and the Match-box."

Major Charrington reported that some ditches had been filled in and others piped. His proposal that the matter be referred to the Rural District Council was agreed. At the next Council meeting the problem of surface water at Garlands further down Riding Lane was reported. This was on 22nd April 1936 and it was agreed that better drainage was required to carry it away. This matter was also referred to the Rural District Council.

It was the problem of "sewage running over a footpath near Chapel Cottage, Stocks Green Road" that came to the attention of the Council on 19th July 1937. The Clerk was asked to pass on the complaint to the Rural District Council's Sanitary Inspector. At the Council meeting on 18th October 1937 it was agreed to ask the Inspector to request the owner of land in the area "to have his ditch cleared to give free passage from the Old Barn". At the same time, the owner, Cdr A W Tomlinson, was asked to erect a stile on the footpath.

The Rural District Council continued to receive complaints from the Parish Council about drainage. On 9th December 1937 two were referred to the Rural District Council – "a gully in Powder Mill Road" needed clearing out whilst there was a problem with surface water "in places near Vines Corner". The Surveyor promised to visit Riding Lane at a time when there was heavy rain as the Parish Council's meeting on 20th April 1938 considered the problem of flooding in parts of the Lane. This problem remains in places in the early 21st Century!

Housing

From time to time the Parish Council considered the increasing demand for additional Council housing in the village. On 20th July 1931 Mrs Houghton proposed that a letter be sent to the Rural District Council …

> "… asking for more Council Houses of a smaller type and lower rental to be erected in Hildenborough."

Dr Fraser proposed that a waiting list of applicants for council houses should be set up.

On 25th July 1932 the Council agreed unanimously to a proposal by the Vicar, the Reverend L G Chamberlen, a member of the Council, that …

> "… the Rural District Council be asked to complete the four houses in Powder Mill Road with as little delay as possible…"

On 17th October a letter from Tonbridge Rural District Council was read to the Parish Council …

> "… stating that they had applied to the Ministry for sanction to build six houses in Powder Mill Road."

Housing was mentioned in the Council Minutes on 22nd October 1934 when Mr C Kemp successfully proposed, with Mr J Mackney seconding, a Resolution…

> "… that an application be sent to the Rural District Council asking for not less than four new houses to be erected in Hildenborough similar to those in Leigh Road."

It seems that housing was a matter considered by the Parish Council's Footpaths Committee as the same meeting referred the naming of "New Council Cottages" to the Committee. On 21 January 1935 the Committee …

> "… recommended to the Rural District Council that the new council houses in Powder Mill Road be named Turley Cottages."

Some ten years before, on 17th April 1925 the Parish Council instructed the Clerk to approach the Rural District Council …

> "… with the object of re-naming 14 of their houses in Shipbourne Road to 1-14 'Garlands' and the houses in the Powder Mills Road 1-8 'Whittakers'."

At that time Riding Lane was known as Shipbourne Road. On 26th February 1926 the Rural District Council was asked that "the three new Council houses just recently completed" in Mount Pleasant should be named 'Hook Cottages'.

At their meeting on 22nd April 1936 the Council passed a Resolution proposed by Mr C Kemp and seconded by Mr W J Webber…

> "… that the Rural District Council be asked to erect no fewer than six more working class homes in the Parish."

On 19th October Mr Mackney, a member of both the Parish and the Rural District Councils, informed the Parish Council that …

> "… the Tonbridge Rural District Council were considering proposed plans for building council houses in Riding Lane…"

At the Parish Council meeting on 18th January 1937…

> "… Mr Mackney was asked to report to the Rural District Council that steps be taken to reserve land for Council Houses adjoining those at Riding Place, Riding Lane."

The Rural District Council, apart from being responsible for the provision of Council houses, also dealt with the numbering of properties. On 18th January 1932 the Parish Council asked the Clerk to discuss with the Rural District Council the numbering of houses in Mount Pleasant. Numbering was mentioned at the Council's meeting of 15th April 1937. Apparently nothing had been done about Mount Pleasant as the Rural District Council was now to be asked about …

> "… the numbering of houses in Mount Pleasant and Hilden Park Road… it was felt that the cost of this work should not be borne by the householders."

At the same time the Rural District Council was …

> "… asked to label the following roads – Hilden Park Road, Hilden Avenue and Oaklands Avenue."

The Rural District Council was concerned about the need to name new streets and to have properties properly numbered. At the Parish Council's meeting on 17th January 1938 a letter from the Rural District Council about the matter was read to the Parish Council. The Parish Council …

> "… agreed not to oppose the Tonbridge Rural District Council's application to the Ministry for powers to name new streets and re-name others, and to number houses in the Rural Area."

Lighting

The Parish Council from time to time considered the question of street lighting for the village. At the Council meeting held on 15th November 1926 the Chairman, Mr G W Johnson, gave details of an estimate that he had received from "Tonbridge Urban District Council for 15 electric lamps for lighting the village". The meeting agreed that "a special Parish Meeting be called for the purpose of adopting the Lighting Act". This meeting, held on 3rd December, was told by Mr Johnson that the cost of installing the 15 street lamps would be £230. These would have a running cost of £44-5-0 per annum. The possibility of gas lighting was raised and it was decided to delay any decision for a year.

On 27th January 1927 the Council considered the result of the public meeting and instructed the Clerk, Mr E B Budding, to get estimates …

> "… from the Tonbridge Gas Co., also from Tonbridge Urban District Council for 20 lights of gas and electric light respectively extending from Watts Cross to Hilden Park Road."

It was reported to the next Council meeting on 17th February that the Gas Company …

"... wished to know in the event of the Council providing lighting for the Village with gas, whether the lamps would be kept alight all night, also would they be lit during the summer months. The Clerk was instructed to inform them that they would only be lit from lighting up time to 11 o'clock pm and not at all during the Summer months."

The estimates were received but no details are recorded in the Minute Book except that the Council meeting on 21st April 1927 instructed the clerk ...

"... to write to the Electric Light Co. and Gas Co. asking if the estimates received would hold good for another year."

A letter from the Tonbridge Gas Co. was read to the Council at the meeting held on 19th July 1927 stating that "the estimate for the price of gas would remain good for another year". The Company had purchased some second hand lamp columns which would be offered to the Council. The Clerk ...

"was instructed to write thanking" the Company for their offer but in view of the "fall in prices" ask the Company "to cancel the purchase of these second hand columns."

The next meeting of the Council did not take place until 1st November 1927 when it was decided to call a Parish Meeting to discuss lighting. Members unanimously agreed to recommend the adoption of the Lighting Act of 1833. There was no further meeting until 12th January 1928 and, curiously, there is no reference to the outcome of the Parish Meeting which had been held on 22nd November. Fortunately there is a record of the meeting in the separate Minute Book for Parish Meetings.

At the Parish Meeting the Chairman, Mr G W Johnson, explained that its purpose was to consider adopting the Lighting Act thus allowing "for lighting the main road through the Village". The Vicar, the Rev'd L G Chamberlen, proposed the adoption of the Act on behalf of the Council "with the necessary rate to be incurred thereby". He faced opposition from future councillors Dr D B Fraser and Major C E W Charrington. They considered ...

"... it more dangerous to pedestrians where there were street lamps, by people knocked down by motor cars more so than where the roads were in darkness."

Major Charrington believed that by "not having the lights the rates were kept down".

Voting was in favour of the Vicar's proposition by 21 votes to 20 but the Resolution failed as a two-thirds majority was required to adopt the Act.

In late 1928 a further attempt was made to adopt the Lighting Act. At a Council meeting on Saturday 20th October unanimous support for the adoption of the Lighting Act was reaffirmed and a Parish Meeting called for 13th November. Once more it was the Vicar, the Rev'd L G Chamberlen who proposed the adoption of the Act but this time a Poll was called for. The result is recorded in the Minutes of the Council's meeting on 21st January 1929 – 211 votes in favour with 156 against but there are no details given of the meeting or comments about the result. As there was no two-thirds majority the lighting scheme for the village did not go ahead but there are few references to the topic at subsequent Council meetings apart from comments about the siting of "Distribution Pillars". For instance, in September 1930 there were complaints that the "Pillar on the corner of Shipbourne Road ... was considered dangerous". Following a response from "the Electricity Works" the Council insisted that the transformer either be removed or a light to be placed on or nearby it. The dispute remained unresolved and on 10th November 1930 the Council referred the matter to the County Council. This "pillar", described as a danger to the public, was situated at the "Shipbourne Road, London Road junction", that is at the junction of Riding Lane and the B245.

The County Council's reply was reported to the Council on 19th January 1931. The County Council had sent a letter to the Urban District Council asking for the transformer to be moved and "erected in another position that will not obstruct pedestrian traffic". There is no record of the Urban District Council's response to this suggestion.

On 15th April 1935 the Council had a discussion about street lighting and it was decided to set up a "sub-committee ... to investigate the matter in the ... Crown Lands to the Green Rabbit" area – from what in 2016 was the BP Garage to Orchard Lea, the site of the Green Rabbit, a restaurant demolished in 1975. The "Street Lighting Committee" reported to the Council on 15th July saying that it wished to meet with an official from the Rural District Council or the County Council. In the meantime it was asked to investigate the cost of providing lighting in the area.

At its meeting on 20th January 1936 the Council was told that, according to a Ministry of Health Report, street lighting should be a matter for the County Council. It was agreed that for the time being no further action should be taken although at the Annual Parish Council Meeting on 22nd April a Lighting Committee of six of the nine councillors was set up. This Committee reported to the Council on 20th July 1936 but it was agreed that a scheme for lighting ...

> "... be left in abeyance in view of (the) possibility of road widening, a by-pass, uniformity of lighting and other factors."

The Minute is significant as it is an early reference to the idea of a "by-pass".

The Lighting Committee was clearly very active, holding three meetings between 18th June and 13th July 1937 and the Council received a report on them on 19th July. The Minutes state: "Full particulars - see Committee Minutes". Sadly these, apparently, no longer exist but, fortunately, a cutting from a local newspaper has been included in the Minute Book giving information about the Lighting Committee's recommendations:

1. A Parish Meeting should be held to consider plans for lighting the whole village.
2. Should it be decided not to light the whole village, a meeting ought to be held "for those residing in the Crownlands to the 'Flying Dutchman'" area to discuss lighting for that part of the village.
3. It was considered that 21 lamps would be required for the Crownlands area with 87 for the remainder of the village.
4. The Clerk was instructed to obtain estimates for the installation and maintenance of lamps from both the gas and electricity companies.

The Clerk reported on 18th October 1937 that he had received tenders from the "Gas Company" and was waiting to hear from the Electricity Company. A representative, "Mr Graham, the South Suburban Gas Company's expert on street lighting" attended the Council meeting on 23rd November 1937. It was agreed that the Lighting Committee should "decide on the main road points where ... lighting was absolutely necessary".

A Parish Meeting was held on 12th January 1938 to consider the adoption of the appropriate Act to permit the extension of street lighting in the village. Approval was given by 109 votes for to 5 against but a poll was demanded. Held on 2nd February 1938, parishioners were asked to agree:

> "that the Lighting and Watching Act, 1833 be adopted by the Parish of Hildenborough."

498 votes were in favour with 85 against, a majority of 413. At the Annual Parish Meeting on 23rd March 1938 it was agreed to ask the Rural District Council "to become the Authority to light the Parish of Hildenborough".

Traffic Matters

For decades the Parish Council has been concerned about speeding through the village and from time to time attempts are made to have various speed limits imposed. These attempts continued until 2015 when the 30mph limit was finally extended along the B245 from the Tonbridge boundary to Foxbush.

At the Council Meeting of 20th July 1936 it was reported that ...

"... parishioners had asked if a speed limit could be imposed from Watts Cross through the Village to link up with Tonbridge."

Mr John Mackney, the Vice Chairman, proposed that an application should be made for a speed limit to be imposed from "Zareba" at Watts Cross. However, Dr D B Fraser successfully moved that the sign be placed at the "Flats", formerly a row of cottages, now the site of a car showroom and a petrol station.

The Flatts (sic) had been mentioned in the Council meeting Minutes for 19th April 1926 when Mr Mackney reported that there had been complaints about ...

"... the numbers of cars and charabancs which pull up on the side of the footpath, along by the Flatts, on Saturdays, Sundays and holidays during the Summer months, and passengers getting out and causing a nuisance."

It was agreed to refer the matter to the police with a request for an additional police officer for the Parish as ...

"... it is considered that the main road through the village is not sufficiently or properly patrolled."

The Parish Meeting held on 15th March 1937 asked the Council to consider the idea of "Belisha crossings" and on 15th April it was agreed that an application for crossings should be made for the following points:

Crownlands (near the site of the BP Garage)

The Flying Dutchman   The Half Moon   The War Memorial

The "Belisha crossings" were named after Leslie Hore-Belisha, the Transport Minister from June 1934 until May 1937.

A cutting from the "Tonbridge Free Press" stuck into the Minute Book reports on the Council meeting of 19th July 1937. Application for a speed limit through the village had been made. In the meantime there were to be no "Belisha crossings" as ...

"...it was not the policy of the Ministry to approve pedestrian crossings where there was no speed limit."

Parish Councillor Mr A B McIvor referred to a petition calling for a 30mph speed limit through the village at the Council's meeting on 20th April 1938. He explained that the petition had been passed on to Sir Adrian Baillie, Bt, the MP for Tonbridge - he had won the seat in a by-election on 23rd March 1937 – and that had been placed before the Ministry of Transport. Mr McIvor ...

"... asked that Kent County Council and the police be informed of the fact and to seek their support."

In the early 21st Century the Parish Council has been very concerned about traffic problems along Stocks Green Road and at that meeting in April 1938 a letter from the County Council was read. This gave reasons why "no path could be made at Stocks Green Road" but the Minutes do not record details from the letter.

On 19th July 1938 a letter from the County Council with reference to speed limits and "Belisha crossings" was read to the Council. It was hoped to establish crossings at Crownlands and the War Memorial. The Clerk, Mr F G Balcombe, was asked to write to the County Council requesting a prompt decision about the proposed speed limit through the village...

"... to 50 yards north west of the War Memorial on Route A21 Hildenborough and to press for crossings ... at 'The Flying Dutchman' and the 'Half Moon'."

In the Autumn of 2015 that 30mph speed limit along the B245 (ex A21) was finally imposed!

The Approach of War

The 1930s were years of increasing concern about the rise of Nazi Germany and as early as 1936 the Minutes mentioned preparations that were being made in case hostilities should break out. In October the Parish Council was informed that Tonbridge Rural District Council was considering "Air Raid precautions". The following April the Parish Council set up a committee "to discuss Air Raid precautions" whilst Mr J G Barns was asked to continue to serve on a committee set up by Tonbridge Urban District Council. In April 1938 the Parish Council decided that all nine councillors should serve on a committee to consider "matters relating to ARP." The Parish Council would look at the possibility of establishing an ARP storage depot on the Recreation Ground.

The record of the last meeting mentioned in the Minute Book for 1924-1938 is dated 19th July 1938. The Clerk, Mr F G Balcombe,

> "... pointed out that the whole of the Council had decided to become the ARP Committee for the Parish"... but that "no meetings had been held and he had placed the matter on the Agenda in order that a chairman be elected and any matters discussed."

The Council Chairman, Mr F Burton was elected committee Chairman and a discussion followed:

> "Mr Buss was of the opinion that the Council should know to some extent how it stands in relation to ARP. There was the question of shelters, Fire Brigades and several other things they were at the moment ignorant about and it would be interesting to know to whom they had got to look to for guidance etc.."

Councillors were told that a public meeting was being held in the Drill Hall next evening in connection with ARP under the chairmanship of a Rural District Councillor. It was agreed to ask "certain questions" at that meeting.

Snippets from the Minutes

The Clerk was instructed "to write to the Autocar Co. that complaints were being made of their irregularity and unpunctuality of the Autocars on this route to and from Tonbridge".
15th November 1926

"Mrs Houghton reported that the water tap which supplies the tenants of the Club Cottages was defective as there was always a small stream of water coming out on to the roadway which was a public road." The Clerk was instructed to contact Col. Harris, Surveyor to Tonbridge Rural District Council. 20th April 1928

The Council was given notice of the transfer of the license of the "Grenadier" public house in Riding Lane from W J Honisett to G E Southin. 21st October 1929

Mr Southin was the landlord at the time of the destruction of the "Grenadier" by a bomb in 1942.

"Mrs Tasker Brown asked about a Boundary Stone near the bottom of Coldharbour Lane which was gradually sinking. Col. Warner said he would find out about it with a view to having its existence preserved." 19th January 1931

Col. C E Warner, the Council's solicitor, was present at the Council meeting on 19th January 1931.

"A letter dated 29th November 1930 was read from the Autocar Services Ltd. regretting the damage to the Village Green caused by one of their buses on 26th November and promising to put the damage right as soon as the weather would allow."
19th January 1931

"Mrs Houghton reported that Mr R F Hodder had tendered his resignation as schoolmaster, and that a scheme had been adopted whereby any child at school could obtain a pennyworth of milk daily."   19th January 1931

Mrs Houghton, a Councillor, had been appointed "Minor Local Authority Manager" for the Hildenborough Church of England School for 3 years until 30th June 1933. She presented Reports on the school to the Council and was re-appointed for a further 3 years in 1933 and 1936.

"Dr Fraser opened up a discussion regarding Air Trips at the Old Barn – it was decided to leave the matter for the time being."   20th July 1931

"The Council wishes to congratulate the school managers and the headmaster on having adopted a special cap for the boys and girls of the school. This promotes esprit de corps among the children and a pride in their school with a desire on their part to bring to it a credit and distinction."   26th October 1931

"Authority was given to the Vicar to permit Mr Barkaway to turn sheep into the playing field."   26th October 1931

"The Vicar moved, Mr Webber seconded that a letter be sent to the Tonbridge Urban District Council asking for the electricity charges to be reduced in the parish."
                                    18th January 1932

On 21st March 1932 the Council objected to the "proposed cancellation of the Green Line licence" to provide a coach service to London. The Council hoped that there would be an alternate "half hourly service by Redcar to and from Victoria and by Green Line to and from Oxford Circus". These comments would be sent to the Ministry of Transport.

"The license of the "New Cock" was due for transfer from J Turnbull to L M Wade on 23rd August 1932."   25th July 1932

The 'New Cock Inn', latterly 'Thirst and Last', situated on the B245 approaching Nizels Lane from the village, was replaced by housing in 2005.

"The Clerk was instructed to put a notice in the Pavilion to the effect" that "cycling on the cricket pitches or round the pavilion was forbidden."   25th July 1932

"The Council had no objection to the proposed New Road from Meopham Park to the Plough Inn as submitted by the Tonbridge Town Planning Committee."
                                    17th October 1932

A petition was received containing forty signatures asking "the Council to support an application allowing Ashby's Underriver – Tonbridge service to pick up on the Main Road." It was agreed to write to the Traffic Commissioners supporting the petition together with a call for a more frequent service.   7th December 1932

"The report received from Mrs H G Hills re: Leigh Charities was read. During 1932 two women received grants of 17/6 each, one woman received 15/- and five families had received 5/- grocery tickets each."   16th January 1933

"Mr Mackney reported that he had attended the funeral of the late Miss E Lawson. He felt it a duty that the Council should be represented in view of the fact that the late Miss Lawson had done so much good in the village during her lifetime."   20th April 1933

Mr Mackney of Limes, Mill Lane was the Vice Chairman of the Council. Ellen Lawson of Bourne Place had died on 17th April 1933 aged 96.

On 16th April 1934 the Clerk was authorised to pay 3/10 to "J M Sturgess" for "Tithe Queen Anne's Bounty". This was a half yearly payment – but what was Queen Anne's Bounty?

Mrs Houghton, as the Council's representative on the School Managers' Board was asked to bring to the Board's attention "the lack of storage facilities for bicycles and to see if a cover could be provided for same." 20th January 1936

On 22nd April Mrs Houghton reported "that the cover for scholars' bicycles was receiving attention".

Mrs Houghton reported "that one girl had gained a scholarship to County School, Tonbridge. Two boys had gained scholarships to Judd School. On July 4th the school won the trophy for the Folk Dancing Competition open to Kent." 20th July 1936

On 18th January 1937 the Council adopted the following Resolution which had been drafted by the Council's solicitors, Messrs Warner, Son & Brydone:

"That the Hildenborough Parish Council do hereby consent to the granting by the Minister of Health for a Provisional Order under the Gas and Water Facilities Act 1870 and the Gas and Waterworks Facilities Act 1870 Amendment Act 1873 empowering the Tonbridge Waterworks Company Limited to construct additional waterworks, making further provision with regard to the supply of water, authorising the Company to raise additional capital and for other purposes."

"The Vicar's invitation to the Parish Councillors to attend the Coronation Service as a body was accepted." 15th April 1937

The Vicar, the Rev'd W H Bass, was a Councillor.

"No objections were raised by the Council in reference to N Jempson's application to the Licensing Meeting for an application to apply for and hold an excise Licence to sell wine at the 'Plough', Hildenborough." 17th January 1938

"Mr Buss moved, seconded by Mr McIvor that a letter be sent to the Ministry asking for permission to become affiliated to the Kent Council Social Services." 20th April 1938

Part 5 – 1938-1952

List of Councillors and Officials

The next section was originally published by the Parish Council in 2012 entitled **Notes from Hildenborough Parish Council's Minutes 1938 – 1952** and is reproduced with minor amendments.

This little publication is dedicated to the Councillors and the Clerk who served the Parish at various times between the years 1938 and 1952

Mr JG Barns	Mr PH Gwyther
The Reverend WH Bass	Mr ASC Harris
Sir Thomas Butler	Mr T Holmes-Wood
Mr F Burton	Mrs L Houghton
Mr FH Buss	Mr J Mackney
Mr AW Challen	Mr AB McIvor
Mrs DMC Charrington	Miss G Moore
Mr NJ Coomber	Mr AGT Oakley
Mr JKF Coutanche	Mr BK Smith
Mrs KNW Davison	Miss EM Turnbull
Lt Col RHV Fairer-Smith	Mr WJ Webber
Mr E Francis	Mr EA Woodhams
The Reverend EWE Fraser	

Clerk to the Council:	Mr FG Balcombe	1929-1964
Chairmen:	Mr F Burton	1938-1946
	The Rev. EWE Fraser	1946-1950
	Sir Thomas Butler	1950
	Mr AGT Oakley	1950-1955

Introduction

Many residents will be familiar with the history of Hildenborough through the work of Kay Cope and Joan Dash who produced "Hildenborough A-Z", published by the Parish Council in 1994 to mark the 150th anniversary of St John's Church and the centenary of the Parish Council. The Council published a revised edition entitled "This is Hildenborough from A-Z" in 2007. A wonderful reference book, it includes numerous facts about the village during World War II. Study of the Parish Council Minute Book for the period from October 1938 – March 1952 provides a formal yet enlightening supplement. Curiously, there is no reference to the outbreak of war or to the Queen's accession to the throne on 6th February 1952.

The Minute Book was maintained in beautiful handwriting by Mr F G Balcombe who was Clerk to the Council for an amazing 35 years from 1929 until 1964. There is an entry in "A-Z" about Mr Balcombe together with a photograph of him as Hildenborough's first "lollipop man". His Minutes provide a valuable insight into life in war-time Hildenborough, a time still recalled by a few residents. Times were very different yet some of the problems were the same as now – flooding, the blocking of footpaths, vandalism, the recreation ground, speeding traffic and lighting for example. The Minutes provide a vivid insight into wages and other costs of the time.

Mr Frank Burton was Chairman of the Council from 1938 until 1946. The nine members met at the Institute in Riding Lane, the Drill Hall (replaced by the Village Hall in 1971) or the Pavilion. Meetings always opened with prayers and during the war years were held at irregular intervals. Sometimes they had to be postponed or adjourned because of the threat of an air raid.

Hildenborough's Fire Brigade

The Council meeting of 17th October 1938 was concerned with implementing the Fire Brigades Act of that year. Tonbridge Rural District Council was to take over responsibility for fire brigades from parishes with effect from 29th January 1939. Later meetings recorded that the Hildenborough Fire Brigade was not to be a "sub unit of Tonbridge". Firemen were allowed to retain their uniforms – do any survive today? Most of the equipment was transferred to the Rural District Council for which the Parish Council received £100. This was subject to strict controls! The Ministry of Health, according to the Minutes of 22nd August 1939, agreed that the money could be deposited with the Post Office Savings Bank but ministerial consent was required before it could be spent!

"A-Z" gives details, plus a photograph, of the village brigade which was based at what is now the kitchen area of the Village Hall. There was a charge for attendance at a fire as the Minutes for the October 1938 meeting make clear. The Council's Fire Brigade Committee reported that an account for £3 had been sent to a resident for the attendance of the village brigade.

The Years 1938 and 1939

Speeding traffic through the village is a cause for concern today as it was in 1938. At the October meeting it was reported that the County Council had failed to get an extension of the speed limit from the Green Rabbit Restaurant (now Orchard Lea) to a point 50 yards beyond the War Memorial. The Council was told that the Ministry of Transport had rejected the plan on the grounds that "the length of road cannot be deemed to be a built-up area". It was decided to refer the matter to the local M.P., Sir Adrian Baillie, Bt..

Other matters considered at the October 1938 meeting included:

▶ A scheme for street lighting. This had been rejected at a village poll in 1937 but the Council felt that it should now be reconsidered.

▶ Drainage problems at the Recreation Ground.

▶ A resolution to be put before a Parish Meeting:
"That a sum not exceeding £600 be asked for by a loan for the provision of and putting in order the necessary Playing Fields for the parish ...."

▶ "Damage at Recreation Ground ... the Clerk was instructed to ask the Police to keep a watchful eye on the property".

The meeting of 22nd November 1938 accepted the Report of the Lighting Committee that "the lighting authority of the Parish Council be handed over to Tonbridge Rural District Council". The same meeting agreed that sheep should be allowed to graze on the Recreation Ground.

On 27th January 1939 it was reported to the Council that "the School is now for

Juniors only, the Senior children having been transferred to Tonbridge". At the same meeting, the surveyor was "asked to proceed with the work of preventing flooding at Riding Lane".

The Minutes for 11th April 1939 give a hint of what must have been at the back of everyone's mind – the possibility of war. The Council agreed that the full Council should form the A.R.P. (Air Raid Precaution) Committee. At the same meeting the problem of drainage at the Recreation Ground was discussed. The Recreation Ground Sub-Committee was authorised to proceed with 'stone picking" and rolling on the Recreation Ground and the Minutes for 3rd May record that 17/- (85p) was paid for "stone picking".

"There would almost be a riot …"

The May 1939 meeting was concerned with street lighting with Mr Lee, Clerk to the Rural District Council, in attendance to outline the lighting scheme for the village. It was agreed that "the months for lighting should be from 1st September to 30th April and the time should be ½ hour after sunset till 11pm". Mr Lee also attended the Council Meeting of 17th July when he explained that the Rural District Council's scheme was "not in conformity" with the Ministry of Transport's Report on street lighting along "Group A roads". For an 'A' road the lamps "would have to be 25 ft. in height instead of 18 ft. and the number of lamps increased from 17 to 45". The Council agreed to support the Rural District Council's protest to the Ministry, pointing out that the scheme would be prohibitively expensive. The matter was extensively reported under the headline:

"There would almost be a riot if lighting scheme was altered says Hildenborough Parish Councillor". (Courier 17 July 1939)

Following the outbreak of war on 3rd September, on the 29th the Parish Council dropped further action "until more settled conditions prevailed".

Money Matters

At each Meeting the Council approved various payments – these give an idea of monetary values at the time. Examples:

17th July 1939	– Increase from 3/6 to 5/- (17½ p to 25p) per week the payment for keeping the Recreation Ground lavatories clean.
	– Wages: the Recreation Ground caretaker was paid £4=11=0d (£4.55p) for six months' work.
15th April 1940	– £3=15=0d (£3.75p) for work on the Recreation Ground – "rolling, grass cutting, harrowing etc. with harrow, two horses and one man".
	– Hire of the Drill Hall for the Annual Parish Meeting - £1.
20th May 1940	– Keeping "the grass down on and around the cricket pitch for about £2 for the season".
15th July 1940	– 26 hours' work at the Allotments ("hedges, ditches etc".) at 1/- (5p) per hour.
21st October 1940	– Payment of the Clerk's quarterly salary of £7=10=0d (£7.50p). On 20th October 1941 it was reported that "the District Auditor" had approved 10% "War Bonus" for the Clerk.
	– It was agreed that troops could use the football pitch and pavilion free of charge

Over the years the Clerk's salary, paid quarterly, was steadily increased. In May 1946 it went up from £30 p.a. to £50 p.a. In April 1950 it was increased to £75 p.a. and to £90 p.a. in January 1952.

The Outbreak of War

Following the declaration of war, the Councillors at their Meeting on 29th September 1939 were concerned with contingency plans. The Drill Hall was felt to be unsuitable as a First Aid Post and it was recommended that "the model cowshed at Foxbush" be considered as an alternative. The provision of allotments, "Food Control", Civil Defence and Air Raid Precautions were amongst matters discussed. There was concern about the absence of protection "for those who may be travelling on the main road during an air raid warning". A Member "was of the opinion that proper provision had not been made for the protection of working-class school children in the event of air raids". The Chairman explained that instructions had been sent to schools by the Kent Education Committee.

All Councillors served on the Air Raid Precaution Committee which, on 15th July 1940, reported that Kent Education Committee was unable to provide "specially constructed air-raid shelters" but that "small mesh wire screens" would be put over the windows "in certain rooms". This was deemed to be unsatisfactory and a letter was sent to the Minister of Education and, subsequently to the local M.P., Sir Adrian Baillie, Bt.. At the Council Meeting of 21st January 1941 it was reported that a shelter to accommodate 159 pupils had been approved. Problem: there were 229 pupils on the roll and the Education Committee was asked about what was to happen to the other 70 children. On 17th March a copy of the letter was sent to the Ministry. One Councillor opposed this, stating that "the woodland at the Scout Hut was adequate protection for those attending school".

The Years 1940 and 1941

During 1940 and 1941 the Council devoted most meetings to matters relating to the war, for example:
- The establishment of nine "War Savings" groups.
- A letter was sent to the Rural District Council "asking if they would give assurances that any conscientious objector employed by the Rural District Council should not receive any increased pecuniary interests or advantage for the duration of the war".
- A section of the W.V.S. had been formed to work with the A.R.P. Wardens and "do social work".
- It was reported that "members of the public had dug a trench on the village green".
- Scrap metal dumps were set up.
- Dumps of lime "for the use of cottagers and allotment holders at a cost of 1/3 (6p) per cwt" (a hundred weight equals about 50.8kg) were set up ... "fetch it and pay on collection". Over ten tons of lime were ordered.
- The provision of sandbags and the establishment of sand dumps.
- The appointment of two people "to advise on the cultivation of gardens and allotments".
- Mr N. Guilford M.R.C.V.S., offered his services "for advice relating to casualties among animals as the result of enemy action".
- "In the event of a Trader being Blitzed" the Pavilion would be used "for storing foodstuffs".
- Commander Tomlinson, owner of The Old Barn, was "Food Director for the Parish". Leaflets "would soon be given to all householders explaining the conditions relating to emergency foodstuffs". This was considered at the meeting of 20th October 1941 when, significantly, the word "invasion" first

appears in the Council Minutes.

- Concerning the "front gardens of Council Houses in Riding Lane ..." the Rural District Council was requested to "ask two of the tenants to take over the land for cultivation".
- The activities of the Cricket Club were suspended "for the duration of the war". However, in October 1941 it was agreed to allow "Hollanden Park" to play hockey on the Recreation Ground for a fee of two guineas (£2.10p) per season. "Permission was given for the grass to be cut and carted away for silage".
- The Brownies were given use of the Pavilion for one evening a week for a fee of 2/6 (12 ½ p) for the season.

The Stirrup Pump Controversy

The provision of stirrup pumps became a contentious issue. On 15th July 1940 the Council, after consultation with the Fire Brigade, the Rural District Council and the District Auditor, decided that a dozen be purchased. At the next meeting an estimate of 22/6 (£1.12 ½ p) each was accepted. Arrangements for storing the pumps were considered. Operators would be trained and those storing the pumps would have "a notice fixed to their gate or house". Plans were also made for a "Demonstration of a Gas Bomb and the De-contamination of the general public" at the Recreation Ground on 23rd August.

Three stirrup pumps were received but the cost was 30/- (£1.50p) each. This was above the estimate so the rest of the order was cancelled and it was agreed to approach the Rural District Council which was now able to supply pumps. On 21st January 1941 it was reported that the District Auditor had authorised the purchase of twelve pumps from the Rural District Council. The first six arrived in March, the rest to follow. Thus, the saga of the pumps had dragged on for eight months! In August 1945 they were sold for 7/6 (37 ½ p) each.

The Pavilion

The Pavilion, opened on 4th June 1932, features regularly in the Minutes and was often the venue for Council Meetings. On 15th April 1940 it was agreed to seek estimates for re-painting and for the repair of damage caused by vandalism e.g. to the lead pipes. It was decided to "put a notice in the Pavilion to obviate the damage." The painting and other repairs were subsequently done at a cost of £18=16=0d (£18.80p). The meeting on 20th January 1941 heard that there had been "wilful damage" done to the Pavilion. "One lad had confessed to being a party to the damage but there were others". Efforts would be made to recover the cost of the damage from the offenders. According to the Minutes of 17th March this was done. In July 1942 it was reported that the Pavilion would "shortly become a rendezvous for Special Constables".

On 4th June 2012, during celebrations to mark the Diamond Jubilee of HM Queen Elizabeth II, the Chairman of the Council, Mr M Dobson, unveiled a plaque inside the Pavilion commemorating the Jubilee and the opening of the Pavilion exactly eighty years before.

The Impact of War on Footpaths

The Council had a very active Footpaths Committee which was concerned that paths ploughed up for cultivation during the war should be protected and restored after it. On 20th October 1941 a Member referred to "a footpath through land approaching

Coldharbour Lane and asked that something should be done to make certain that the footpath is maintained after the war". Under Defence Regulations footpaths could be ploughed up or blocked but notice had to be given. Such matters were dealt with by the Kent War Agricultural Executive Committee (K.W.A.E.C.). The Council Meeting of 24th November 1941 suggested that where a footpath was ploughed up "a furrow should be cut each side of the footpath". The following July it was reported that five more footpaths had been ploughed up and the Council was concerned that one was ploughed without notice. The K.W.A.E.C.'s attention was drawn "to the amount of land now covered with thistles in the Parish."

The Council continued to be concerned about footpaths throughout the war and in the years following. In March 1944 it was agreed that:

"... owners of footpaths which had been ploughed up under the W.A. Committee's instructions should be informed that the Parish Council reserve the right to see that those footpaths become Rights of Way as soon as possible after the Act ceases to be in force".

In June 1950 the Council began work on a complete survey of all footpaths in the Parish in accordance with the Survey of Footpaths Act 1949, and the "National Parks and access to the Countryside Act, 1949". By December the survey had been finished and maps and observations sent to the Rural District Council.

From the Wartime Minutes

During the last three years of war Council Minutes often cover matters relating to the hostilities. Twice the Council adjourned in haste – on 18th January 1943 and on 18th October 1943 because of air raid alerts. Some of the items considered by members:

- Letters of congratulation were sent to Lt. W. H. Rees, R.N. and Pilot Officer B. Goodale in March 1942. They had received awards "for gallantry in action". No details were given but perhaps someone today knows about these awards. What were they? Under what circumstances were they given?
- 16th April 1942 – as the "Service Road on Foxbush Building estate" was being used as a parking space for military vehicles, had it been requisitioned by the military?
- 18th November 1942 – there was a request to the Home Guard to stop exploding bombs during exercises near to built-up areas.
  17th January 1944 – it was agreed that Army Cadets could use the Recreation Ground on Sunday afternoons for "Football or other Games".
- 19th April 1944 – a letter from the Rural District Council referred to the closure of surface shelters at Crown Lands (near the present BP garage) and the Village Green.
- 16th October 1944 – work on repairing a "footbridge at Mill Field" had not been done as the "builders were busy on Bomb damage".
- 16th October 1944 – the Kent War Agricultural Committee was to be approached for labour from Italian P.O.W.s "to carry out work at the Allotments and the Recreation Ground". There is a reference in the Minutes of 20th October 1947 to a payment of £31=2=1d (£31.10p) to the Committee for "Labour P.O.W.".
- 17th April 1945 – a resolution was passed asking a Parish Meeting "To discuss the advisability of Building a new Hall, and whether this should take the form of a War Memorial".

Efforts were made to support "the Salvage Drive" run by the Rural District Council but there were problems. On 19th October 1942 the Council was told that "certain lads were collecting paper and books for what might be their own personal gain." It was stressed that in order "to benefit a saving on the rates" the public should be persuaded to give salvage "to the dustmen".

"Posts and wires" at the Half Moon were discussed at the same meeting. Newly erected "posts and wires" at the Inn were considered to be "a public danger". These had already caused "minor accidents" and "with the 'Black Out' it is possible that serious accidents are inevitable". The Rural District Council was asked to secure the removal of this danger. Consideration of the matter on 18th January 1943 was interrupted by an "alert" and in view of the fact that most of the Members were A.R.P. workers "the meeting was adjourned". When it resumed on 10th February the Council agreed to ask the Rural District council for the "requisition of the iron for munitions", at the same time pointing out that the posts were considered to be a "Public Danger".

A letter was read to the Council on 27th September 1943 from the Ministry of Works stating that "the chains round the War Memorial had been scheduled for removal", presumably to be melted down for munitions. The Council wrote to the Ministry opposing the plan.

"Dig for Victory"

As part of the war effort, every encouragement was given to the cultivation of land for food, for example through the Gardeners' Society and by the use of allotments of which there were several in the village. There were plots on the site of what is now Mount Pleasant Court and on land south of The Cock Inn there were also allotments.

At the 17th January 1944 meeting the Council agreed to pass on to the Gardeners' Society circulars on "Potato Eelworm" and the "Dig for Victory" campaign. Enthusiasm for allotments had waned by January 1952 when the Council heard from the Allotments Committee that more than half the plots were vacant and "over £30 debit had been shown over the last 10 years". The situation hadn't improved since June 1950 when it was reported that "expenditure nearly always exceeded income" and it was agreed to pay for the vacant plots to be cleared of weeds. It was agreed to spend £12 for work on the allotments but that application should be made to the Ministry of Agriculture to sell the land. It was felt that "the allotments were a long way from the village and new houses now had larger gardens". Although not named, these Minutes presumably referred to the plots south of The Cock Inn.

Elections

Conventional elections were not held during the war. If a vacancy arose amongst the Council of nine, Members nominated candidates and by open vote chose one to fill it. As the war came to an end plans were made for the first post-war election. The Council had asked Kent County Council that the Parish be divided into two Wards – East, with seven councillors, and West with eight – but this was rejected. The County Council agreed that the number of councillors should be increased to eleven. In November 1945, following a request by "six local government electors", the Council successfully proposed to Kent County Council that the next election should be by ballot rather than by a show of hands.

The first post-war election was held on 1st April 1946 with twenty-four candidates for eleven seats at a cost of £40=13=4d (£40.67p). Councillors served for three years and any casual vacancy was filled by the unsuccessful candidate with the highest number of votes. At the Annual Council Meeting on 17th April elections to the Council's Committees were held – Finance, Footpaths, Health and General Purposes, Recreation Grounds, Allotments,

Lighting with an ad hoc committee to consider "Victory Celebrations". It is noticeable that in the days before stricter controls there was no Planning Committee. In the Minutes of 20th October 1947 there is a reference to a planning matter when the Rural District Council's attention was drawn "to the erection of a Hut such as Ford's Fotos at Masters' Café " – had the Council passed plans for this hut on the site of what is now Weald Court?

The next elections were held on 14th May 1949 at a cost of £38=12=2d (£38.61p). As in 1946 these were hotly contested with seventeen candidates for the eleven seats. Curiously, the Chairman of the retiring Council, the Vicar, the Rev. E. W. E. Fraser, did not stand for re-election. Nevertheless, in his absence, the Vicar, although not a Councillor, was unanimously chosen as Chairman at the Annual Council Meeting on 20th May. The local press reported that:

> "Proposing the Vicar, Sir Thomas Butler said there was no-one who could fill the bill as well, let alone do better".

The Vicar accepted nomination and Sir Thomas was elected Vice-Chairman. Mr Fraser remained Chairman for a year before standing down. Sir Thomas Butler was elected to replace him at the Annual Council Meeting on 26th May 1950, a post that he held for only a few months until he left the district. Mr A. G. T. Oakley replaced him.

The Victory Celebrations

The Victory Celebrations on Saturday 8th June 1946 were organized through a series of committees – "Teas, Ground, Sports, Side Shows, Bonfire, Social and Dance". There would be 17 races for children and three for adults with a total of £20 for prize money. For younger children there were pony rides. For adults and children over 13 there was to be a show in the Drill Hall where there would "be 50 seats reserved for elderly persons or others and probably conveyance for those who might require it". Tickets were available from Mr Balcombe's shop, "Cobblers", opposite the Village Green.

"Window Bills" gave details of the programme:

10.30 a.m. – noon	Sports
2 p.m.	Sports, side-shows and pony rides
4.30 p.m.	Children's tea
6 p.m.	Other attractions
8 p.m.	Entertainment (at Drill Hall)
10 p.m.	Bonfire
10.30 p.m.	Dance (at Drill Hall)

These were the days of rationing and application "to the Food Office for supplementary rations" was made. It "was agreed to cater for 500 persons plus the number of children attending the tea". It was suggested "that about 100 of the bigger children should go to the Gospel Hall".

It was subsequently reported that the celebrations had cost £39=19=6½d (£39.98p).

Raisins, Sultanas, Peas and Pears

With food rationing, "food parcels from the Dominions" were especially welcome. At the Council Meeting of 1st January 1946 a committee was set up to help the Rural District Council representatives with the distribution of the food and the Minutes for 3rd May give details of "parcels received from the people of South Africa":

25 lbs raisins, 25 lbs sultanas, 2 tins of peas, 2 tins of pears

"The Clerk offered to weigh out 50lbs of fruit and distribute to those whose names had been selected" by the committee. It is not clear how the tins of peas and pears were divided up!

Welcome Home!

A committee to arrange for a Welcome Home "to those who had served during the war" was established on 3rd July 1946. On 8th October the Council agreed to the committee's suggestion that "the expenses be covered by subscriptions, sponsored by the Parish Council". On 5th December it was confirmed that there would be "a dinner and concert at The Old Barn on 22nd January 1947". It was reported that "the Home Guard was placing funds at the disposal of the Committee".

On January 6th 1947 the Council heard that it was estimated that about 300 would be present. Commander Tomlinson, owner of the Old Barn, reported that "he could manage the catering, but was experiencing difficulty in hiring sufficient equipment for over 150". It was agreed to "borrow plates etc. from other sources". The Minutes do not give details of the event itself but on 19th March 1947 "the thanks of the Council to those who gave their help ... and also to the firm who so kindly gave cigarettes" were placed on record.

The War Memorial

At the same time as providing a "Welcome Home" for returning servicemen and women, the Council turned its attention to the War Memorial. On 19th June 1946 it was agreed that "steps should be taken to have the names of the fallen ... engraved on the present Memorial Stone at an early date". The meeting on 28th April 1947 heard that the memorial needed attention – the chains around it and the masonry needed repairing and cleaning. Provision had to be made for the names – at present the only vacant spaces were at the rear. The matter was referred to the Kent County Council, trustees of the charity which even today is responsible for the memorial site. On 20th October an estimate for the engraving work of £38 was accepted but the problem of repairs was unresolved. Estimates were to be obtained and sent to the County Council. The work having been done there was a "short dedication service of the names of those who fell during the last war "on Armistice Sunday, 7th November 1948".

"Vicar prefers Sunday Games to Cinema – Better ThanWatching Bad Films, He Thinks"

(Courier 24 October 1947)

Generally, Council Minutes are bland statements of decisions but accompanying the Minutes for 20th October 1947 is a cutting from "The Courier" for 24th October which quotes some of the views expressed at the Meeting.

One of the matters discussed was a proposal to allow cricket and other games to be played on the Recreation Ground on Sundays. The Vicar, The Rev. E. W. E. Fraser, the Council Chairman, was reported as saying that whilst nothing should be done to make it more difficult for people to go to Church, young people are better employed playing healthy games on Sunday rather "than lounging about on street corners or sitting in stuffy cinemas watching questionable films". He said:

"We ought not to be merely negative. If people do not want to go to Church, it is not for us to impose Christian laws on others".

The matter was referred to the forthcoming Parish Meeting. This approved the proposition that games could be allowed on Sundays "out of Church Service hours". Bye-laws had to be amended and submitted to the Home Secretary for approval.

The newspaper report of 24th October, under the by-line "snub for British Legion", referred to a request that a Legion representative be co-opted on to the Council's Housing

Committee. A Councillor was quoted as saying that the Parish Council was quite capable of attending to the housing wants of the Parish without help from the Legion. The request was rejected as was the Legion's plan to erect a hut on the Village Green for use as a temporary headquarters. According to the report, the Clerk, Mr F. G. Balcombe, remarked that the "top part of the Green could be built on". Members thought that the Green was in a bad state and allowing the request would make it worse.

The Underriver Bus

According to "A-Z", the 'bus service to Underriver has run since 1932 but "The Courier" reported in the 24th October 1947 edition that a letter to the Council from an Underriver resident stated that a petition signed by 59 residents had been sent to Messrs Ashline who ran the service requesting improvements. "The Courier" reported the problem:

"The early morning 'bus arrived at Tonbridge too late for shopping purposes and the 2.10pm return 'bus was too late for those who had to be home for lunch". (Courier 24 October 1947)

Messrs Ashline's reply was quoted:

"The present 'bus service was still unprofitable and it was necessary to have at least 12 passengers on the inwards and outwards journey to cover the bare cost. Buses often travelled half empty".

Two Councillors were appointed to meet Messrs Ashline.

No doubt the fuel crisis of the time added to Messrs Ashline's problems and by chance, the cutting from "The Courier" includes a quotation from the Tunbridge Wells Gas Manager "at a meeting of the Housewives' League":

"Fuel Frivolity"

The Ministry of no Fuel and hardly any Power – or, as we playfully like to call it, The Ministry of Foul and Pure ..."

A 30 m.p.h. speed limit through the Village?

At the October 1947 Council Meeting another attempt was made to secure a 30 m.p.h. speed limit from The Green Rabbit (now Orchard Lea) to the War Memorial, a matter which had been raised before. The request was made to the Police and the Kent County Council. The latter, in a letter dated 20th November, stated that "members were unable to see their way to take any action" in relation to the request. The Council decided to refer the matter to the local M.P., Mr Gerald Williams. He replied in January 1948, enclosing a letter from the Transport Minister, Alfred Barnes, M.P., stating that he did not consider an extension of the 30 m.p.h. limit through Hildenborough was warranted.

Councillors did not give up on their attempts to get a 30 m.p.h. speed limit through the village and a further application was sent to the County Council in August 1949. In October the Parish Council pointed out that the limit was "more than ever necessary, particularly as the convent school was now at Foxbush". On 18th January 1950 the Council was told that the County Council had approved the proposal. Members requested that it be implemented "as soon as possible". This was not to be as a letter from the County Council dated 8th July 1950 stated that:

"The Minister has now intimated that after very careful consideration of the proposal he does not feel that a case for the speed limit has been established as the amount of development fronting the road is insufficient to justify this important traffic route being deemed to be a road in a built-up area".

The matter was again raised on 23rd February 1952 when a site meeting was held near

156

the War Memorial. The County Councillor together with the Chairman of the Roads Committee, a surveyor and a technical adviser and a representative of the Clerk attended on behalf of the County Council. The Police were represented by a Superintendent from Maidstone and an Inspector from Tonbridge. The Rural District Council was represented and five Parish Councillors together with their Clerk attended. It was agreed to support another application for the speed limit. Again, nothing was achieved and subsequent requests rejected but in 2015 it was finally agreed to impose a 30mph limit from Foxbush through the village.

The Minutes show that there was another problem with speeding. In July 1946 the Council had received complaints "that Army Vehicles travelled Philpotts Road at a high and dangerous speed. There had recently been two accidents ...". The matter was referred to the Police. In April 1950 the Council again took up the problem of army lorries speeding along Philpotts Road to and from Gaza Barracks.

Pedestrian Crossings

Council records show that Members were frequently concerned about pedestrian crossings. In November 1947 there was a request to move the crossing near the War Memorial to a point near the 'bus stop outside the Church. An application was made for a crossing "at the Flying Dutchman near the Leigh Road".

In 1951 there was considerable concern about "the removal of the Pedestrian Crossing at St John's Church". An "informal meeting" was held at the Drill Hall on 17th October attended by 55 residents. Representatives from the County Council, the Rural District Council and Tonbridge Police were invited to speak. A Parish Council meeting that same evening agreed to send a strong letter of objection to the County Council who had removed the crossing "before the scheme has been submitted to, or approved by the Minister of Transport, or even before the expiration of the period allowed for the submission of objections". In support, the letter made numerous comments, pointing out that at Summer weekends 2,000 vehicles an hour used the road (then the A21) which had "no speed limit". In a letter dated 19th November 1951, the County Council informed the Parish Council that the Ministry of Transport had approved "the retention of the crossing place near St John's Church in substitution for that north of the "Half Moon Public House".

Rejection of a Plan for Playing Fields

At a Council Meeting in October 1947 a letter from the Council's Solicitors, Messrs Warner & Co, was read. It stated that the application for a loan to purchase land for playing fields at Crown Lands, an area of approximately four acres, had been refused by the Ministry of Health:

> "The Minister does not feel justified in consenting to a loan for the purpose at the present time".

Discussions about the scheme had been started in 1937 but interrupted by the war. There had been problems with access to the site (near the "Boiling Kettle", the present BP garage) and the solicitors in a letter dated 5th April 1945 stated "that the District Valuer considers the price proposed to be given to be too high as the land is practically flood land".

The Drill Hall and Institute

On 16th July 1946 the Council met as a Committee to consider a letter from Mr Edwin Hendry, Chairman of the Trustees of the Drill Hall and Institute. He said that the Trustees

had agreed to offer the Hall and the Institute to the Parish Council...
"...for such sum as shall clear all the Trustees' liabilities".
It was reported that these liabilities were approximately £100. The following week the Council agreed to open negotiations with the Trustees.
On 24th November 1947 the Council passed the following Resolution:
"That this meeting in accordance with the Resolution passed at the Parish Meeting on 12th November 1947 accept the offer dated 5th November 1947 of the Trustees of the Drill Hall and Institute property to transfer the ownership of the said property to the Parish Council".
The Deeds were finally handed over to the Council at a ceremony in the Vicarage on 13th June 1949. The buildings were eventually replaced by the current Village Hall, opened in 1971.
Early in 1950 the Drill Hall had been renovated and heating with coal was replaced by gas radiators. With effect from 1st April 1950 the Parish Council revised the hire charges for the Drill Hall. Examples:

1 hour with light and heat	15=0d	(75p)
Each subsequent hour	7=6d	(37½p)
1 hour without light and heat	10=0d	(50p)
Each subsequent hour	4=6d	(22½p)
1 hour with light only	12=0d	(60p)
Each subsequent hour	5=6d	(27½p)
1 hour with heat and no light	13=0d	(65p)
Each subsequent hour	6=6d	(32½p)

There were discounts for regular bookings and reduced charges for hiring for a whole day e.g. a 12 hour day £3=10=0d (£3.50p), a 9 hour day £3. There were separate charges for the Committee Room, depending on whether heat and/or light was required. The charge for 3 hours without heat or light was 4=0d (20p). It was agreed that the caretaker's wages "will be increased by 3/- (15p) per week and no commission will be allowed for money collected for lettings".
In June 1950 the Council passed a Resolution about the sink in the Institute's kitchen. A filter was to be fixed "to prevent food going down and stopping the drain, the K.E.C. (Kent Education Committee) to be notified of this and to ask the cooks to be more careful in future" as the kitchen was being used for school meals. At the request of K.E.C. the Council agreed in October to the installation of a second kitchen sink. The kitchens caused further problems when in April 1951 urgent work was authorised as "the floor has collapsed". K.E.C. made a grant of £12 towards the cost of the "new concrete floor" of £78=19=9d (£78.99). The Drill Hall had further difficulties in January 1952 when the Social Club explained that the "roof was leaking in the Bar, the lavatory and the Billiard Room, also the floor of the small room was needing repairs". The work was done at a cost of £5=9=3d (£5.46).
An example of the hirers of the Hall at this time was the Rabbit Club. In December 1951 permission for the let was given "on condition the Hall was left in clean condition."

The Library

In March 1950 the Council decided to explore the possibility of having a branch library at the Institute and in April the County Librarian agreed to operate a Library in the Committee Room on Mondays from 2.30 – 4.30p.m. and Fridays from 5 – 7 p.m. The charge of £15 would include lighting, heating and cleaning for a year. In December it was agreed to install a new gas light fitting in the Committee Room. In Autumn 1951 the

Library's opening hours were extended to include Tuesday afternoons at an additional annual charge of £7=10=0d (£7.50p). In January 1952 the Council accepted the supervisor's request "for an additional gas jet and lamp to be fixed in the Library room". In March the Council agreed to ...

> "... the installation of a gas fire in the Library Room, the whole of the heating for the Council's lettings would then be gas heating and in future no coal would be required".

80 Applicants for the post of Caretaker

On 30th January 1952 the caretaker of the Drill Hall and Institute resigned with effect from 9th February and the Council had to find a replacement in a hurry. In the interim the Clerk agreed to undertake the work. A sub-committee was appointed to fill the vacancy for the £3 per week job. Their advertisement read:

> "Hildenborough Parish Council require Caretaker and handyman. Cottage available 2/3 bedrooms".

On 15th February a recommendation for an appointment was made to the Council. There had been eighty applicants and eight were short-listed. It was reported that some applicants had been rejected as they had too large a family for the cottage which went with the job. The new caretaker didn't take up his duties immediately as extensive repairs to the cottage were required. The Clerk continued with the work whilst these were being done.

A sign of the times: all the other Minutes between 1938 and 1952 were written with pen and ink but those for 15th February 1952 were in the new "biro"! This invention by the Hungarian hypnotist Lasalo Biro appears to have been first sold in this country in 1945 – price 55/- (£2.75p)!

Oakhill House

On 14th March 1944 a Council meeting was held to discuss the proposed purchase of Hollanden Park, including Oakhill House, by Messrs Elliott and Spears "for business purposes". Mr Spears attended and answered Members' questions and the Council then unanimously passed a Resolution in support of the planned purchase. It considered that "the surroundings will be preserved" and that the business would be "an asset from a rateable point of view and would give employment to quite a number of local residents". Oakhill House was used as a lampshade factory and was to be acquired by Fidelity in 1986 soon after an application to demolish it was refused.

Post War Housing Schemes

It was in March 1944 that the Rural District Council asked the Parish Council to consider possible sites for houses under the "Post War Housing Schemes". On 3rd April Members agreed to ask the Rural District Council's Housing Committee "to do their utmost to secure more than eighteen houses in the Parish under the above schemes". A list of the suggested sites:

1. Continuation of Council Cottages, Riding Place, Riding Lane.
2. North side of Mount Pleasant Road (opposite Park View) Hubble's Land.
3. Next to Writtle Cottages, Coldharbour Lane.
4. Rear of Turley Cottages (Stocks Green).
5. Continuation of Grove Wood Cottages, London Road.
6. North side of London Road (The Flats).

The Rural District Council had proposed "to acquire three acres of land forming part of Burnt House Meadow near Club Cottages", Riding Lane, but the Council was informed in July 1944 that the Rural District Council had decided "to seek the approval of the Ministry of Health to the acquisition of two acres of land owned by Mr S. L. Hubble facing Mount Pleasant and 0.92 acres of land opposite the school, Riding Lane" instead of the Burnt House Meadow site.

Improving the Pavilion

At a Council meeting on 4th November 1943 estimates were accepted for providing electricity for the Pavilion. The Electricity Company would be paid £3=10=0d (£13.50p) for "laying a twin service". For the provision of "wiring, lamps etc." an estimate of £10 was accepted from "Messrs Gilbert and Stamper". A "second hand heating lamp" was to be obtained for 25/- (£1.25p) and the Clerk was instructed to purchase "a boiling ring" at a "reasonable cost".

Over the years the Pavilion had suffered damage, mainly due to "bomb damage", and repairs were authorised in May 1946 with the Clerk asked to "make enquiries on these matters from the proper authority" – presumably with a view to obtaining compensation for damage caused by enemy action.

In January 1948 the Council accepted an offer from the Cricket Club to paint the front of the Pavilion "on condition that the Parish Council purchased the paint, brushes etc. Labour would be free". The cost of the paint etc. came to £2=14=1d (£2.70½ p). It was reported that several windows had been broken and that "the Police were making enquiries". Clearly, apart from painting the Pavilion, the Cricket Club together with the Football Club, did a lot of voluntary work on the Recreation Ground as they were formally thanked by the Council the following October.

The last significant entry in the Minutes relating to the Pavilion was for 30th January 1952 when the Clerk reported that "the sum of £27=5=0d (£27.25p) had been recovered from the insurance for Fire Damage at the Pavilion" but no details were given.

Lighting up the Village

Before the war the Parish Council had been concerned with a lighting scheme for the village. In 1938 it had requested that the Rural District Council take over responsibility for lighting and a scheme was drawn up. The Ministry of Transport raised objections and the matter was dropped at the outbreak of war. On 1st January 1946 the Parish Council asked the Rural District Council "to proceed with the street lighting for the Parish of Hildenborough as soon as possible". In response the Council was asked if it wished to revise or extend the 1939 scheme. The Parish Council set up a committee to look into the matter.

Negotiations with the Rural District Council led to the Parish Council in July 1946 expressing concern about the cost of the cast iron lamp standards suggested. Perhaps for "side roads" concrete standards could be used. Later that month it was agreed to write to the Rural District Council stating that it was felt that "the capital expenses seemed to be on the high side". The Council was asked if "there is any possibility of the Ministry taking over the lighting of the Main Roads". In October the Parish Council agreed "that spun-concrete lamps be used and not cast iron posts, for street lighting at Hildenborough when the Ministry sanction the work to be done".

On 6th January 1947 the Parish Council was told that the Ministry of Transport "considered that the main road would require another 27 lamps costing approximately another £850-£900". The Council's scheme, approved by the Rural District Council, involved "a rate of approximately 4½d (2p). The total rate of the enlarged scheme would be approximately 7½d (3p)." The Parish Council agreed to ask:

"In view of the Government's proposed scheme to take over the Transport and Electricity undertakings would the Rural District Council recommend the advisability of postponing the lighting of the main road pro tem …".

Discussions about the number and types of lamps dragged on for months. The cost was a major concern but the matter of a lighting scheme was left to the Rural District Council. Lighting ceased to appear as an item in the Minutes except where there were specific concerns e.g. in March 1950 the Council requested the Rural District Council to install a street lamp at the junction of Church Road and Mount Pleasant, the estimated cost "not to exceed £20". The Rural District Council agreed to the new lamp. Later that year members of the Parish Council were asked for ideas about possible sites for additional lamps. These would be submitted to the Rural District Council. By January 1951 four had been erected at "Hilden Farm Estate" and one at Vine's Corner. A request by a resident for street lighting "in Foxbush Estate" was rejected by the Rural District Council. The Parish Council, in January 1952, sought an extra lamp at the Hilden Estate and one at Riding Park.

The Recreation Ground

The Recreation Ground was acquired by the Parish Council in 1931 and has always been a major concern. The Minutes tell how the problems of today featured in earlier years – maintenance, drainage, letting of the ground, vandalism etc. A Recreation Ground Committee had the task of reporting to the full Council.

As long ago as October 1938 drainage was a problem and a meeting of interested parties was to be held and a loan sought to cover the cost of solving it. In November it was reported that a loan might not be necessary as the Council appeared to have sufficient funds in its account held by the Rural District Council and it was agreed to go ahead with a drainage scheme. Details of the scheme are vague but there are references in the Minutes to lengths of iron pipe and to a "catch-pit". Apart from the "catch-pit", it was reported on 11th April 1939 that the drainage work had been completed. It was indicated in May that "the catch-pit" had been installed.

At the April 1939 meeting it was agreed to obtain estimates for "Rolling etc. and the removal of stones". Accounts for payment agreed in May included:

Rolling grass   7=0d (35p)
Stone picking   17=0d (85p)
Catch-pit etc.   12=0d (60p)

A year later the Council declined an Estimate of 3/- (15p) per hour for "Rolling, grass cutting, harrowing etc." to include "harrow, two horses and one man". It was felt that the work should be done for a fixed sum of £3=15=0d (£3.75p) rather than for an hourly rate. In May 1940 it was agreed that an offer "to keep the grass down on and around the cricket pitch for about £2 for the season" should be accepted.

The Minutes of 12th August 1940 show that it was agreed to pay 1/- (5p) an hour for the cutting of hedges, cleaning out ditches, repairing broken fences and other "necessary work". Over the years there are various references to the cost of work done at the Ground. In October 1945, for instance, an offer to undertake hedge trimming and ditch cleaning "at 1/- per rod" (5p per 5½ yards) was accepted.

In the Minutes for 17th April 1946 the Council considered complaints about "dogs, cycling and horse riding at the Recreation Ground" and decided that bye-laws should be considered. In the following months there are references to equipment and maintenance but details are not always given. There is more information in the Minutes for 19th March 1947 when various purchases were approved and work to be done agreed. The "sand pit" was to be renewed and "1 set of Heavy Iron Swings, 4 seats, 1 set swings, 2 seats and 8 chains to be purchased from Hirsts of Halifax". A "gang mower", approximate cost £100, would be bought. The Football and Cricket Clubs agreed to pay their annual rent of £5 p.a. for four years in advance to help with the purchase of the mower. £10 was allocated to the Ground Committee "to have the ground dredged and rolled".

At their meeting on 14th January 1947 Councillors received copies of the Bye-laws and it was agreed to put up notice boards stating "Cycling prohibited and dogs not allowed except on a leash". A notice by the "small swings" would say "Only for children up to 6 years of age". That meeting gave the Ground Committee "power to act with reference to a surround of barbed wire at the pond." The account from "Hirsts of Halifax" of £63=18=11d (£63.95p) was approved for payment.

By January 1948 it was felt that the purchase of a wheelbarrow was necessary. A shed would be erected to house the mower and other equipment. The wheelbarrow was duly purchased at a cost of £5=10=0d (£5.50p). For the year 1948 it was agreed to pay £5 "per time for mowing the Recreation Ground".

Gang-mowing for the "Rec"

In December 1948 the Council considered Estimates from Kent Education Committee for work on the Recreation Ground and the Village Green by their "Gang-mower service":

Gang mowing   6/6d (32½p) per acre
Harrowing   7/6d (37½p) per acre

The offer was accepted although extra labour would be needed for "Hedge Cutting, Ditching etc.". If the new system was satisfactory "it was agreed that the Gang-mower should be overhauled and sold". In March 1949 it was decided to offer the Council's Gang-mower to Underriver Cricket Club for £75 without a guarantee "as it stood". If the Club declined the offer the mower was to be repaired at a cost of £20 and then offered for sale at £100. In April, as the Cricket Club didn't want to buy the mower, it was agreed to offer it "to the Colony" (Princess Christian's) for £75 without a guarantee. Still unsold, it was agreed in June to advertise it for sale. In October it was reported that "a gentleman had viewed the mower and would probably write at a later date". It is not known if he ever did!

Kent Education Committee agreed to mow the Recreation Ground for 1950 and the Minutes for June show that a payment of £31=4=0d (£31.20p) was made for the work in 1949. In August 1950 the Council accepted an Estimate of £24=18=0d (£24.90) "to take down from the Village Green and re-erect and make good the shelter on the Recreation Ground". This referred to the old air raid shelter.

Vandalism at the Recreation Ground was reported at the Council Meeting on the 23rd May 1951:

> "It was reported that there is no abatement of the damage done to the Council Property at the Recreation Ground. It was agreed that the Clerk should have an interview with the Superintendent of Police (Tonbridge) asking for a special observation to be kept, should any offender be caught the Council would be prepared to prosecute".

A Miscellany from the Minutes

"In reference to a gate at Hawden Farm, it was agreed … to write to the present owner of the Farm asking him if he would restore the gate to its former state in order that cycles and perambulators could pass through". **3rd May 1939**

PART 5 − 1938-1952

Officers of the National Fire Service attended a Council Meeting on **16th April 1942** to explain what services the Parish was entitled to under "The National Scheme": "At the moment there were 3 full time men in Hildenborough and 9 voluntary but there was no guarantee that the latter would answer the siren. There were no messengers here, and having no siren in the Parish it was not always certain that their services were needed. It was reported that there was a crew on duty or available for duty 3 nights a week."

It was reported "that the grit was being stolen from roadside dumps and it was considered that was a matter for the Police". **10th November 1942.**

From time to time the Council considered requests for public seats: "… a request has been made for seats of some description in the Riding Lane area to rest wayfarers". **17th April 1946.**

"Sanitation" was a concern at the Council Meeting of **14th July 1947** when a Resolution was passed:
"That the attention of the Rural District Council be called to the fact that there appears to be insufficient lavatory accommodation at Masters for the number of Coaches calling there twice daily".
The "Masters' Tea House" was on the site of what became B&Q and is now Weald Court. At one time travellers were served by three "tea rooms" in the village along the route of what was then the A21 – the "Boiling Kettle" (now the BP Garage), the Green Rabbit (now Orchard Lea) and Masters' Tea House.

"It was agreed to make an application to the Post Office Engineer's Dept. for a kiosk to be erected in the area of Stocks Green Road and Leigh Road". **20th October 1947.** This is presumably the one remaining red 'phone box that stands at the junction of Leigh Road and Brookmead. In early 2017 the box was under threat of closure by BT as statistics show that it is rarely used. In the previous year it was only used three times.

"Complaints were received with reference to the unpleasant taste of the drinking water in the Parish". **9th March 1948.**

There are frequent references in the Minutes to Pillar Boxes – requests for additional ones and problems with the collection times. The Council supported a Petition …
"… for the requisition of a Pillar Box at some point in Coldharbour Lane between London Road and Hildenborough Hall" (now The Raphael Centre). **21st April 1948.**

The Council fought for years for the Village Police Constable to be on the telephone. It was agreed …
"… that the Chief Constable of Kent be informed through the Superintendent of Tonbridge Police that the Village Constable is not on the telephone and to be asked that the 'phone be put into his residence as soon as possible". **16th October 1944.** The reply: the Police Authorities … "… were not prepared to have the 'phone installed at a War Reserves premises". **15th January 1945.**

The Council passed a Resolution requesting …
"… Police Authorities asking them to persuade the Telephone Engineer to speed up the installation of the 'phone at the residence of the Village Constable". **20th May 1949.**
Another request was sent in June 1949.

An example of the impact of rationing was recorded on **21st April 1948** when the Council agreed to apply to the "Petroleum Board" for extra "Petrol Units" to assist those who were using their own cars in connection with the August Bank Holiday Fête in aid of the Memorial Hall Funds.

"The Police were instructed to enforce the Litter Bye-law as complaints had been received about ice-cream wrappings and other rubbish on the main road through the village". **18th July 1949**.

The Council accepted "An Estimate for tuning the Piano" at the Drill Hall "the contract would be 24/- (£1.20p) per year for tuning four times per annum". 5/- (25p) would be charged for the use of the piano for "concerts and dances etc. ...". **24th January 1951**.

Estimates were considered for "work on a proposed Car Park at Riding Lane" but a decision was delayed "as there was a possibility that soil etc. would continue to be dumped on the site and so relieve the cost later". **17th October 1951**.

HILDENBOROUGH PARISH COUNCIL

PARISH MEETINGS

The Council kept two books of Minutes. One recorded proceedings at Parish Council meetings whilst the other covered Parish Meetings. An Annual Parish Meeting was held each Spring but Parish Meetings were called from time to time to consider specific topics. Such meetings were usually summoned by the Council but six electors could requisition a special Parish Meeting.

The book containing the Minutes of Parish Meetings also contained a record of village celebrations held to mark special occasions.

Part 6 – 1894-1924

The Local Government Act, 1894, which established Parish Councils, laid down rules about meetings of the Council and of the Parish. The Minutes of Council Meetings were recorded in one book whilst another recorded the Minutes of Parish meetings. The Council held its own Annual Meeting at which officers and committees were elected by Councillors but there also had to be an Annual Parish Meeting. Additional Parish Meetings could be called as required.

Initially a Parish Meeting was convened annually to elect nine councillors and a chairman of the Council but from 1901 the elections of councillors was held every three years with a Chairman elected annually by the Parish Council. Sometimes the election took place at a separate meeting but in later years the Annual Parish Meeting was held immediately afterwards. At this Annual Meeting the Council would give an account of their previous year's work, as happens today.

Apart from the Annual Parish Meeting additional meetings could be called:
  - By the Chairman or any two councillors
  - By six parochial electors. This happened in July 1948 in order to discuss the proposed closure of the glass factory in Stocks Green Road.

The 1894 Act laid down where Parish meetings could be held:
  - In certain circumstances in the Parish Church or the Vestry Room
  - In any public baths provided under "the Baths and Wash houses Acts"
  - In "licensed premises" but only when no other venue was available
  - If there was no suitable "public room" (eg in a village hall), meetings could be held, free of charge …
      > "… in any suitable room in the school house of any public elementary school receiving a parliamentary grant and in any suitable room maintained out of any local rate."

The room must not be used as "part of a private dwelling house".

Only electors registered in the parish were entitled to attend and vote at a parish meeting. There was a quorum of only two and the attendance at meetings usually varied from single figures to approaching 100. There was a record attendance of 288 in 1949 at a meeting called to discuss the possibility of Hildenborough being transferred from Tonbridge Rural District Council area to that of the Urban District Council.

Hildenborough's first Parish Meeting

The inaugural Parish Meeting was held on Tuesday 4th December 1894 at 6.30pm in the School Room.

The Minute Book for Parish meetings provides a record of such meetings from 1894 until 3rd March 1956, a period of 62 years. The book also contains accounts of various Parish celebrations e.g. Coronations, Jubilee and Peace celebrations.

At that first meeting the room "was completely filled with electors". The Overseer of the Board of Guardians, Mr Edwin Hendry ...

"... inaugurated the business of the Meeting by announcing that it was called to bring into operation the Local Government Act of 1894 and the business that evening was to elect a Chairman and a Parish Council of nine Members."

Mr Hendry proposed Mr Charles Fitch Kemp of Foxbush as Chairman, a proposal that was carried unanimously. The Act stated that the Chairman must either be a Councillor or a person qualified to be a Councillor. In the early years of the Council the Chairman was generally not a councillor and Mr Kemp was not nominated as a candidate at that first meeting. In accepting office Mr Kemp declared that now...

"it was very desirable that they should elect nine good men and true to represent the Parish."

Mr Fitch Kemp then proceeded to conduct the election of nine councillors. Voting would be by a show of hands although a secret ballot could be requested. This would entail a secret ballot of the entire electorate, something which would incur significant costs. This Council would serve for 15 months until the first Annual Meeting in March 1896. Co-option by the Council would fill any casual vacancies.

The Chairman asked for nominations to be handed to him. In accordance with the Act, fifteen minutes were allowed for this. Those nominated then faced questions from the electors. Examples -

– Should Parish Council meetings be open "to the Public and the Press"?
– At what time should meetings be held?
– Were the candidates in favour of allotments in the village?

There were 16 nominations. Each elector had 9 votes and the show of hands for each candidate in alphabetical order led to the election of the following:

Thomas Bassett	Great Forge Farm	Farmer
Richard A Bosanquet	Mardens, Philpots Lane	Merchant
Thomas Collins	Marchwood, Fairhill	Agent to Lord Derby
Roger Cunliffe	Meopham Bank	Banker
John Francis	London Road	Inspector of Weights and Measures
Edwin Hendry	London Road	Grocer
Charles Hitchcock	Mount Pleasant	Cricket ball maker
Horace H Hitchcock	16 Lansdown Road, Tonbridge	Cricket ball maker
George W Johnson	Mountains	Civil engineer

There were demands for a poll but these were withdrawn after some discussion. Mr Fitch Kemp pointed out that the 9 chosen only held office for 15 months – they would "hardly have time to do either much harm or good". He declared his satisfaction with the result of the meeting ...

"... and said they might all go home feeling assured that the Parish would not be set on fire for the next 15 months."

Several of the councillors then addressed the meeting, each pledging to work for the good of the Parish as a whole. Mr Charles Hitchcock summed up the mood ....

"... if they were all united they might make their village better and brighter. There was room for improvement and he hoped to see it brought about."

Mr Fitch Kemp concluded the meeting by declaring that they were ...

"... solely anxious that this Act should be worked so as to be a benefit to the great bulk of the parishioners, and no niggardly feeling with regard to taxation would prevent them going hand in hand with the working classes and doing anything that was required for their comfort and their enjoyment, or that would add to the pleasure and happiness of their lives."

The Chairman referred to a number of issues which the Council would need to consider e.g. the erection of a "Public Building", the extension of the allotments, and the improvement of the roads. All the Parish must be taken into consideration including "those who lived at Nizels and the recently attached part of Leigh". He went on to say of the councillors ...

"... let them be thoughtful, impartial, considerate and kind, don't let them think if differences arose on the Council, that necessarily the man who was adverse to them was an enemy or opponent. Give and take was a good motto if they wanted to get along, and if that feeling animated the Members of the Council as he hoped and believed it would, they would never lack the confidence and regard of the parishioners at large."

1895-1896

Rent Rises?   The Institute

The second Parish Meeting was held on 25th March 1895 with 30 parishioners present. The meeting considered several topics which were currently under review by the Council.

- The condition of the roads
- Allotments. The Chairman referred to "the kind and generous spirit" in which Lord Derby, a significant landowner, had met the Council about a possible site for allotments.
- The acquisition of a "parish building". Perhaps "the old Institute" could be acquired from the current owner, Mr Charles Barkaway.
- "a bathing place"
- Lighting in the village. Would the Tonbridge Gas Co. "bring their mains to Hildenborough"?

Mr Horace Hitchcock, a councillor, reported that there was "an opinion abroad" that expenditure on the roads and the proposed hall might lead to landowners raising "the rents of their cottages". One parishioner commented that he considered "that for a village their rents were very high". Mr Fitch Kemp , the Chairman, pointed out that such expenses were for the benefit of all and that "all ratepayers must contribute their quota". He continued ...

"... if they took the railway and about eight or ten of the property owners they would find that the vast proportion of any expenditure by the Parish Council would come out of their pockets."

He suggested that ...

"... it was only reasonable, as cottage owners would benefit by these improvements that they should be asked to contribute towards the expenditure."

The next Parish meeting was held at the "National Schools" on 31st October 1895 with Mr Charles Fitch Kemp in the chair and 26 parishioners present. The purpose of the meeting was to consider the proposed purchase by the Parish Council from Mr Charles

Barkaway ...
"... of the freehold house and premises at Hildenborough known as the
Institute and certain land adjoining thereto."
It was agreed to seek ...
"... the consent of the County Council and such further consent as may be
necessary for raising a loan for the amount of the purchase money of the said
premises together with the expenses attending the said purchase and loan."
The first annual election of Parish Councillors was held on 9th March 1896 with Mr C
Fitch Kemp presiding and 73 "Parochial Electors" present. 9 candidates were chosen on
a show of hands from 12 nominees. They were declared elected after some discussion.
Should there be a poll? This demand was withdrawn but it was claimed that the Council
was not "sufficiently representative".
The 1896 Annual Parish Meeting was held on 1st April with only the chairman, Mr
Fitch Kemp and 13 parishioners present. The meeting was informed that the County
Council had refused to sanction the purchase of the Institute. An appeal to the Local
Government Board had been unsuccessful with the Board stating that it "had no power to
interfere".

The Diamond Jubilee, 1897

The Annual Parish Meeting of 18th May 1897 followed immediately after the election of
the new Council. The 70 parishioners present heard details from the Chairman, Mr
Charles Fitch Kemp, of how Queen Victoria's Diamond Jubilee would be celebrated in the
village. There then followed in the Minute Book 19 foolscap pages quoting a glowing
account of the festivities in the "Tonbridge Free Press" of 3rd July 1897. The weather had
been kind and the celebrations a great success. The account refers to ...
"...popular rejoicings the like of which we make bold to assert could not be
equalled in any village in Kent. The good feeling existing between all classes
has long been a characteristic of this village and the liberality which the gentry,
headed by the noble squire of 'Foxbush', have always displayed was exemplified
on the present occasion by the provision of a fund sufficient to entertain the
whole of the inhabitants in lavish style."
"The noble squire of Foxbush" was the Council Chairman, Mr Charles Fitch Kemp.
Under his leadership the Council organised the celebration and the account tells how...
"A festive appearance was imparted to the village by the display of bunting at
various points notably at Foxbush where the Union Jack surmounted the
mansion."
The 'Half Moon' and 'Flying Dutchman' were suitably decorated. Businesses were closed
"and the employers of labour ... generously gave their men a half holiday."
Mr and Mrs M C Morris, the headteachers at the "prettily decorated" school, organised
the presentation on 28th June of "a beautiful medal" to each of the 196 children present
by Mrs Kemp, wife of the Council Chairman. Mrs Kemp and her party were welcomed by
the Vicar, the Rev'd R L G Pidcock and a rendering of "Auld Lang Syne". The National
Anthem was sung and the proceedings ended with the Jubilee Hymn 'King of Kings'"
together with "a few kind words to the children" from Mrs Kemp. All were "much pleased
with the thoughtful kindness of the lady of Foxbush".
The main festivities took place on 29th June on the Oak Hill Cricket Ground (now
Westwood). At the entrance gate was "a handsome archway bearing Her Majesty's
gracious Jubilee message":
"From my heart I thank my beloved people. May God bless them. V.R. and I".

On top of the archway was a portrait of the Queen bordered by flags and the royal colours. From the archway there was an avenue of …

> "… poles covered with birch boughs with lines of small flags on either side and larger ones at each summit. Facing the London Road there were Venetian masks from which hung the Royal Standard and Union Jack."

Flags decorated the field and in front of the cricket pavilion was another portrait of the Queen.

All residents aged 16 years and above were invited and 530 tickets were issued. Two adjoining marquees were erected, "combining to make a magnificent dining saloon." Entrance was via a pretty archway and the interior of the marquees was decorated with flags and shields. "Choice plants from Foxbush and Mountains" and cut flowers from various local gardens added to the decoration.

The task of catering was entrusted to Mr W Austin of Tonbridge …

> "… who attacked it with praiseworthy zeal and achieved a most complete success. To show the admirable nature of the preparations we may state that forty waiters were employed and that the good things provided included lamb roast and boiled beef ham veal and ham pies with tarts jellies, blancmange and tartlets supplemented with cheese and salad beer lemonade and ginger beer ad lib." (sic)

Music was provided by the Royal Military Band from Tunbridge Wells. Before the dinner "the Old Hundredth was sung by the company upstanding and Grace was said by the Vicar," the Rev. R L G Pidcock.

After dinner, "the National Anthem having been heartily rendered," the Council Chairman, Mr Fitch Kemp proposed "the toast of the day 'The Queen'." He then delivered a speech praising the Queen and reviewing some of the events of her sixty year reign. His address was frequently interspersed with cheers and cries of "hear, hear!" Following the toast, the band led the singing of the National Anthem.

Other toasts followed. Mr Bosanquet proposed a toast to "the Old Residents". In his speech he took his listeners on a journey through "the lovely little village of Hildenborough". He lived in Philpots Lane and not far away was "Noble Tree Cross". What, he asked, "would Hildenborough be without the two dear ladies who resided there." (cheers). He sometimes thought…

> "… Hildenborough was not half grateful enough for all its blessings, that the people did not know all the good they got and that it was not till the grave closed over some lady in the parish that the naughty boys, young and old, knew what they had lost."

Mr Bosanquet then referred to 'Mountains', home of the Johnson family. He said that he did not often quote the Scriptures …

> "… but he could not help thinking of the verse 'I will lift up my eyes unto the hills from whence cometh my help'. How many there were in Hildenborough, especially old people and widows, who knew what it was to go to Mountains and the kindly friends that lived there."

On his tour of the village, Mr Bosanquet next came to Foxbush, "home of the squire" (Mr Fitch Kemp). Hollanden in Coldharbour Lane was mentioned – the home of the Hardwick family, now the Raphael Centre. He referred to "the great hospitality" shown at the Trench, home in Coldharbour Lane of Thomas Kingscote. Mr Bosanquet gave …

> "… the toast of 'the old residents' coupled with the names of their noble Chairman, Mr Kingscote and Mr George Johnson, a noble son of a noble father. The toast was received with enthusiasm and cheers and the band played 'The Old English Gentleman'."

Mr Kemp replied to the toast and to applause appealed to everyone...

"... to do all they could to not only maintain the position of this country amongst the nations of the world but by their industry, probity, integrity and prudence live good and virtuous lives and be an example to those amongst whom they lived."

There followed brief speeches from Mr Kingscote and Mr G W Johnson, the latter speaking on behalf of his father, Mr J H Johnson of Mountains, who was unable to attend due to ill-health. The next toast, proposed by Mr Kemp was to "The industries and progress of Hildenborough". He said that 50 years ago ...

"... there was very little to make life enjoyable in Hildenborough and very little company however much they might desire fellowship. The time rolled on and the industry of ball making unique in itself had its birth place in Hildenborough. The industry had gone on growing and growing..."

He mentioned several people by name including Mr Horace H Hitchcock, cricket ball maker, and Mr Charles Crowhurst, a carriage builder. Mr Hitchcock, in response, said that they had "in Hildenborough almost everything that made life worth living". Mr Robert Wingate of Oakhurst mentioned the building of the Church and the local school, the establishment of the Parish Council and "the creation of a relief station which saved people going all the way to Tonbridge".

The Vicar, the Rev'd R L G Pidcock proposed the next toast – "The Hildenborough Parish Council". He said that the Parish Council...

"... was a body of representatives elected by the intelligent and thinking men to serve their interests and manage their affairs."

The Vicar commented that Hildenborough's Parish Council, unlike some others, although only founded recently, had worked hard to improve the state of the parish. He looked, for example, to ..

"... those streets at Mount Pleasant which were a disgrace to any Parish"

but whose condition had been improved (cries of "hear, hear"). The Council had tackled the need for allotments and had taken the lead in arranging the Jubilee celebrations. It was considering plans for a recreation ground and a swimming bath. He did not agree with those who considered that a recreation ground would soon become "a bear-garden". Members were looking at the possibility of acquiring the Institute.

The Vicar mentioned "with pleasure" that he found that many villagers "belonged to some benefit society" and he urged all men to make some such provision. Amidst "roars of laughter" he suggested that young women should decline offers of marriage from men who had failed to take this step. Finally, he exhorted those present ...

"... to live good, upright and conscientious lives, so as to set a good example to the rising generation ..."

The next speaker was Mr John Francis who pointed out that at the start of the Queen's reign in 1837 "the word Hildenborough was not then coined". He found "the first mention of Hildenborough in 1843 or 1844" and if they continued to progress as they had done since then, Hildenborough would become a borough and the Chairman the first Mayor.

Three final toasts followed – to "The Sports", to "The Ladies" and to "The Vicar, Mrs Pidcock and family".

The account of the dinner, which was to be followed by sports, does not say how long it lasted. With no microphones, it must have been difficult for those present in the marquees to hear but they would have been able to read a full account of proceedings in the local press.

There was a wide variety of events during the afternoon of sports with cash prizes in most for the first three. There was what was said to be a novel event...

"... what was described as a Phiteezi race for which a special prize was offered. The competitors divested themselves of their boots which were heaped up in the centre of the course and the men, on arriving at this point, had to pick out their own, put them on and continue the journey to the winning post. One of the greatest troubles appeared to be to find the right boots and when these were discovered they were either laced up all the way or the laces were tied in knots, or in some way the competitors had hindrances to overcome. This event created great merriment and the winner loudly cheered."

The nature of the "special prize" for the Phiteezi race was not disclosed but details of the prizes for other events were given:

150 yards	Boys under 12	1st prize 2/-	2nd 1/6	3rd 1/-
100 yards	Boys under 12	1st prize 2/-	2nd 1/6	3rd 1/-
100 yards	Skipping race - girls under 16	1st prize 3/-	2nd 2/-	3rd 1/-
100 yards	Sack race	1st prize 3/-	2nd 2/-	3rd 1/-
150 yards	Boys under 14	1st prize 2/-	2nd 1/6	3rd 1/-
150 yards	Girls under 16	1st prize 2/-	2nd 1/6	3rd 1/-
100 yards	For veteran men (over 50)	1st prize 5/-	2nd 2/6	
100 yards	For veteran women (over 45)	1st prize 4/-	2nd 2/-	
100 yards	Egg and spoon race for women	No prizes mentioned		
400 yards	Open race	1st prize 5/-	2nd 3/-	3rd 2/-
	Throwing the cricket ball	1st prize 5/-	2nd 2/6	

(Conversions to decimal currency: 5/-, a crown, five shillings = 25p
4/- = 20p   3/- = 15p   2/6, half crown = 12½p   2/-, a florin = 10p   1/6 = 7½p)

Whilst the sports' events were taking place, preparations were made for tea ...

"... and just after half past five another happy party of about 550 partook of a very liberal spread comprising ham and beef sandwiches, bread and butter, cucumber and lettuce."

Beforehand Grace was sung and at the end the children sang the National Anthem. Three cheers for the Queen followed.

After tea there was dancing to the music provided by the military band whilst the children could watch a Punch and Judy show or enjoy swings. The day ended with ...

"... the fireworks when Mr H A Powell of Tonbridge, Agent for Brock & Co. of Crystal Palace fame gave a really excellent display and a hearty rendering of 'God Save the Queen' brought to a close one of the happiest days ever spent by the inhabitants of Hildenborough."

1898 – 1903

In March 1898 and 1899 there were nine nominees for the Council in each year and these nine were therefore elected unopposed. The Annual Parish Meeting followed immediately after the annual election meeting. The Chairman, Mr Charles Fitch Kemp, gave a review of the work of the Council during the past year and parishioners then had the opportunity to raise issues of concern:

- Roads, especially in the Mount Pleasant area
- "the kerbing of the footpath on the high road and the probable extension of the same between Mr Barkaway's shop and the Flying Dutchman" – the shop was on the corner of Half Moon Lane.
- Drainage at Oak Hill

– The proposed purchase of the Institute

Only 14 parishioners attended the Annual Parish Meeting on 30th March 1900 and there is no reference to an election. Some new matters were raised:

– Tonbridge Fire Brigade and the links with the parish
– The possibility of having gas lighting on the road to the station
– A proposal to construct a footpath from Foxbush Corner to the station.

There was another uncontested election in March 1901 at a meeting attended by 20 parishioners. The new Council was to hold office for three years instead of one year as before. The election meeting was followed immediately by the Annual Parish Meeting which began with ...

> "... a vote of sympathy to Mrs Pidcock and her family on the death of the Vicar of Hildenborough."

Apart from the proposed footpath from Foxbush Corner to the Station, the only other matter raised was "Roadside Wastes".

Little interest was shown in the Annual Parish Meeting held on 11th April 1902 with only 11 parishioners present. For the first time at an Annual Meeting there is a record of a statement of accounts being presented. Mr Robert Wingate, the councillor who acted as Honorary Treasurer reported that at the end of the financial year the council had a balance in hand of £52-1-5. The meeting discussed the problems with the Tonbridge Joint Burial Committee and with the local Fire Brigade but the main item on the agenda was the forthcoming Coronation of Edward VII and Queen Alexandra. After considerable discussion it was agreed...

> "... that a Committee of upwards of 40 of the leading parishioners should be formed to consider the due celebration of Coronation festivities in this Parish."

The Celebration of the Coronation of King Edward VII and Queen Alexandra

The Coronation had been delayed by several months as the King had been taken ill with appendicitis and the celebrations in the village were finally held on Saturday 9th August 1902. The Minute Book contains an account of the day.

> "The village was profusely decorated" with "streamers of flags" suspended from the telegraph poles. At the Vicarage there was an arch of evergreens surmounted with a crown. On one side were the words "Long may they live" and on the other "Long may he reign". From the Church spire floated a new white ensign "being the first occasion on which the correct flag had been flown".

The entrance to Foxbush, home of the Council Chairman, Mr Charles Fitch Kemp, was ...

> "... decorated with the Royal Coat of Arms, emblems, flags and lights with the letters ER in fairy lamps, a very artistic arrangement and the work of Mr Mist" of Ightham.

The entrance to Mountains, home of the Johnson family, was similarly decorated. Streamers, flags, bunting and fairy lamps were everywhere...

> "... one and all of the villagers, as well as the occupiers of the larger houses, had united in making the place as bright and attractive as possible."

The day began with the celebration of Holy Communion at the Church conducted by the Vicar, the Rev'd James Stone. At 1.30pm there was a service of thanksgiving at which the sermon was based on the text ...

> "... thou shalt set a crown of pure gold upon his head"
> Psalm 21v.3

Following the service there was a procession of parishioners including the school children and the Boys' Brigade to the cricket ground for an afternoon of sports. An additional attraction was the Punch and Judy show. Music was provided by Mr H Manning and the Maidstone Invicta Band. Mr W Austin of Tonbridge had successfully provided the catering at the Diamond Jubilee festivities in 1897 and he did the same for these celebrations. Mr Mist from Ightham erected the marquees where the teas were served. He was also responsible for the decorations around the ground.

The Minute Book records that the event was attended by …

"… nearly all the parishioners with the exception of some of the old bed-ridden parishioners, who were presented with a small sum of money."

Upwards of 1,100 tickets had been given out, around 800 for adults, the rest for children. "The following are the statistics as regards the teas. Provisions for the teas:

168 lbs ham	290 lbs beef	90 lbs mutton	124 loaves
224 lbs cake	Total number fed: 1,147"		

There was a wide variety of sports' events

50 yards boys	50 yards girls	Three –legged race
150 yards Boys' Brigade under 14		220 yards Boys' Brigade over 14
Slow bicycle race		
100 yards Open handicap	under 14	100 yards handicap (open to the Parish)
Throwing the cricket ball	under 18	over 18
Egg and spoon race	boys	girls
Thread and Needle race	married	single

High jump
100 yards Pipe and Tobacco race (over 40)

Sack race	Boot race
Quarter mile Open championship	Half mile Handicap

Wheelbarrow race – 50 yards
120 yards veterans' race (over 35)

Girls' skipping race	women's race

Tug of war (The "Ball Makers beat the Institute and the Single beat the Married")

Was the "Boot Race" the same as the Phiteezi Race held at the Diamond Jubilee celebrations?

There seem to have been two outstanding athletes at these sports – "Macey" and "Palmer":

Macey	–	100 yards handicap	2nd
	–	Quarter Mile Open Championship	1st
	–	Half Mile handicap	2nd
Palmer	–	220 yards Boys' Brigade over 14	2nd
	–	High Jump	1st
	–	Sack Race	1st
	–	Quarter Mile Open Championship	2nd
	–	Half Mile Handicap	1st

Prizes were donated. These included a Cup, a cricket ball, cruets, a copper kettle, carvers, a tea pot. Cash totalling £6 was donated for the purchase of other prizes.

During the interval between the children's and adult teas, Mr Fitch Kemp of Foxbush, the Council Chairman, addressed those present. He reminded them of the recovery of the King from his attack of appendicitis and said that …

"… they all ought to give thanks to God for preserving the King's life and enabling him to be crowned."

He asked for everyone...
> "... to pray to Almighty God to bless their illustrious monarch and their no less illustrious Queen, and prosper their children."

At the conclusion of the programme ...
> "... an excellent display of fireworks was followed by a torchlight procession from the ground back to the village."

The Annual Parish Meeting held at "the National Schools" on 25th March 1903 was attended by 22 "parochial electors". They heard a Report from the Chairman, "Mr C Fitch Kemp, JP, DL" on the work of the Parish Council over the past year. Reference was made to the –

- New building at the Institute
- Allotments
- The Education Act, 1902 – which transferred control of the school to the County Council, Mr H H Hitchcock had been appointed under the Act to "the Committee" overseeing the school
- the prolonged negotiations with Tonbridge Urban District Council about the Fire Brigade
- Lighting the village

The meeting passed a Resolution of "hearty thanks and commendation" to the Headmaster of the local school, Mr M C Morris. Earlier in the month he had rescued a child from drowning in a nearby pond. This prompted a discussion about ...
> "... providing some swimming accommodation for boys and men in the parish,"

a matter which had been under consideration since the formation of the Parish Council in 1894. The council "would keep the matter in view during the year."

There was a Report on the successful Coronation celebrations for which the total cost to the Parish was £151-10-5.

1904 -1911

1904 was election year and the triennial election meeting was held on 7th March with 23 electors present. As in recent years there was an uncontested election of the nine councillors and the Annual Parish Meeting followed immediately afterwards.

The Treasurer, Mr Robert Wingate reported on the accounts whilst the only other matters raised were the "inferior bricks which had been placed by the District Council round the Institute" and the provision of lighting in the village. It was resolved...
> "... that a hearty vote of thanks be accorded by the Parish to Mr Powell for supplying a lamp to light the street corner leading to Shipbourne Road" (now Riding Lane)

Even fewer parishioners attended the Annual Meeting on 7th April 1905. The 14 present heard that the negotiations with Tonbridge Urban District Council over the Fire Brigade had still not concluded – "the present position was not a pleasant one". The Chairman, Mr Fitch Kemp, referred to the problem of the water supply in the village – "still far from satisfactory". The Water Company had repeatedly ...
> "... stated that they were going to lay longer mains down the road and also make arrangements for considerably increasing the water pressure."

The lack of pressure ...
> "... was experienced especially in the outlying parts of the Parish and also in respect of the water supply to the Church organ, the insufficiency of which was becoming quite notorious."

The meeting, which only lasted for 30minutes, considered three matters raised by those present:

1. Allotments. For the period from April 1896 to April 1905 the income from rents was £120-3-10 and the expenditure £120-17-8, thus leaving a balance of 13/10 (69p) owing to the council.
2. "Dust raised by motors passing through the village". The Chairman considered that …
   "… the passage of the motors down the High Road in the Summertime caused an intolerable nuisance and rendered it impossible for people to live in comfort in houses which were adjacent to the road."
3. The planned footpath to the station. Perhaps the money for this would be better spent in keeping the footpath "on the High Road in decent condition."

The Vicar, the Rev'd James Stone, presented a Report on behalf of the Trustees of the Leigh Charities. A share of the income was to aid those living in the Hollanden portion of the village, previously part of Leigh Parish. The Trustees' meeting on 21st November 1904 heard that a total of £6-12-6 had gone to 17 residents whilst 8 others "received two 4d loaves quarterly".

The Annual Parish Meeting on 28th March 1906 was also poorly attended. There were only 13 parishioners present to hear Mr Fitch Kemp's review of the year after which he referred to the General Election. He said that he was sure that …

"… he was only voicing the wishes of all present whatever their views might be when he said that he hoped Parliament would shew (sic) the wisdom, judgement and patriotism required for the proper government of this Country and the maintenance of the Empire."

(Following the resignation of Arthur Balfour's Conservative government in December 1905 and its replacement by a Liberal administration led by Sir Henry Campbell Bannerman, an election was called. This was held between 12th January and 7th February 1906 and resulted in a Liberal 'landslide': Liberals 400 seats, Conservatives 157, Irish Nationalists 83, Labour 30).

The water supply was again mentioned at this meeting as was the state of the "High Road". It was agreed to draw the attention of the County Council …

"… to the disgraceful state of the High Road running through the village with a view to obtaining the improvement of the road and the abatement of the dust nuisance."

1907 was election year and 36 parishioners attended the election meeting on 4th March which was followed by the Annual Parish Meeting. The election was contested for the first time since 1897 with 10 nominees for 9 seats. One of those missing from the new Council was the late Mr Robert Wingate of Oakhurst who was not only a councillor but also the Council's Treasurer. The Annual Parish Meeting resolved to send a message of sympathy and condolence to his family. It then considered the perennial problems of:

- The poor condition of the roads and "the dust nuisance caused by motors"
- The fire brigade
- The water supply. There were problems with burst pipes and disturbances caused by the laying of new pipes.

The Chairman, Mr Fitch Kemp, concluded the meeting by referring to…

"… the proposed visit of an old resident (Mr Thomas Kingscote) who was coming to address them on the important subject of the proper observance of Sunday and he ventured to hope that there would be a large attendance of parishioners."

(Mr Kingscote had lived at The Trench in Coldharbour Lane.)

The Annual Parish Meeting of 6th April 1908 didn't attract much interest as only 9 parishioners were present. It was notable for being chaired by Mr G W Johnson of Mountains in place of the late Mr Charles Fitch Kemp of Foxbush, the Chairman since the Parish Council was established in 1894. Mr Johnson reported that a Memorial Tablet had been placed in the church:

> "To the Glory of God and in Memory of Charles Fitch Kemp, DL, JP of Foxbush for 38 years the Trusted and Beloved Warden of this church. His broad sympathy, wise judgement and ripe experience drew to him the hearts of all men and bound them to one another, in concord and mutual good will. Full of years and honour he passed to his rest on the eve of All Saints 1907 Aged 78 This Tablet is dedicated by Parishioners and Friends."

The new Chairman reported that he had some good news to report as a settlement had been reached with the Urban District Council over the Fire Brigade. There was further good news in that the County Council, through the Rural District Council, had agreed...

> "... to tarring of London Road to abate the dust nuisance."

He also announced that ...

> "... the footpaths through the village were to be thoroughly repaired by the County Council."

Attendance at the 1909 Annual Parish Meeting was once again low with only 10 parishioners at the School on 29th March. The sad loss of "one of their oldest Councillors, Mr John Francis" was recorded. The Chairman, Mr G W Johnson, reported that the village Fire Brigade was properly equipped following the settlement with the Urban District Council and the Tonbridge Brigade. "A wakeful eye had been kept upon the main roads, which were now in good order". This good news was then followed by more sad news as at the end of the meeting, the Clerk, Mr M C Morris, the Councillor who had succeeded Mr Johnson as Clerk in 1907, said that he had just heard of the death of Mrs Hitchcock, wife of Council member Mr Horace Henry Hitchcock. Mr Hitchcock, famed as a cricket ball maker, had been a member of the Council since its inauguration in 1894.

The Election Meeting on 14th March 1910, followed by the Annual Parish Meeting, saw the highest attendance for many years. The Chairman, Mr G W Johnson, addressing the 49 electors present...

> "... congratulated them upon the revival of interest in the public life of the parish betokened by the large gathering."

He referred to the retirement from the Council of Mr Hitchcock and to the death of Mr William Holmwood, a Councillor since 1899.

There was no contest for the 9 Council seats with 3 new members joining the council. Amongst the matters raised at the Annual Meeting:

- The Auxiliary Fire Brigade was working well
- The Leigh Charities - £3-9-6 had come to Hildenborough whilst 13 people had received two 4d loaves each
- The state of the main road was described as 'a disgrace'
- Footpaths – many were in poor condition
- The water supply, especially in the Egg Pie Lane area

Only 11 parishioners came to the 1911 Annual Parish Meeting on 7th April. The Chairman, Mr G W Johnson, reported on the Council's work during the previous year. Allotments were mentioned and Mr Johnson praised the work of the Fire Brigade...

> "... he complimented the firemen on their smartness at two fires which had occurred during the year."

The main business of the meeting was a discussion about celebrations for the Coronation of George V and Queen Mary. With so few present it was decided to call a public meeting to which all parishioners would be invited by circular letter.

The Clerk, Mr M C Morris, reported that at the end of the financial year the Council had a credit balance of £23-4-10. In the absence of the Vicar, the Rev'd James Stone, the meeting was informed that ...

> "... ten poor persons in the Hollanden district had received £3-1-6, twelve had received the quarterly bread and two tickets for coal and groceries had been given." This was from the Leigh Charities.

About 85 parishioners came to the special meeting at the end of April 1911 to discuss plans for the Coronation celebrations. It was agreed ...

> "... that the Coronation be celebrated by a high tea, to which all parishioners should be invited, by sports, dancing, and a torchlight procession; and that the cost, not exceeding the amount realised by a twopenny rate, be defrayed out of the funds available to the Parish Council."

A Committee of 46 was elected to make the arrangements – the work would be done through five sub-committees.

The Coronation Celebration of George V and Queen Mary, June 1911

As with previous celebrations, the entire village was decorated. There was a ceremonial arch to the entrance of the cricket ground where the celebrations were to take place. Near the 'Half Moon Inn' there was a fine floral arch topped off by "a patriotic device and a blaze of fairy lights". Mr R Brown and his team were responsible for a spectacular arch but misfortune befell them:

> "For two days, he and his men laboured in the erection of an elaborate archway opposite the Church. They left the finishing touches for the Coronation morning, in blissful ignorance of the fact that the Post Office motor coach was preparing a specially lofty load for its journey to Hastings ... unfortunately it got mixed with Mr Brown's skilfully arranged wires, and chaos was the result. The builder was the recipient of general sympathy in thus having his labour rendered in vain."

The account of the celebrations, beautifully written up in the Minute book, is based on a report that appeared in the "Free Press" on 30th June 1911. The decorations are described in some detail...

> "... Venetian masks, surmounted by huge flags lined the temporary carriage way to the cricket ground and surrounded the pretty sports course. The pavilion front bore a crown and the Royal initials outlined in fairy lamps, and the bandstand was most skilfully draped and enclosed with Japanese lanterns and artificial flowers."

The houses and shops were all decorated and there were arches over the entrances to Foxbush, Mountains and Oak Hill whilst "Pembroke Lodge was a study in white and gold".

The Celebrations were spread over two days. They began at the School on the Wednesday afternoon. The proceedings started with ...

> "... A modified form of the ceremony of 'trooping the colours'... and some of Elgar's famous Coronation part songs were tastefully rendered by the scholars."

The Council Chairman, Mr G W Johnson, and the Vicar, the Rev'd James Stone, delivered short addresses. Mr Johnson then distributed commemorative mugs, paid for by the Parish, to the children. As a personal gift from him, Mr Johnson presented "beakers" to the heads of households where there were no school children.

Next day the celebrations began "with a merry peel on the Church bells at half past five." There was a service of Holy Communion at 8am and at 1.30pm "an enormous congregation assembled for a thanksgiving service" –
> "The service was a delightful one. The choir gave an exquisite rendering of the anthem 'The King shall rejoice' while the conclusion of the service was marked by an impressive singing of the 'Te Deum'."

Following the service a procession was formed "and a way was made to the cricket ground to the stirring strains of the Band of the 4th Royal West Kent Regiment under Bandmaster Bartram."

The Sports' events followed. There were the usual running races, some just for members of the Boys' Brigade, plus traditional events such as the tug-of-war, the egg and spoon race, the sack race and the thread and needle race. There was "throwing the cricket ball", a "Band Race" and a skipping race. There were some close finishes...

> "... notably in the race for boys under 12 where, after a dead heat, R Johnson defeated G Clements by what, at Epsom would be called a short nose. The ladies' tug-of-war produced a most desperate struggle and afterwards the most lively arguments. It was generally agreed, however, that the ladies with the most dainty figures were also the best pullers."

The prizes "were handsome ones, and were subscribed for by the leading residents of the parish".

Unfortunately, drizzling rain rather spoiled the events on the sports field but the tea that followed was served, as at previous celebrations, in huge tents. As before, Mr Austin of Tonbridge was responsible for the catering.

> "Hildenborough" declared the report on the celebrations ..." when it entertains its parishioners does not restrict its hospitality to the young or to the old or to the poor. Rich and poor, young and old, all sit down together. So it was on this occasion, and the delightful mixing of the company at the festive board was quite one of the charms of the day."

The report continued ...

> "Every table was a top table and every guest was 'above the salt'. In all 1,182 persons partook of the substantial meat tea provided ... There was no speech making at the meal – another unusual charm – but after the distribution of the prizes by the Dowager Marchioness of Downshire, Mr G W Johnson made a short, but most impressive patriotic address."

The Dowager lived at Nizels – now a golf club.

The rain interfered with the dancing that followed the tea. The music was provided by the Regimental Band ...

> "... who nobly stuck to the band stand while the rain ran in streams over their folios. And still the dancers danced merrily on, and they expressed disappointment when the programme was cut short by a shower heavier than usual."

The celebrations ended with a torch and lantern-light procession from the cricket ground to the Church ...

> "... the long lines of waving lights produced a very fine effect. In fact, this was one of the most popular features of the day. Arrived at the Church, the band struck up the National Anthem in which the whole assembly joined. Then followed 'Auld Lang Syne' and – home."

The weather had "left much to be desired" throughout the day but despite this, the celebrations had been greatly enjoyed by all.

1912-1924

The 1912 Annual Parish Meeting, held at the school on 27th March, was poorly attended with only six parishioners present to hear the Chairman, Mr G W Johnson present his review of the past year. The Coronation celebrations had been a great success, giving "complete satisfaction to the whole population". The main topics considered by the Council had been –

The Fire Brigade   Allotments   the Hawden footpath

The Vicar, Rev'd James Stone, reported on the Leigh Charities: 10 residents had received a total of £3-2-0, 13 had been given quarterly bread whilst one person had received a pension of five shillings a quarter.

The perennial topic of the state of the roads was again raised. The condition of the "High Road" was "dusty" whilst the section between the 'Flying Dutchman' and Hilden Park was dangerous due to "the partially filled in ditches". These problems were passed to the County Council.

The attendance was much better on 17th March 1913 when Mr Johnson presided over the election meeting attended by 102 parishioners. This was followed by the Annual Parish Meeting but only 18 stayed for that! There were 17 candidates for the 9 seats on the Council and the election was by a show of hands for each candidate as they were named in alphabetical order There was a demand for a poll of all electors, a secret ballot, but with the cost estimated to be £50, the demand was dropped.

At the subsequent Annual Parish Meeting, the few remaining parishioners heard a review of the past year from the Chairman, Mr G W Johnson. Like his predecessor, Mr Fitch Kemp, Mr Johnson was not a councillor but had been called upon by the Council to chair meetings. The usual topics were raised – the Fire Brigade, the Leigh Charities, the Hawden footpath to Tonbridge and allotments. In addition, a plea was made for more cottages to be built.

The 1914 Annual Parish Meeting, held on 31st March, was attended by 32 parishioners. The question of more cottages was again raised and it was reported that the Parish Council was in discussion with the Rural District Council about plans for new cottages. The Council had recommended that the Rural District Council...

> "... build at least 4 cottages for men earning low wages, say less than 20/- (£1) per week."

The Leigh Charities, the Fire Brigade and allotments were topics discussed. One allotment holder complained that "he was losing vegetables from his allotment". The main discussion related to the "sanitary condition of the village".

Mr Reginald Nevins of Pembroke Lodge expressed concern at the risks to health of the state of some cottages in the village. He felt that the Rural District Council and the sanitary authorities were not doing their job properly...

> "... several cottages ... were not supplied with proper sanitary arrangements."

Mr Nevins feared that poor sanitation could lead to "an epidemic of illness in the village." On the proposal of Mr Nevins, the meeting passed "with one dissentient" the following Resolution:

> "That the Parish Council be requested to take immediate steps to bring pressure to bear upon the Proper Authority to have the cottages in the village supplied with proper water-closet accommodation, the closets furnished with water-cisterns and mechanical means of flushing the closet pans, the improper accumulation of refuse removed, the Village Baker supplied with water from the Tonbridge Water Co. and rendered safe from effluvia from drains or privy and the Village otherwise put in a wholesome and sanitary condition."

The 1915 Annual Parish Meeting was held on 21st April under the shadow of war. There were seven parishioners present to hear the Chairman, Mr G W Johnson, report that a sub-committee of the Council had been set up to consider the "sanitary condition of the village" and to liaise with the Rural District Council. 4 cottages had been built by the Rural District Council which had a scheme to construct a further 12. A meeting had been called to enrol Special Constables and, at the request of the Rural District Council, the Parish Council had set up a sub-committee in connection with the National Relief Fund.

The next Annual Parish Meeting, held at the Institute on 3rd April 1916 was attended by 16 parishioners. It was overshadowed by the war with Mr Johnson, the Chairman, commenting that ...

> "... owing to the War we had all been and were passing through a very anxious time, and he might almost say there were more important matters to consider than some of the Parish affairs."

Mr Johnson reported that –
- The Special Constables had done their work very well
- Arrangements had been made in case of an air raid
- The order "as to lights in houses" should be obeyed "for the safety of the whole Parish ..."
- The Allotment Committee had powers to employ labour to care for plots whose holders were away on war service.

There were problems with the renewal of the lease "of the allotment ground on Great Forge Farm" (Riding Lane) and a special Parish Meeting was held on 14th August 1916 to consider the situation. The 26 parishioners present passed a Resolution referring the matter to the County Council and to the Board of Agriculture.

The war dominated the 1917 Annual Parish Meeting held at the Drill Hall on 26th April with eleven parishioners present. As usual, the Chairman, Mr G W Johnson, reviewed the past year. "He was ready to swear in more Special Constables" and stated that directions had been received for action should an emergency be declared. A War Savings Committee had been set up in the village with current membership of 157. Reference was made to National Service with Mr Johnson stating ...

> ".... that it was the opinion of the Government that all men between the age of 40 and 61, save those working on Agricultural and A and B volunteers should enrol."

(The conscription of younger men had been introduced in 1916.)

The meeting heard that all the allotment plots were under cultivation and that the Great Forge Farm lease had been extended until after the war. Seed potatoes were being supplied to parishioners through the County Council Agricultural Committee. Arrangements would be made for the spraying of the potatoes. 50 parishioners had asked for potatoes and the Council had purchased 4 tons 2cwts at a cost of £56.

The Vicar, the Rev'd James Stone, raised the problem of litter in the village. For example, a nuisance ...

> "... was being caused by people throwing their rubbish and old tins etc. in the small wood below the Schools."

The Chairman pointed out that offenders could be prosecuted. There was no need for a litter problem...

> "... especially as there was a scavenger appointed by the Rural District Council to collect the refuse."

It was reported that the Rural District Council ...

> "... had apparently established a place for the deposit of refuse further up Riding Lane."

This needed to be confirmed.

The 1918 Annual Parish Meeting was held on 26th March with Mr Johnson, the Council Chairman, reporting to the 8 parishioners present. The question of the Great Forge Farm lease was being considered by the "Food Production Department of the War Agricultural Committee". Derelict land at Hilden Park was being cultivated by parishioners and the Council was renting other nearby plots of land for allotments.

It was reported that there were now 31 Special Constables and that the "War Savings Association" had 210 members who had subscribed about £180 during the "Special Week".

52 parishioners attended the Election Meeting on 17th March 1919 to elect 9 councillors. The 9 candidates were duly elected unopposed with Mr G W Johnson one of them. Hitherto he had been the Council Chairman but not an elected councillor.

The Annual Parish Meeting followed and, after a review of the past year, those present considered ...

> "... the subject of a War Memorial."

What form should this take? Amongst the suggestions:
- The Drill Hall to be replaced
- Ground to be acquired for a recreation ground
- A monument listing the names of the fallen
- A list of the names of the fallen in the Church
- A "Memorial Cross"
- Almshouses
- Incorporate rooms in the Village Hall "for Technical and Domestic Education for young people" together with Swimming Baths. A letter ...

> "... was read from Mrs Hills – Bourne Place – offering £500 towards a suitable scheme and Mr G W Johnson also promised a probable sum of £400."

A special Parish Meeting was held at the Drill Hall on 23rd June 1919 with 31 parishioners present to discuss :
1. The advisability of purchasing "the London Road" allotments
2. Peace celebrations

Subject to a suitable price being agreed, it was resolved to purchase the allotments situated beyond Watts Cross on the road to Sevenoaks.

In respect of the Peace Celebrations the Chairman introduced the discussion by pointing out ...

> "...there is considerable feeling in the parish that this is not a time when there should be unlimited rejoicing – as at the Coronation."

He said that the following suggestions had been made –
1. A thanksgiving service - for all
2. Some form of garden fête - for children
3. A supper for returning soldiers
4. A flower show

Colonel Warner said that he entirely agreed with the sentiments expressed by Mr Johnson – "adults were not out for convivialities". A lengthy discussion followed before it was agreed that there shall be ...

> "... a thanksgiving service – open air if possible – and an open air entertainment for children."

Donations towards the cost were invited with the balance to be paid out of the rates.

The meeting then discussed the plan for the supper which would be for returned military personnel. It was agreed that the only other invitations would go to Parish Councillors with the cost paid for by "private subscription".

Only 10 parishioners attended each of the 1920 and 1921 Annual Parish Meetings on 8th April and 30th March respectively. Mr Johnson, the Chairman, presented a review of the past year at each meeting. Amongst the matters discussed:
- Allotments
- Street lighting, with a request for lighting at street corners
- "bad smells at Crossways Corner"
- Footpaths, especially along the main road
- The "dangerous state of the ditch at Watts Cross"
- The Fire Brigade – new uniforms had been purchased and 3 hydrants installed
- Housing – "two sets of cottages were being erected by the Rural District Council".

At the 1921 meeting ...
> "Mr Francis mentioned the very unsatisfactory state of the footpath along the London Road. He maintained that one of the busiest roads in Kent should have a good footpath for the safety of pedestrians."

At that meeting Mr Johnson commented ...
> "... upon the good feeling which was characteristic of this Parish."

The Parish Meeting, attended by 29 parishioners, held on 22nd March 1922 in order to elect 9 councillors made history: for the first time a woman was elected. Mrs M H Brown (Mrs Tasker Brown) of Watts Cross was one of the nine candidates elected unopposed. At the same time, Mr Johnson did not seek re-election but was to remain Chairman of the Council.

After the election there followed the Annual Parish Meeting with the Chairman's review of the past year. There was a new agreement with the Urban District Council over the Fire Brigade. He said that unemployment...
> "... was not a serious problem in the Parish at present as it had been relieved by individual help."

As in previous years the state of the footpaths along the main road was discussed and a Resolution passed directed at Kent County Council. Sections of them remained in a poor state: the Parish Council complained regularly yet nothing was done to improve their condition.

13 parishioners attended the 1923 Annual Parish Meeting at the Drill Hall on 21st March. Once more the state of the footpaths in the village was considered and there was a suggestion that ...
> "... a footpath should be constructed on the London Road from Watts Cross to the New Cock Inn."

The Inn, now developed for housing, was near the large garage for commercial vehicles which borders Nizels Lane. Funds for this project might be obtained from the Ministry of Transport. The proposal was referred to the County Council.

Footpaths were again discussed at the Annual Parish Meeting on 31st March 1924 attended by 9 parishioners. Amongst other topics:

1. It was reported that "two boards had been placed by the Kent County Council showing motor traffic that it is dangerous to pass through the village at speed of more than 8mph".
2. "The ancient custom of Beating the Bounds was performed on 3rd November 1923". There is a full account of this, recorded by Mr Edwin Francis, in "This is Hildenborough from A-Z", originally published by the Parish Council in 1994. A revised edition appeared in 2007.

Part 7 – 1925-1956

1925-1930

The 1925 Annual Parish Meeting was preceded by the triennial election of 9 councillors by a show of hands. On this occasion the meeting on 16th March, attended by 41 parishioners, had a choice of 10 candidates. The Council Chairman, Mr G W Johnson, presided and opened the proceedings by calling for nominations. Fifteen minutes had been allowed for this and the opportunity to question the candidates followed. A poll, a secret ballot of all electors, an expensive procedure, could be demanded after the show of hands but as was usual no poll was requested. The first woman on the Council, Mrs M H Brown of Watts Cross, originally elected in 1922, was one of those re-elected. Mr Johnson himself was not a candidate but was re-elected by councillors as the Parish Council Chairman.

The Annual Parish Meeting heard the customary review of the past year from the Chairman. There was little of significance to report at this meeting or at that held on 22nd March 1926 when only eleven parishioners were present. Both meetings were held in the Drill Hall in Shipbourne Road (now Riding Lane).

33 parishioners attended a special Parish Meeting on 3rd December 1926 called to ascertain…

> "… the views of this Parish on the question of lighting the village with electric light, and adopting the Lighting Act" to permit this.

The Chairman, Mr Johnson stated that …

> "… he had received an estimate from the Tonbridge Urban District Council for 15 lights put on to the new cable which is being laid - £230. Running cost per annum – £44-5-0."

There was a discussion about where the lamps would be placed. Would gas lighting be preferable? Would a "Private Electric Lighting Co." put in light at a much lower cost? It was agreed to defer any decision for 12 months.

At the same meeting the following Resolution proposed by the Vicar was passed unanimously:

> "That the Parish Council be asked to take the necessary steps to purchase these two pieces of land for a playing field for the children of the village."

This referred to land at Mount Pleasant, now the Village Green. The Vicar, the Rev'd L G Chamberlen, MC had told the meeting that he had received an offer from …

> "… Mrs Baker of Tonbridge of a piece of land, situated in Mount Pleasant, for £100, and another smaller piece adjoining belonging to Mr William Williams of Sevenoaks for £75."

Only 9 parishioners were present at the 1927 Annual Parish Meeting on 23rd March to hear the Council Chairman's report on the past year. The Fire Brigade under Commander Tomlinson had been brought "to an efficient state" and had attended two fires – a "stook fire in Coldharbour … and a chimney fire at Pembroke Lodge". The Council had completed the purchase of the larger plot of land at Mount Pleasant whilst purchase of the smaller plot would be completed in May. Meanwhile, "the Council have commenced the levelling and draining" of the land.

Mr G W Johnson, as Council Chairman, presided over a Parish Meeting held on 22nd November 1927 attended by 42 other parishioners. He explained that the purpose of the meeting was …

"... to further consider and vote on the adoption of the Lighting Act of 1833 for lighting the main road through the Village."

The Vicar, the Rev'd L G Chamberlen proposed the adoption of the Act "with the necessary rate to be incurred thereby". Dr Fraser, seconded by Major Charrington, moved an amendment to reject the proposal ...

"... on the grounds that he considered it more dangerous to pedestrians where there were street lamps, by people being knocked down by motor cars more so than where the roads were in darkness."

Major Charrington added that "not having the lights the rates were kept down". Another parishioner commented that the number of lamps proposed – 20 – was inadequate.

A vote was taken on the Vicar's original Resolution with 21 in favour and 20 against. It failed as a two-thirds majority was needed to adopt the Act.

One other matter was considered at this meeting – "omnibuses". Two rival companies were ...

"... running their omnibuses simultaneously instead of at suitable intervals," this causing "inconvenience to the public".

A Resolution was passed unanimously asking the Licensing Authority to withdraw their licence...

"... until they were willing to arrange their services to suit the convenience of the public".

The local MP was asked ...

"... to support the Bill authorising the Southern Railway to run Motor Omnibus services".

Copies of the Resolution were to be sent ...

"... to the Ministry of Transport, the County Council, the MP for the Division, the Chairman of the Tonbridge Petty Sessions, the Tonbridge Rural District Council and the Local Press."

34 parishioners were present at the Drill Hall for the triennial election of councillors on 13 March 1928. 12 names were put forward and a show of hands determined the 9 chosen. One, Mrs Louisa Houghton, was only the third woman to join the Council.

After the election meeting, the Annual Parish Meeting was held. The Council Chairman, Mr G W Johnson, reported that the work on ...

"... the ground at Mount Pleasant was proceeding, but it must be left to the Council whether it should take the form of a lawn with trees and seats or a children's playground."

It was reported that Mr Walter J King had "retired from the Council after 30 years of faithful work". In proposing a vote of thanks to him, Mr F H Buss said that "he looked upon him as the Father of the Council". The Chairman said "he thought that he was the 'Father' as he had served ten years as honorary Clerk, a greater number of years as Chairman". Mr Buss "then said we should have to look upon the Chairman as the Grandfather (laughter)".

Only 16 parishioners attended the 1929 Annual Parish Meeting on 20th March. Commander A W Tomlinson, "as Chief of the Fire Brigade" gave a report on the Brigade's activities over the past year:

"The Brigade had been called to four fires, one false alarm to test the time taken to turn out, four Wet Drills and sixteen Dry Drills, stores and appliances in good order. The Second Officer and the men had carried out their duties with zeal and ability."

Other matters raised at the meeting included –

- The new Village Green : was it going to be fenced off?
- Should the seat set into the church wall be of stone or wood?
- Footpaths: the path from Garlands to Coldharbour was very overgrown.
- Allotments: did they now pay for themselves?
- Main drains at Watts Cross

Ill health prevented Mr G W Johnson, the Council Chairman, from presiding over the Annual Parish Meeting on 30th March 1930 and the 16 parishioners present elected Mr F H Buss as Chairman for the evening.

The meeting heard that the Council had a credit balance of £14-6-7. It was reported that the Fire Brigade had been called out once during the past year. Consideration was being given to the installation of additional fire hydrants in the village, one…

"… at Leigh Road below the Black Arch to cover Selby Farm, the Meadows and the Cottages by the Arch," the other just beyond the Lower Cock Inn.

Other matters raised:
- A complaint about the rubbish at "the west end corner of the Churchyard".
- An overgrown hedge at Woodfield Avenue
- The "Boundary Stone in Coldharbour Lane near Barley Corner was being lost sight of". Could it be raised?
- Apart from one Councillor, Mr Tasker Brown, the meeting agreed that the War Memorial should be cleaned.

A "Special Parish Meeting" was held on 30th October 1930 with over 90 parishioners present plus representatives of the County and Rural District Councils. The purpose was to discuss giving permission to the Parish Council to purchase land for a recreation ground. A loan would be required and authority was sought to sell land used for allotments, if necessary, to raise some money.

The Vicar, the Rev'd L G Chamberlen, proposed three Resolutions which were passed unanimously:

1. "To approve the purchase by the Hildenborough Parish Council of the field and shaw adjacent to the National Schools owned by Mr Barkaway under Section 69 of the Public Health Act, 1925, not exceeding £1,250.
2. "To consent to the Hildenborough Parish Council incurring expenses or liabilities in respect of the said purchase which will involve a loan, provided that should the money be obtainable from other sources at a more advantageous rate than under the conditions of the Act such an offer should be accepted if otherwise suitable."
3. "To agree to the sale by the Hildenborough Parish Council if need be of the Allotments on Sevenoaks Road."

During the discussion on these Resolutions the question of "Sunday Games" was raised – the Chairman, Mr G W Johnson, said it would be for the Council to decide. Dr Fraser pointed out that …

"… along the north west boundary of the field there ran a stream which was impregnated with active sewage."

This complaint would be investigated.

The cost of any purchase by the Council was very important:

"…the rateable value of the parish was £13,273 and a 1d rate produced £65. The present rate was 2½d which brought in £162-0-10."

The following were making grants to help with the purchase costs:

The Kent Playing Fields Association	£150
The National Playing Fields Association	£40
The Carnegie Trust	£120
TOTAL	£310

1931 – 1936

On 9th March 1931 63 electors met at the Drill Hall for the triennial election of Parish Councillors. As was customary, voting was by a show of hands and 9 candidates were chosen from the 13 nominees. Once again, the Council Chairman, Mr G W Johnson, was not a candidate but was later asked by the new council to continue as Chairman. There followed the Annual Parish Meeting with Mr Johnson presenting a review of the past year.

The next Annual Parish Meeting, on 21st March 1932, was attended by only eleven parishioners and the Minutes give little information about the Chairman's review. Even fewer attended the next meeting on 29th March 1933 when rather more detail was given:

- Dr Fraser's offer of some laurels for the Recreation Ground had been gratefully accepted as had Mr Mackney's gift of 50 spiles. Mr Mackney had arranged for the field to be rolled.
- More Council houses had been built in "Powder Mill Road".
- There was a drainage scheme for the Watts Cross area.
- Efforts were being made to obtain more land for allotments.

The next triennial elections were held on 7th March 1934 at a meeting attended by 34 parishioners. There were eleven candidates for the nine seats with the result being declared following a show of hands. There was no demand for a poll. The Annual Parish Meeting followed with the Chairman presenting the customary review of the past year. The question of "Sunday games being played on the Recreation ground" was raised but it was decided to hold a special Parish Meeting to consider it. 68 parishioners attended this on 19th March when the following Resolution was considered ...

> "... that the Recreation Ground be open on Sundays for games to be played only by parishioners."

The Resolution was defeated by 34 votes to 21.

With the Silver Jubilee of King George V and Queen Mary approaching, a special Parish Meeting was called for 28th February 1935 to consider how the event should be celebrated. 51 parishioners attended with the Parish Council Chairman, Mr G W Johnson, presiding. The Council had established a Jubilee Committee under the leadership of Dr D B Fraser.

Dr Fraser reported that under the guidelines laid down by the Ministry of Health, the Jubilee Committee recommended the spending of up to £50 of Parish money and that a fund be established for private donations towards the cost of the celebrations. He said that the Committee had been guided by two definite principles:

> "Firstly, that special attention should be paid to making the day attractive and memorable for the children. Secondly, to give expression to His Majesty's wish that the occasion should not be marked with unduly lavish expenditure."

Suggestions from the Committee included :

Morning –   a Parish Service
            Presentation of medals to the children
            Perhaps the planting of a tree
            "Approval had been obtained from the School Managers to allow the Buildings to be used by those who would like to bring their food with them."

Afternoon - Maypole dancing
            Sports for adults and children
            Punch and Judy show
            Tea for all children aged 4-14 years old with the presentation of a mug to each child.

Possibly a "comic football match"

Evening -   "At 7pm we hope to be able to arrange for the broadcasting of the King's speech."

During intervals – community singing and dancing

8.45 pm – fireworks and a bonfire.

"Music during the afternoon and evening to be provided by Mobile Unit Loud Speakers."

Dr Fraser estimated that the cost of the programme would be £75 but £25 should be allowed for contingencies. He recommended that arrangements should be made by a group of sub-committees. The meeting adopted several Resolutions:

- "That this Parish in a spirit of loyalty, joy and thankfulness for 25 years of His Majesty's reign propose to hold celebrations on 6th May of this year."
- £100 could be spent "from the rates."
- there should be sufficient medals to provide one for each child
- those aged over 65 should have a souvenir mug
- Tonbridge Rural District Council should invite all Parish Councils in the District to join in sending a "Petition of Congratulations" to His Majesty the King."

It was agreed to set up sub-committees to cover:

    Sports   Fireworks and bonfire   Entertainment   Refreshments

A fifth sub-committee was set up "to go into the matter re: a Village Hall and Hospital Bed". This sub-committee would consider what to do with any surplus funds raised by donations. Perhaps money should go towards establishing a bed at "Tonbridge Hospital" or to a "New Parish Hall".

In the Minute Book there is a cutting from the "Tonbridge Free Press" with a lengthy report of the Jubilee celebrations on 6th May 1935 which were clearly a great success:

"All the simple glamour and care-free jollity, so characteristic of a country village and fête, attended the Jubilee celebrations at Hildenborough. The village was gaily decorated with bunting and flags and the celebrations proceeded smoothly from the planting of the tree in the morning to the lighting of the bonfire at night."

The activities were along the lines proposed by the Jubilee Committee. At 10am the Parish Council Chairman, Mr G W Johnson "planted a cedar tree at the main entrance of the recreation ground". After the tree planting the presentation of mugs to children aged 4 to 14 years was made by Mrs Henry Hills. She said ...

"... she hoped they would value them and grow up good citizens of our wonderful Empire."

At 11am the procession formed up for a march to the Church for the thanksgiving service conducted by the Vicar, the Rev. E H Wade. It was led by the band and members of the Church Lads' Brigade followed by a bugle band, the children, the Fire Brigade, Girl Guides and Brownies, amongst others.

The report highlighted the success of the procession of the May Queen and the Maypole dancing:

"Altogether the ceremony was one which the villagers will long remember with pleasure and one of which the equal would be hard to find in the district."

Barbara Hitchcock ...

"... was a charming May Queen, gracefully attired ... her ankle-length dress of white silk, with train."

The afternoon was devoted to sports for both children and adults. There were the traditional distance races together with events like the tug-of-war. That was won by the team from "The Grenadier", the Riding Lane public house which was destroyed by enemy action in 1942. There were several novelty events including the egg and spoon race, obstacle races, a flower pot race for women, a slow bicycle race, a sack race and skipping races. W Bagley won the adults' high jump with a jump of 5ft whilst there was a tie for the boys' event with the winners jumping 4ft 3ins.

Tea for the children was held at 5pm in the Drill Hall and in the Gospel Hall. Community singing preceded the successful relay from a loudspeaker of the King's speech. Dancing and fireworks followed. Major Charrington presented a quantity of beer for residents to enjoy and the celebrations ended with the lighting of the bonfire at 10pm.

The Special Parish Meeting to plan for the Jubilee celebrations had been followed by the 1935 Annual Parish Meeting attended by 32 parishioners on 18th March. There were questions about expanding the street lighting from Crownlands (Hilden Park Road area) up to the 'Green Rabbit' (now Orchard Lea) and about the suggestion that the new Recreation ground should be fenced. Dr Fraser had reported on the plans for the Jubilee and the question of how to use any surplus funds was discussed. The meeting resolved ...

"... that subscriptions be invited on behalf of The Queen Victoria Cottage Hospital, Tonbridge as a Jubilee Memorial."

The suggestion was that, funds permitting, a bed at the hospital should be endowed.

In the absence of Mr G W Johnson, Mr John Mackney of Limes Farm presided over the 1936 Annual Parish Meeting held on 25th March. 21 parishioners were present. In his review of the year Mr Mackney referred to the success of the Jubilee celebrations. Amongst other matters discussed:

- The footpath to the station had been made up as had the path at the corner of Riding Lane and the "Main Road"
- A call for the lighting of the whole village was referred to the Council
- Poor drainage at "Hilden Park Estate"
- New sand was needed for the Recreation Ground sandpit and the swings needed to "be tested and greased, and new handles ... placed on the small see-saw".
- The possible rolling of "the whole of the Recreation Ground"

Mrs Louisa Houghton, the Council's representative on the School Management Board presented the Manager's Report:

- 75 children had milk daily
- Attendance at the school was one of the highest in the Tonbridge area
- For National Savings the children had saved £90, up from £65 last year.

Mrs Houghton was asked if she was ...

"... satisfied that classes should have to receive instruction on licensed premises."

The Headmaster, Mr L R A Fitz, replied that ...

"... three of His Majesty's Inspectorate had seen the room and considered it to be adequate for education to be conducted there."

1937 – 1939

George V had died on 20th January 1936 and his successor, Edward VIII, had abdicated on 11th December 1936. On 3rd February 1937 a special Parish Meeting was held to consider what form the celebrations marking the Coronation of George VI and Queen Elizabeth should take. 27 parishioners met, under the Chairmanship of the Council Chairman, Mr G W Johnson.

It was decided that the arrangements should be similar to those for the Silver Jubilee celebrations in 1935. It was agreed:

"that the Parish in a spirit of loyalty celebrate the Coronation of the King and Queen on Wednesday 12th May 1937."

As the Minutes of the meeting record, of these celebrations…

> "… Generally speaking it was to be almost a repetition of the celebration held at the Silver Jubilee."

Amongst the decisions taken:

- A 2d rate would be levied to meet the cost
- A parade of local organisations would be held half an hour before the Church service at noon.
- A commemorative tree would be planted at the Recreation Ground
- By 11 votes to 5 the meeting voted that medals should be given to the children
- Children and the over 65s should receive a commemorative mug
- There would be a tea for the children
- Printed numbered programmes would be sold
- A sports' programme would be held
- There would be "a Punch & Judy, fireworks, bonfire and dancing in the Drill Hall at night. There would be no community singing".
- Prizes would be awarded for the best decorated premises
- Mr Fitz, the Headmaster, would arrange an entertainment to be given by the children
- Major Charrington's offer of free beer was gratefully accepted
- A committee was set up to organise the celebrations.

As with the Jubilee Celebrations of 1935, the Minute Book contains cuttings from local newspapers about the local Coronation celebrations:

> "Hildenborough had a great day, with every item supported to the full by the entire village. The morning found every man, woman and child was in his or her best clothes. They anticipated the day's events with great eagerness."

There is a detailed account of the day's events which included Maypole and Morris dancing but which had begun with a church service at St John's. The 1935 May Queen, Barbara Hitchcock, was present for the crowning of the new Queen, Joan Fox. The new May Queen "well and truly planted the tree" at the Recreation ground. The newspaper reported…

> "And when the tiny tots were tucked away, tired out and soon fast asleep, the adults were listening with wrapt attention to the broadcast of the King's speech, and subsequently parading in fancy dress and receiving their prizes.
>
> Came night. The rejoicings at Hildenborough, so sincerely English, were coming to an end. But not quite. The Drill Hall has never been so packed as when what seemed to be the whole village made their way to the Hall to dance until the early morning hour."

As in 1935, Major Charrington's free beer was served to all residents!

During the afternoon there was an extensive programme of sports for the children and, after tea, for the adults. These events were followed in the early evening by fancy dress parades for children and for adults. Details are given of the winners of the children's fancy dress:

William Wilson	"Cup Final Result – a crippled footballer"	1st
Jean Killick	Victorian lady	2nd
Phyllis Batten	Gipsy	3rd
George Wickenden	Dutchman	4th
Sheila Owen	Shredded Wheat	5th

Following their parade, the children "were given milk and free bags of cakes during the evening".

Following the broadcast of the King's speech at 8pm there was the adult's fancy dress parade. The winners were:

- Mr H Bennett   Rajah   1st
- Miss Gleed and Miss Simmons   Red Riding Hood and the wolf   2nd
- Miss Springate and Miss Bew   Miller and windmill   3rd

The weather for the day was reasonably kind although rain prevented the planned open-air dancing. However, it did not prevent the lighting of the bonfire and the display of fireworks which preceded the dancing in the Drill Hall. The bonfire and fireworks were under the direction of the Hildenborough Fire Brigade, named as:

"Messrs F G Balcombe, A Upton, E Quinnell, D Seal, W. Woodgate, J Stroud and G Smith."

Commemorative medals were presented to the children in the morning whilst they received a Coronation mug at their tea in the afternoon. Residents over 65 also received a mug with "Mr Thompson of Froxfield, London Road" aged 100 the oldest recipient. "Rose Elizabeth Swan , aged 4 days" of Mount Pleasant was the youngest.

The plaques on the trees planted to commemorate the 1935 Silver Jubilee and the Coronation in 1937 disappeared over the years but were replaced in 2015 by the Parish Council.

The 1937 triennial elections took place at the Drill Hall on 15th March with 79 parishioners present to choose 9 councillors from the 11 candidates. As usual voting was by a show of hands and, as at all previous elections, no secret ballot of the whole parish was demanded. The elections over, the Annual Parish Meeting was held immediately afterwards with the Chairman, Mr G W Johnson, presenting his review of the past year. He referred to footpaths, allotments, the Fire Brigade and the forthcoming Coronation. Ominously, he also mentioned "Air Raid Precautions".

Mrs Louisa Houghton, the only woman Councillor, had been re-elected at the top of the poll earlier in the evening. She reported to the meeting on behalf of the school managers. She had ...

"... paid many visits to the school re: milk supply, needlework, games and for the examination of registers."

She went on to say ...

"About half the scholars were taking milk and several necessitous cases supplied free. The school had been visited by 4 HM Inspectors and 2 from the Kent Education Committee. The doctor had visited twice and the nurse four times.

Four scholarships won, 1st prize for folk songs, 1st prize for folk dancing, won 3 athletic cups.

The attendance was over 93%, the highest for 25 years. 87 to 90 books taken each week from the Library.

A cycle shed had been built for 20 cycles and the School Master had initiated visits of the officer of the Juvenile Employment Bureau, Tonbridge. Many boys and girls had been placed in situations that they themselves wanted."

Amongst other matters raised by parishioners:

- The need for "Belisha Crossings" (Leslie Hore-Belisha, MP, Transport Minister from June 1934 until May 1937 was a keen advocate of pedestrian crossings).
- The suggestion of a seat "opposite the Boiling Kettle" (now the BP Garage)
- The possibility of draining the Recreation Ground
- The suggestion that "a platform be erected for pedestrians to walk on where the floods came up in Riding Lane".
- Flooding at Garlands (Riding Lane). Mr G Martin "stated that water was under his

kitchen floor".

During the years 1938 and 1939 the village was much pre-occupied with the question of street lighting. A special Parish Meeting was held on 12th January 1938, attended by 142 parishioners, a record attendance for a Parish meeting in Hildenborough.

The meeting was asked to consider the adoption of the appropriate Act to permit the extension of street lighting. It considered the cost of installing and maintaining the lighting and whether such lighting should be by gas or electricity. At this stage it was agreed to adopt the Act and leave consideration of its implementation to a later date. On a show of hands, by 109 votes to 6, the Act was adopted but a Poll of all electors was demanded. This was held on 2nd February 1938 …

"… on the following question, viz: That the Lighting and Watching Act, 1833, be adopted for the Parish of Hildenborough".

The result of the Poll was:

498 votes in favour   85 against   Majority in favour 413

The cost of the Poll was "£13-11-8".

The following month, on 23rd March 1938, the Annual Parish Meeting was held with only 17 parishioners present. Mr G W Johnson who had been associated with the Council since its inception in 1894, had resigned as Chairman the previous December. At various times he had been a Councillor, Clerk to the Council, Treasurer and from 1907 until his resignation in December 1937, Chairman. He was succeeded as Chairman by Mr Frank Burton and it was Mr Burton who presided over the meeting and gave the Report on the past year. He mentioned –

– The success of the Coronation celebrations
– Footpaths: a map marking all the footpaths was being prepared
– That the Council wished to see the drainage of the Recreation Ground by the end of 1939.

Anxiety about the possibility of war led Mr Burton to report that…

"…Air Raid Precautions had occupied their attention. 16 wardens and the members of the Fire Brigade had gone through their gas course, as had most of the Special Constables. Shortly a house would be used to demonstrate how premises could be made gas proof etc. …"

Various matters were discussed at the meeting:

– Lighting: it was agreed to ask the Rural District Council "to become the Authority to light the Parish of Hildenborough" following the vote at the previous month's special meeting.
– Signatures were being collected "house to house" on a petition calling for a 30mph speed limit through the village. This would go to the MP, the County Council and the Ministry of Transport. There was a call for pedestrian crossings.
– There was a call for "a footpath in Stocks Green Road where the houses are situated".
– Flooding in Riding Lane
– Complaints about the refuse collection
– The cleaning of the War Memorial stonework
– The Recreation Ground: did the Cricket Club intend to use it? Work was in hand for "concreting around the swings etc."

In the first years of the 21st Century the Parish Council secured the registration of the Village Green at Mount Pleasant as "common land", thus giving it added protection from possible development. In 1938 there had been such a threat. On 12th May a Parish Meeting, chaired by Mr Burton, was held with 44 parishioners present to consider a plan…

"... for the proposed erection of a Parish nurse's house, clinic and garage." Strong "objections to the building either on the Green or at the Recreation Ground" were registered. By 23 votes to nil the proposal was opposed.

There was another Parish Meeting later in 1938, this time to discuss the Recreation Ground. On 2nd November 50 parishioners met under the Chairmanship of Mr Frank Burton, Chairman of the Parish Council. The meeting considered plans for drainage at the Recreation Ground and the possibility of obtaining land for playing fields in the Crown Lands (Hilden Park) area. In each case it was estimated that the cost would be around £300. By 21 votes to 11 the following Resolution was passed:

"That a sum not exceeding £600 be asked for by loan for the provision of and putting in order the necessary Playing Fields for the parish of Hildenborough."

The last Annual Parish Meeting held before the outbreak of war took place on 27th March 1939 with 53 parishioners present. The possibility of war was a preoccupation and Mr Burton, the Council Chairman, gave a report on ARP (Air Raid Precautions) work. Wardens had carried out the task of distributing and fitting gas masks. Numerous other matters were considered by the meeting including:

- Drainage at the Recreation Ground (which was proceeding) and the possible purchase of land for a playing field at Crown Lands. No application had yet been made for the loan to cover the cost.
- There was a request for more frequent refuse collections.
- The Ministry of Health had granted an Order permitting the Rural District Council to proceed with a lighting scheme for Hildenborough following consultations with the Parish Council.
- Under the Fire Brigades Act, 1938, the Rural District Council had assumed responsibility for fire protection for the rural parishes. Hildenborough's Fire Brigade was not retained on grounds of cost and from 1st April 1939 the Tonbridge Brigade would assume responsibility for Hildenborough.

The Vicar, the Rev'd W H Bass, in the absence of Mrs Houghton, presented the Report of the School Managers:

- Attendance had been 95%
- 3 scholarships and 3 cups had been won
- School National Savings Certificates amounted to £106-0-4 during the year.
- The school in Riding Lane was now a "Junior School" with older children now "conveyed by 'buses to and from Tonbridge schools".

1940-1956

Only 21 parishioners were present at the next Annual Parish Meeting held in the Drill Hall on 26th March 1940. Topics relating to the war were amongst those discussed:

- A vote of thanks was passed expressing gratitude "to those in charge of evacuation reception and also to those who had received children".
- Major Kingham "addressed the meeting on the War Savings Campaign". He congratulated Mr Fitz, the Headmaster, on his work with Savings' Groups. Mr Fitz reported that "there were up to the moment 9 Groups".

The meeting heard that the Recreation Ground had been drained and paid for without the need for a loan. The street lighting plans would not be put into effect until after the war. It was confirmed that the village Fire Brigade had been taken over by the Rural District Council. Next year 1940/41, there would be a 1d reduction in the general rate.

Mrs Houghton reported to the meeting on behalf of the School Managers:

- "20 seniors went to Tonbridge"
- "Education was about back to normal."
- The health of the scholars was excellent
- Four scholarships had been won
- One girl had attended for 6 years with 100% attendance
- The playground had been repaired
- Over £5 each week was subscribed to the War Savings.

The 1941 Annual Parish Meeting was held on 24th March with 13 parishioners present to hear the review of the year past. Several matters relating to the war were considered:
- School shelters
- Stirrup pumps
- Care of animals in wartime conditions
- It was reported that in the village "there were 270 Fire Watchers and 60 Fire Fighters"
- Mr E Francis and Mr D W King had been chosen as honorary consultants and would give advice in conjunction with the Royal Horticultural Society on matters relating to cottage gardens and allotments
- The distribution of lime for gardens
- It was agreed to send a request to the Rural District Council for the installation of a siren in the village

Problems associated with the war also featured in discussions about the school:
- "if an 'alert' was on at dismissal time the teachers saw the children home"
- "Is it considered seemly that the First Aid Point should use the same premises as the School Canteen, considering that all their equipment is getting spoilt by the steam and would be quite unfit for use in case of emergency?" was a question put by one resident.

For the School Managers, Mrs Houghton reported that four girls and one boy had won scholarships. "Two-thirds of the children were taking milk". Two new teachers had been engaged. "Excellent work" was being done in connection with the canteen and savings certificates".

The meeting also considered the relationship with the "Tonbridge Joint Burial Board". Hildenborough paid £11 pa to the Board although Hildenborough residents now used the local churchyard rather than that in Tonbridge. Reports were received from the Drill Hall Trustees and from the Trustees of local charities.

At the Annual Parish Meeting held on 23rd March 1942 attended by a dozen parishioners, in addition to the usual Reports from the School Managers and from the Trustees of Charities, matters in connection with the war were considered:
- Mr Fitz, the local Headmaster, reported that there were now 12 War Savings Groups in the Parish. Nationally, "Warships Week" had raised £35,476.
- Mr Fitz had undertaken...
  "... the post (unpaid) as O C Water Supplies in the event of an emergency". He has "a map showing all the wells in the Parish,"

The matter of emergency water supplies was raised at the next Annual Parish Meeting on 19th March 1943 when the 17 parishioners present agreed ...
  "... that samples of water from wells scheduled suitable for drinking purposes should be tested."

At the meeting there was disquiet about the protection of the village by the Fire Service. It was agreed to send the following Resolution to the Minister of Home Security (Mr Herbert Morrison, MP):

"That the full facts concerning the inadequate facilities for the protection allowed by the National Fire Service to this Parish should be brought to your notice."

The next Annual Parish Meeting, held on 29th March 1944, was also only attended by 17 parishioners. The need for additional housing in the village was discussed. It was reported that the "AR Precautions... were in a healthy state" but a councillor, Mr F H Buss...

"... reported that the shelter near the Boiling Kettle was locked during raids." Mr Burton, the Chairman, undertook to investigate.

Mrs Houghton gave a detailed report on behalf of the School Managers. She...

"... gave particulars regarding attendances, scholarships, school dinners, milk, health, savings and dental treatment."

The meeting agreed...

"... to place on record the appreciation of the Foster Mothers, who looked after evacuees."

The 1945 Annual Parish Meeting on 27th March was attended by 47 parishioners and the Chairman, Mr Frank Burton, gave the customary review of the past year's work by the Parish Council. The village had been promised 18 houses "under the post war housing scheme" but the meeting agreed that the Council should ..

"... press for more houses to be built in Hildenborough, as the proposed 18 were totally inadequate compared with the allocations to other villages of similar size."

There was a discussion about ....

"... the Constitution, powers and representatives of the Trustees of the Drill Hall and Institute."

It was agreed that the Trustees and "the Committee of the men's club" should meet and discuss the subject of an agreement etc. It was suggested that...

"... if there was a surplus of cash perhaps the Trustees would consider painting the interior of the Drill Hall."

Reports were received from the School Managers and from the Trustees of "Leigh United Charities" and "the Charity called Hills for the Hildenborough Nursing Association". There was a discussion about the acquisition of land for another recreation ground and a Resolution was passed asking the Parish Council ...

"... to proceed to acquire land at the rear of Hilden Park Road."

It was pointed out that the area would need adequate drainage.

Until this meeting there was never any suggestion that "party politics" intruded into the work of the Parish Council but on this occasion there was a complaint that the Council had co-opted a new member to fill a vacancy. "Allegations were made that the procedure had been illegal" but the Chairman stated that it was in order for the Parish Council to fill any vacancy by co-option rather than leaving the matter to a Parish Meeting. One parishioner...

"... gave notice that the County Council would be informed that the political truce was not honoured at the Parish Council Meeting."

It is not clear why the County Council needed to be informed of this.

The meeting then went on to pass a Resolution by 19 votes to 1 that ...

− The number of Parish Councillors be increased from nine to fifteen.

− The "Hilden Area" be made into a separate ward.

The Resolution was to be forwarded to the County Council with the request that the changes should be implemented in time for elections scheduled for April 1946.

With the end of the war in Europe in May 1945, a special Parish Meeting was held on

29th May with 117 parishioners present. Mr Burton, the Council Chairman, explained that the purpose of the meeting was …
  "… to discuss the advisability of building a new hall and whether this should take the form of a 'War Memorial'."
He described the project and said that financial help could be obtained "from the Council of Social Service". He stressed …
  "… that the Hall should be planned so that it should be capable of future expansion, and that it should be undenominational and non-political."
Two Resolutions were passed:
  1. By 100 votes for, none against – "that this meeting considers it advisable that a Village Hall be built to serve the needs of the whole Parish".
  2. By 81 votes for, one against: "that this meeting considers that the main War Memorial should be the Village Hall, but that as a more immediate memorial the names of the fallen should be added to those engraved on the 1914-1918 War Memorial".
  There then followed a discussion about a possible site. The Chairman pointed out that it…
  "… should be large enough to provide a good car park as well as room for expansion."
A suggestion that the Hall should be built "in the area of 'The Flying Dutchman' was withdrawn and, by 112 votes to nil, a Resolution passed…
  "that a committee should be formed to inquire into a site and report to a Parish Meeting."
A Site Committee of 13 was then elected.
  The Site Committee, under the chairmanship of Major Charrington, reported to a Parish Meeting attended by 65 parishioners on 30th August 1945. It was clear that the committee was divided in its conclusions. Seven possible sites had been examined and five rejected as unsuitable or not for sale. The two remaining sites were:
  1. Hubble's Field in Coldharbour Lane
  2. The present Recreation Ground
Hubble's Field was described as being about 10 acres with access possible from both the Village Green and Coldharbour Lane. "It could be bought for £2,400" but the Local Authority would require anyone developing it to contribute to the "cost of widening and making up Coldharbour Lane for the full frontage of the site at a cost of about £600". Should Hubble's Field become a Recreation Ground as well as a Village Hall, the present Recreation Ground could be sold by the Parish Council to help finance the cost.
  The Site Committee looked at…
  "an area of about 2 acres of woodland and coppice with some small ponds which at present is unused and undeveloped. This unused piece of land is next to the Schools, with a frontage in Riding Lane."
Seven members of the committee favoured this site but five opposed it.
  Mr Burton, the Parish Council Chairman, then read out a Resolution passed by the Council on 23rd August:
  "That should a piece of land, part of the Recreation Ground be required for a War Memorial Hall, subject to the consent of a Parish Meeting, the Parish Council will give it favourable consideration and recommend to the Parish Meeting that the land be given."
The meeting discussed the Site Committee's Report and finally passed a Resolution by 59 votes to nil:

"That this meeting is not satisfied with the preliminary discussion on the sites, and would like to explore further the question of both sites and expenses involved thereto, with the Town Planning Committee."

It was agreed that the Site Committee and the Parish Council should hold a joint meeting to discuss "what information should be passed on to the Town Planning Committee".

On 14th November 1945 a Parish Meeting with 36 parishioners present met...

"to discuss the Division of the Parish into Wards, and the boundary lines of the Wards."

This meeting was a consequence of the suggestions made at the Annual Parish Meeting on 27th March which called for the division of the Parish into two wards and an increase in the number of councillors from 9 to 15. Those present agreed to the creation of the two Wards.

Following examination of "a large map of the Parish" and several suggestions, a Resolution was passed by 126 votes to 5 but not before it had been "read out to the meeting three times":

"That the Boundary dividing line should be North from Tinley Lodge, down the centre of Coldharbour Lane, part of London Road to the 'Flying Dutchman' along Powder Mill Road to the Boundary line of the Sevenoaks Rural District Council South of the 'Plough Inn'."

At the 1946 Annual Parish Meeting held on 14th March in the presence of 45 parishioners there was no mention of the suggested creation of two Wards in Hildenborough. However, the Chairman, Mr Frank Burton reported that at the next election there would be an increase in the number of seats on the Parish Council from 9 to 11. The election, if contested, would be by secret ballot rather than a show of hands at a Parish meeting.

Among other matters raised at the meeting:

- A request for more housing in the village would be sent to the Rural District Council
- The possibility of allotments in the Hilden area
- Subject to the consent of Mr L R A Fitz, the Headmaster at the school, a parents' association should be formed.
- It was hoped that the next Council would make progress with the plans for a new Village Hall.

In 2016 Robin Oakley presented to the Hildenborough History Society a paper entitled "Memories of Living in Hildenborough in the 1940s and 1950s". He is the son of Mr A G T Oakley, Chairman of the Parish Council from 1950 until 1955. Quoting "The Courier" of 19th May 1945, Robin Oakley refers to the V.E. Day Celebrations. The Vicar, the Rev'd E W E Fraser conducted a thanksgiving service whilst "the King's speech was relayed ... to the school playground". Dancing followed. Next day "VE Plus One" day the WVS and Mr Oakley arranged an "impromptu social and dance". Everyone brought their own refreshments although tea and coffee were provided. In the evening there were games, community singing and dancing organised by Mr Oakley and fellow Councillor, Mr Challen. There was a collection towards the cost of the WVS Children's Party to be held at the end of the week. £4-15-3d (£4.76) was raised – any balance to go to the Village Hall fund. At the children's party, Mr L R A Fitz, Headmaster between 1931 and 1952 "produced a delightful children's play and led the community singing".

The events mentioned by Mr Oakley were held immediately after the end of the war in Europe. V E Day was on 8th May 1945 but hostilities in the Far East continued until VJ Day on 15th August and the principal celebrations to mark the end of the war were not held until June 1946. By this time many of the troops had returned home.

A special Parish Meeting, attended by 44 parishioners, was held on 15th May 1946 at the Drill Hall. The agenda: "to discuss V Day Celebrations". The Vicar, the Rev'd E W E Fraser, as Parish Council Chairman, presided and explained that the meeting had been called...

> "... in order that a discussion could take place, and to have the opinion of the meeting as to whether a V Day Celebration to be held on June 8th was desirable or not."

Following the discussion, during which concerns were expressed about the cost, a vote was taken – 16 voting for a celebration, 16 against. The Chairman didn't exercise a casting vote but as one of those against the Resolution in favour of a celebration withdrew his vote, the motion was declared carried. It was felt that the cost would be considerably less than the £100 limit that had been set by the Council.

Having agreed by the narrowest of margins to proceed with the celebrations, the meeting set up committees and appointed volunteers to organise the event. Detailed accounts of earlier Parish celebrations were recorded in the Minute Book but there is no record of this event except for an account of the plans:

- A celebratory tea for all children under 16. Miss Turnbull took on the responsibility of organising the tea and said that "she would be open to receive any gifts of food etc. for the day". The officers of the Gospel Hall would be asked to lend their hall for the tea.
- A committee would arrange sports' events
- There would be side shows and pony rides with money raised used to offset the cost of the day.
- There would be a "social" during the evening, ending with a dance.
- A majority favoured a bonfire
- Volunteers with cars were asked to help transport "the old folk and invalids".
- "a St John's Ambulance unit should be present on the field".

In the years following the end of the war, the question of a Village Hall was considered by the Parish Council and by Parish Meetings. In August 1945 a Joint Committee had been set up at a Parish Meeting with the Site Committee (established the previous May) and the Parish Council combining to consider the options.

A Parish Meeting, attended by 57 parishioners, met on 25th October 1946 to consider the recommendations of the Joint Committee. This had considered two possible sites for a Hall – Hubble's Field and the Recreation Ground. The latter was, by far, the cheaper option and the meeting unanimously passed the following Resolution:

> "that the present Recreation Ground be retained, with the addition of a War Memorial Hall being built upon it."

The Chairman, the Rev'd E W E Fraser told the meeting that since it has been called there had been several developments:

1. A letter dated 23rd October 1946, ie two days before the meeting, from the Ministry of Health stating that consent for a loan would not be granted "at the present time". A loan could only be approved in cases where "the immediate necessity for the purchase is clearly established".

2. It appeared that consent was being given to the proposed development of land "from Leigh Road to the rear of Hilden Park Road" and that "provision had been made for a piece of land there to be used as a community centre". This overlooked "the site which the Council were now negotiating for as a playing field".

3. "The Trustees and Managers of the Drill Hall had made an offer on certain conditions of the Drill Hall, Institute and Buildings to the Parish Council." The Council was now taking legal advice about this offer.

A further Parish Meeting to consider the proposed Village Hall was held on 29th January 1947 but only 17 parishioners were present. The Notice convening the meeting read:

War Memorial Funds
To consider the methods of raising funds
To appoint Trustees
To appoint Officers and Committee and to settle committee's powers

January 1947 proved to be during one of the severest winters on record and it was decided to adjourn the meeting until early March as ...

"... owing to weather conditions there was not a reasonable representation of the Parish present."

The meeting reconvened on 6th March 1947 but only 24 parishioners attended. It was agreed:

"That the whole of the Parish Council be Trustees of the funds only, and not of the building, and that the Council appoint a treasurer for the funds."

It was also agreed to set up a committee with seven members elected at this meeting and a further three nominated by the Parish Council. This Committee would have the power to raise funds and would remain in office until the Annual Parish Meeting in March 1948.

Later that month, on 26th March 1947, the Annual Parish Meeting was held in the presence of 30 parishioners with the Vicar, the Rev'd E W E Fraser in the chair. He gave a report of the work of the newly enlarged Parish Council which had taken office following the election by secret ballot on 1st April 1946. This was the first such ballot since the inception of the Parish Council in 1894. The number of councillors was now 11, an increase of two. The plans to divide the Parish into two wards had not been implemented.

The Chairman's Report included references to:
- The Victory Celebrations
- The proposed War Memorial Hall
- The War Memorial Cross
- The "Welcome Home" dinner for returning service personnel
- Food parcels from the Dominions
- Housing
- Pedestrian crossings
- "improvements at the school and the Recreation Ground"
- The proposed Hilden Park playing fields

Reports were presented to the meeting by the Trustees of the local charities, the Drill Hall and Institute, and the School Managers. A parishioner...

"... spoke of the necessity of a Nursery Class and the allocation of milk for children during the holidays."

The possibility of allotments "in the Hilden Estate area" was raised. This was not a new idea and the Chairman said that, subject to demand, the Council "would do their best to obtain the land for that purpose".

The matter of a Village Hall was taken a stage further at a Parish Meeting attended by 66 parishioners on 12th November 1947. Also present was "Mr H Cogger, Solicitor, Tonbridge". There were three items on the Agenda:
1. "To consider an offer made by the Trustees to transfer the ownership of the Drill Hall and Institute to the Parish Council ..."
2. To consider the matter of games at the Recreation Ground on Sundays.
3. "To consider the interim use of the War Memorial Hall Fund."

"A long and varied discussion took place" on the first item. There was concern about the cost to the ratepayers. It was confirmed that the caretaker's cottage was included in the offer which covered "the freehold of the whole premises". A proposal to accept the Trustees' offer was carried by 52 votes to nil.

There was considerable discussion on the topic of Sunday games but by 25 votes to 19 it was finally agreed that "the playing of amateur organised games in the Recreation Ground on Sundays "be authorised but the games "must be outside the times of the morning and evening Church services".

By 37 votes to 2 the meeting authorised the Parish Council "to use up to 50%" of the War Memorial Hall funds with "a limit of £500" on condition that ...

"... the money may be called in at 3 years as from 1st January 1948, at the rate of 2½% interest per annum, and the balance to be invested as the Trustees decide..."

With the Rev. E W E Fraser in the chair, 25 parishioners attended the 1948 Annual Parish Meeting on 17th March. Mr Fraser's Report covered most of the topics that had been mentioned the previous year. New topics included speed limits, telephone boxes, Ashline's 'bus services and street lighting. The usual reports were presented including one from the War Memorial Hall Fund which showed a credit balance of £1,026-11-1. It was agreed that up to £50 of this money should be spent on engraving the names of the Fallen during the recent war on the War Memorial. This work would be undertaken by "Messrs Higgs & Tye of Sevenoaks".

The meeting re-elected the officers and committee of the War Memorial Hall Fund, filling a vacancy left by a member who had moved away from the parish.

Extracts from a letter from "The Lord Mayor's United Nations Appeal for Children" were read and two people volunteered to help the charity in the village.

A Resolution was passed deploring the Rural District Council's refusal to approve...

"... applications to erect garages on the Leigh Road and Powder Mill Lane frontages of the Hilden Farm Estate."

The Council was asked to reconsider this decision "which is likely to cause hardship and serious inconvenience to residents".

A parishioner asked that the County Council be informed of the poor state of some parts of the road in Riding Lane. Another asked for...

"... a Post Office pillar box and if possible a stamp machine to be put up somewhere in the neighbourhood of the Hilden Farm Estate Office."

In the summer of 1948 an unprecedented event occurred: a special Parish Meeting was requisitioned by six electors. This was...

"To discuss matters relative to the continuation of manufacturing glass products at the Glass Factory, Hildenborough."

128 electors were present at the meeting held on 8th July. Mr Mepham, one of the six, said that 58 of the factory's workers lived in Hildenborough, 42 came from Tonbridge and 22 from the Powder Mills area and it was now under threat of closure.

The Vicar, the Rev's E W E Fraser explained that....

"... when the glass factory came to Hildenborough, there was a guarantee that it would be removed six months after the war end, and it was owed to the residents that that fact should be borne in mind."

Sir Thomas Butler was...

"... concerned about the guarantees he understood had been given to people who bought land and built houses close to the factory site. He felt that a contract should remain a contract..."

The Chairman of the meeting was Mr F H Buss in place of the Parish Council Chairman, the Vicar, who had waived his right to preside. After lengthy discussions, Mr Buss then put the following Resolution proposed by Mr Mepham with the words:

199

"I beg to propose on behalf of this meeting which has been convened by Local Government Electors who are employed at the Medical Glassware Factory, Stocks Green Road, Hildenborough...

"That this meeting recommends the Rural District Council to reconsider the decision on the closing down in June 1950, and to be allowed to carry on for all time. Over 50 electors are employed at the factory, and their livelihood will be endangered, and cause much unemployment in the area."

The Resolution was passed by 81 votes to 7.

"By 8pm the Drill Hall was full and about 70 people overflowed into the Institute rooms where a two-way microphone-loudspeaker system was conducted." These are words recorded in the Minute Book for a Parish Meeting on 9th February 1949 attended by nearly 300 people! For decades such meetings were usually attended by well under 100 parishioners, sometimes by fewer than 20. What attracted such a huge interest that night? The Council Chairman, the Rev. E W E Fraser read the Notice convening the meeting –

1. "To consider the application proposed to be made by the Tonbridge Urban District Council to the Local Government Boundary Commission for the Parish of Hildenborough to be transferred from the Rural District of Tonbridge to the Urban District of Tonbridge.

2. To consider any other matters affecting any alteration of the boundaries of the Rural District of Tonbridge."

Mr B Lee, Clerk to Tonbridge Rural District Council, present by invitation, then explained the Rural District Council's ...

"... record of work which included facts and figures on the following: Area, Population, Boundary Regulations, Housing, Sewerage and Sewage Disposal, House Refuse Collection, Maternity and Child Welfare Service, Planning, Street Lighting and Roads."

After questions, the following three part Resolution was proposed:

1. "That this meeting of Local Government Electors of Hildenborough wishes the Tonbridge Rural District Council to continue to be a separate Local Government Unit and that Hildenborough shall remain part of it.

2. That they object to the suggested transfer of Hildenborough to Tonbridge as they consider that such a proposal would not be in the best interests of the Parish.

3. That the Tonbridge Rural District Council and Hildenborough Parish Council be asked to do everything possible to support the views of this meeting."

Voting on the Resolution was 283 in favour, 3 against with 2 abstentions.

Far fewer parishioners attended the next Parish Meeting, the 1949 Annual Parish Meeting on 16th March with 33 electors present. The Chairman, the Rev'd E W E Fraser, presented a Report on the past year. Amongst the topics mentioned were:

- The Recreation Ground
- A resident police constable
- Telephone kiosks
- Dominion and colonial food gifts (the post-war years were ones of shortages and rationing so such gifts were gratefully received)
- Lectures on Local Government
- The War Memorial Cross and the War Memorial Hall Fund
- Housing
- The Drill Hall and Institute
- Revision of the Parish boundaries
- Street lighting

Various other Reports were considered – from the Trustees of charities, the School Managers, the Trustees of the Drill Hall and Institute, the Trustees of the War Memorial Hall Fund.

The meeting agreed to changes to the powers of the War Memorial Hall Committee. In addition to raising funds, the committee could...

"... explore the proposals for a new Hall and the possibility of obtaining grants towards the cost..."

A secret ballot was held to elect seven members of the committee. It was agreed that their term of office should now be three years, not one as hitherto. This would be the same as the term for councillors who nominated three of their number to serve on the committee.

The 1950 Annual Parish Meeting on 29th March was well attended with 88 parishioners present. This was the last meeting to be presided over by the Council Chairman, the Rev'd E W E Fraser who...

"... tendered his resignation as Chairman of the Parish Council as he wanted to be freer for his work as Vicar"... assuring "the meeting that, as long as he remained in Hildenborough, everything concerning the Parish as a whole will always have his keen interest."

In his final Report for the year past, Mr Fraser mentioned a number of perennial topics such as speed limits, pedestrian crossings and street lighting. New matters touched upon included...

... the gift of a clock for the Drill Hall, the Festival of Britain (scheduled for 1951) and postal services.

The Report was adopted "with applause".

After Reports from various Trustees and the School Managers had been considered, the meeting discussed the problem of housing in the village. Dr C Glaisher, who was "Secretary of the service committee of the local British Legion" reported that the names of ex-servicemen had been removed from the Rural District Council's housing register. He had the names of three from Hildenborough. Mr G Lewis said –

"on the question of housing, there have been ... complaints of old people being exposed to hardship."

It was decided to refer these problems to the Rural District Council.

It was reported that the War Memorial Hall Fund now had a credit balance of £1,505-12-6. There was a lengthy discussion about the prospects for a War Memorial Hall. Should the headquarters of the British Legion be incorporated in the new hall? It was agreed that the Legion's Committee should meet the Hall Committee for discussions about this idea.

There were two items on the agenda of a Parish meeting held on 6th September 1950 in the Drill Hall with 76 parishioners present:

- The proposed War Memorial Hall
- The Festival of Britain, scheduled for 1951, the 100th anniversary of the Great Exhibition.

The Chairman, Sir Thomas Butler, stated that the War Memorial Hall Fund Committee had come to the conclusion that their plan for an entirely new hall was impossible. The cost would be prohibitive and the Committee together with the Parish Council felt that a revised scheme was "more in keeping with present-day conditions".

Plans for this revised scheme had been displayed around the village and were passed round at the meeting. The scheme provided –

- For several improvements to the Drill Hall
- For a separate room for the exclusive use of the British Legion for which a nominal rent would be paid.

    – The Legion to contribute approximately one-third of the funds for the scheme
The estimated cost of the scheme was about £5,500.

    By 61 votes in favour with 3 against, the following Resolution was passed:

    "That the present Hall be enlarged and provision made for the British Legion,
based on the plans that have been presented to the Parish Meeting and on the
conditions recommended by the Parish Council."

    As far as the forthcoming Festival of Britain was concerned, the Chairman suggested
that the event provided the opportunity for ...

    "one extremely good effort for raising money to enlarge the Drill Hall"

It was left to the Council to consider the matter.

    21 parishioners attended the Parish Meeting on 22nd November 1950 chaired by Sir
Thomas Butler who stated that ...

    "... the meeting had been called in accordance with the Order laid down in the
... National Parks and Access to the Countryside Act, 1949."

A survey of the Parish had been completed in order to comply with the Act and all
footpaths had been walked and observations made and recorded. "Newly marked maps
and schedules had been open for inspection for five clear days". The Clerk was asked to
read out "the Schedules from 1-56" and those present were asked to put forward any
comments or objections but there were none.

    By the time of the 1951 Annual Parish Meeting held on 28th March, Mr A G T Oakley
had succeeded Sir Thomas Butler as Parish Council Chairman and he presided over the
meeting. He presented a Report to the 27 parishioners who attended on the past year
whilst the meeting also heard from the School Managers and the Trustees of the various
charities. There is little information in the Minutes about the contents of these Reports.
One parishioner asked the Council to continue...

    "... to press for the extension of the speed limit from the 'Green Rabbit' to the
War Memorial."

(The 'Green Rabbit' was a restaurant, long gone, situated where Orchard Lea now is.)

    There was a discussion about the forthcoming Festival of Britain but enthusiasm for
any village celebrations appears to have been lukewarm. By 17 votes to 2 the following
Resolution was passed:

    "That no action be taken as regards the Festival of Britain in so far as parish
funds are concerned."

    The Council was asked "to give their moral support" to a house-to-house appeal linked to
the Festival in aid of the War Memorial Hall Fund. It was reported that the Fund had a
credit balance of £1,610-4-11.

    There is no record in the Minute Book of any celebrations marking the Festival
although a "treat for children" was suggested.

    Other matters raised included –

    – "more warmth for the Drill Hall"

    – Car parking

    – The County Council was asked to paint the chains surrounding the War Memorial

    The 1952 Annual Parish Meeting, held on 19th March, was sparsely attended with only
24 parishioners present to hear the various reports. Of these there are no details given
except that the War Memorial Hall Fund now had £1,948-19-0 in the bank, an increase on
the previous year of £338. Perhaps this was due to the success of last year's house-to-house
appeal. The committee was re-elected en bloc.

    King George VI had died on 6th February 1952 at the age of 56. The Coronation of
his elder daughter, Princess Elizabeth, as Queen Elizabeth II was scheduled for 2nd June
1953 and a Parish Meeting was called for 11 December 1952 –

- To discuss Coronation affairs
- To levy the necessary rate
- To elect a Coronation Committee

The Parish Council Chairman, Mr Oakley, presided with 31 parishioners present. The meeting reviewed the account of the 1937 Coronation programme before considering the nature of the celebrations for June 1953. There is no record in the Minute Book of the celebrations but amongst the suggestions:

- Kent Education Committee was "giving spoons and beakers to children of various ages attending National Schools". Something should be done for those at private schools together with children under school age.
- It was agreed that the celebrations should be on Coronation Day itself "with something for over 70s to be on a separate day".
- The newly appointed Headmaster of the local school, Mr L R Haisell, thought that "as much as possible should be done for children during daylight".
- A firework display. By 20 votes to 1 the meeting agreed that £25 should be allowed for this with any extra expenditure met by public donations.
- The Parish Church would be floodlit.
- During the afternoon there would be a fancy dress procession, sports for children and adults
- Catering would be on the Recreation Ground "with free ices and refreshments for the children and a children's tea".
- On the Recreation Ground there would be sideshows, "Punch & Judy and Magic".
- A dance band had already been booked together with a "loud speaker unit".

The British Legion offered to be responsible for the arrangements for the dance and the fireworks. "A Coach Tour and Tea or some other enjoyment for the over 70s" was proposed.

The Chairman produced a "tentative budget" and the meeting agreed "that a 2d rate, producing £200, would meet the expenses". The organisation of the celebrations was to be in the hands of a committee set up by the meeting.

Only 18 parishioners attended the 1953 Annual Parish Meeting held on 25th March at the Drill Hall. The Chairman, Mr Oakley, called upon the meeting to observe a short silence as a tribute "to the late Queen Mary who passed away the previous evening".

Mr Oakley presented his annual Report of the work of the Parish Council. It covered "some 20 items" including –

- The Coronation
- Speed limits, pedestrian crossings, street lighting, road names, car parking
- The Recreation Ground, pond, proposed playing field in the Hilden area
- Footpaths, sign posts
- Litter
- The War Memorial Hall Fund, the library, the Drill Hall
- Flood fund
- Allotments
- Post box, 'bus fares
- Rates

There was a request for "a street light at the entrance to Garlands". The Chairman said that this was on the original lighting scheme for the village but no light was possible at present "as there was no cable yet in the area".

Reports were presented to the meeting on behalf of the various trustees representing the local charities and the Drill Hall. It was agreed to provide a kettle for use in the Drill Hall kitchen!

On behalf of the School Managers it was noted that a new Headmaster, Mr L R Haisell, had been appointed in succession to Mr L R A Fitz who had been in post since 1931. It was reported that "about 150 children had the midday meal at school".

The accounts for the War Memorial Hall Fund were presented to the meeting. The Fund's credit balance had increased by about £66 and now stood at £2,015-12-9.

In the Minutes there are few details of the contents of the various Reports presented to the next Annual Parish Meeting on 31st March 1954 with Mr Oakley in the chair and 27 parishioners present. It was agreed to take up the matter of litter baskets at 'bus stops with the Rural District Council but the main item on the agenda related to allotments. It was unanimously agreed that "the 1.576 acres of land" at the London Road allotments be sold. The sale "would be advertised and the best offer, not lower than the District Valuer's price would be accepted".

There appears to have been little of controversy discussed at the 1955 Annual Parish Meeting held on 16th March with Mr Oakley, the Parish Council Chairman, presiding. 20 parishioners were present to hear the usual Reports. In his Report of the work of the Council over the past year, Mr Oakley referred to a lengthy list of topics, including some new ones, considered by Members. He mentioned –

- The Recreation Ground   Ponds
- The Drill Hall, the War Memorial Hall Fund Committee
- Speed limits, "high kerbs", "road patrol for school children"
- Road gritting, footpaths
- Post box, telephone kiosk
- Caravan site
- Train and 'bus services, 'bus shelters
- "slaughter house"

Major C E W Charrington suggested ...
> "... that when the alterations were completed at the Hall, now that it was the property of the ratepayers it should be called the Village Hall and not the Drill Hall."

A new Parish Council was elected in 1955 and Mr E A Woodhams succeeded Mr Oakley as Chairman. Thus, it was Mr Woodhams who presided at the Parish Meeting on 20th July –

1. "to discuss alterations to the Village Hall
2. To elect a management committee concerning the finances together with the methods of raising the balance of the money required."

Mr Woodhams told the 34 parishioners present that ...
> "... the Council had felt for some time that the Hall should be 'more of a community centre'. It should be a village centre rather than a hall run by the Parish Council and the way to do that is to let the people who use the hall manage it."

Estimates had been obtained for the alterations to be done to the Hall, the lowest being £3,385-15-9 from Mr C Woolley. Mr W A Bassett, LRIBA was the architect. A grant had been applied for and the War Memorial Hall Fund had £2,620-12-7 in credit which the Trustees were prepared to hand over towards the cost of the work. Without the grant there was a shortfall of around £750. Five guarantors had come forward with a total of £300 should it be needed.

There was a lengthy discussion about the "scheme of management" of the Hall. The Chairman made it clear that ...
> "... the official Trustees would own the Hall and a Management Committee would run the Hall."

The meeting passed a Resolution –
"That the Hall be handed over to the Charity Trustees and managed by a committee."
The Committee would be made up of representatives of organisations using the Hall. Part of the membership would be elected at the Annual Parish Meeting.

Another Parish Meeting was called to discuss the Hall for 7th October 1955. Chaired by Mr Woodhams, it was attended by 33 parishioners. He reported that the the Council had taken legal advice about the "Trusteeship and management of the Drill Hall". He also stated that a provisional grant of £975 had been promised.

Following the legal advice, the meeting rescinded the Resolution passed at the meeting in July. A new Resolution was proposed by Mr Oakley, the previous Chairman of the Parish Council:
"that the Parish Council remain the Trustees for the property but such property shall be run by the Management Committee."
The Chairman then introduced the Secretary to the Kent Council of Social Service who had travelled from Folkestone to address the meeting on the running of village halls. He produced a model trust deed and explained how the Hall should be managed. A temporary committee was then chosen to carry the matter forward.

The Minute Book recording the Parish Meetings and village celebrations from 1894 ends with a brief account of the poorly attended 1956 Annual Parish Meeting held on 14th March. Mr Woodhams chaired the gathering attended by only 13 parishioners. He reported that the alterations to the Hall had been completed and that a plaque would be placed in it commemorating those who had been lost in the Second World War.

At that time the Library was housed in what was still described as the "Drill Hall" and the meeting was told that about 1,000 books per month were being loaned out.

The "past members of the War Memorial Hall Funds" were thanked for their work in raising the funds which had been used on the Hall improvements. Three charity reports were read on behalf of:
"Leigh United, Hills for Hildenborough Nurses' Association, Sir Thomas Smythe."
Under "Any Other Business" Dr Glaisher asked that the Council ...
"... should in the near future discuss the matter with reference to burials in the Parish. The Churchyard which is the present Burial Ground was becoming filled and alternative sites should be considered."

With Thanks To The Following Subscribers

Valerie Andrews
Mr & Mrs Ayling
Malcolm & Jennifer Baker
Jen & John Bescoby
Richard & Margaret Botten
Shiela & Chris Broomfield
Marshall Browning
Mrs G R Bumstead
Geoff Calderhead
Eric & Judith Chalker (3 copies)
Lee & Clare Cheeseman
Tony & Rosemary Cole
Colin & Sarah Cope
Jac & Mellie Corbett
Mr & Mrs T Crockford
Anne & Patrick Davies
David & Sylvia Davis
Brian & Margaret Dimbylow
Howard & Joy Dolling
Claire & Simon Dunk
Jim Edwards
Mr Robert Flatman &
    Mrs Barbara Flatman
Fosse Bank School
J V Foster
Carol Fox
David Gaskin
Susan and Andrew Gidley
A Goodwin
George & Sue Gorham
Robert & Yvonne Greenaway
Vicky & Dave Grimshaw
Marion & Pearl Hall
Helen Harper & Tom Noone
David Haugh
Mike & Maggie Hewson
Dennis & Brenda Hill
Mrs Julia Honey
Mike & Ann Hutchinson
Kate & Bill Izzard
Jane & Oliver

Elaine Karaiskos
Oliver Kinsey
Claire Knight
Pieter & Constance Kooiman
Ian & Julie Kury
Mrs Pat Lamb
Leigh & District Historical Society
Ken & Sigi Lester
Harriet McNeil
Vic Measday (2 copies)
Celia & William Miller
Richard Mountford
Sally Musson
Maurice Nairne
Peter Nairne
Chris Neal
R H T & L F Neal (2 copies)
David Noakes
Mr Stuart Oakenfull &
    Mrs Rosemary Oakenfull
Richard & Peggy Parsons
Mark & Christina Pavlou
Shirley Pearce
Malcolm Pettit
Evan & Christine Portlock
Kathy Pratt
Trevor & Diane Prockter
Cllr Mark & Mrs Julie Rhodes
Sandy Sandison
Sally Shanks
Ted Shorter
Temlett Family
Elizabeth Toy
Bryan D Vernon
James Eric Wadsworth
David Wallis
D R Ward Builders
Jane Williams
Bryan & Barbara Winter
Ron Woodgate
Anonymous (15 copies)